T0340783

Propaganda Blitz

Propaganda Blitz

How the Corporate Media Distort Reality

David Edwards and David Cromwell

Foreword by John Pilger

First published 2018 by Pluto Press
345 Archway Road, London N6 5AA

www.plutobooks.com

Copyright © David Edwards and David Cromwell 2018

The right of David Edwards and David Cromwell to be identified as the
authors of this work has been asserted by them in accordance with the
Copyright, Designs and Patents Act 1988.

British Library Cataloguing in Publication Data
A catalogue record for this book is available from the British Library

ISBN   978 0 7453 3812 5   Hardback
ISBN   978 0 7453 3811 8   Paperback
ISBN   978 1 7868 0330 6   PDF eBook
ISBN   978 1 7868 0332 0   Kindle eBook
ISBN   978 1 7868 0331 3   EPUB eBook

This book is printed on paper suitable for recycling and made from fully
managed and sustained forest sources. Logging, pulping and manufacturing
processes are expected to conform to the environmental standards of the
country of origin.

Typeset by Stanford DTP Services, Northampton, England

Simultaneously printed in the United Kingdom and United States of America

We've been slandered, libelled, trashed and traduced, ridiculed and reviled by much of 'mainstream' journalism for two decades. And yet, simultaneously, surreally, we have received the unfailing support of someone whose opinion matters more to us than all the rest of them combined. Knowing that the finest political journalist of our time believes in what we're doing has made a huge difference to us. We dedicate this book to John Pilger. Onwards!

Contents

Foreword

John Pilger

When I sat down to write this, Robert Parry had just died. One of America's finest reporters, Parry was, wrote Seymour Hersh, 'a trailblazer for independent journalism'. Hersh and Parry had much in common; Hersh revealed the My Lai massacre in Vietnam and the secret bombing of Cambodia, Parry exposed Iran-Contra, a drugs and gun-running conspiracy that led to the White House. In 2016, they each produced evidence that disputed the claim that the Assad government in Syria had used chemical weapons. They were not forgiven.

Driven from the 'mainstream', Hersh must publish his work outside the United States. Parry set up his own independent news website where, in a final piece following a stroke in December 2017, he wrote, 'Whether they would admit it or not, [Western journalists] believe in a "guided democracy" in which "approved" opinions are elevated – regardless of their absence of factual basis – and 'unapproved evidence is brushed aside or disparaged regardless of its quality.'

This is not how many journalists see themselves. They imagine they set the public record straight and check the excesses of power, which Edmund Burke called a 'fourth estate'. The BBC goes further and ordains itself a divinity on earth, 'speaking truth to power': an exquisite nonsense that has endured since its founder secretly wrote propaganda for a Tory prime minister during Britain's General Strike.

Although journalism – the 'media' – was always a loose extension of establishment power, something has changed in recent years. Dissent tolerated when I joined a national newspaper in Britain in the 1960s has regressed to a metaphoric underground as liberal capitalism moves towards a form of corporate dictatorship. This is a historic shift, with journalists themselves policing the new 'groupthink', as Parry wrote, dispensing its myths and distractions, pursuing its enemies.

Witness the witch-hunts, the campaigns against refugees and immigrants, the anti-Russia and Brexit hysteria, a growing anti-China campaign and the suppression of public discussion of a beckoning world war.

With many independent journalists ejected from the 'mainstream', a corner of the Internet has become a vital source of disclosure and evidence-based analysis: what some would call true journalism. Sites such as wikileaks.org, consortiumnews.com, wsws.org, truthdig.com, globalresearch.org, counterpunch.org, informationclearinghouse.com and zcomm.org are required reading for those trying to make sense of a world in which science and technology advance wondrously while political and economic life regress behind a media facade of spectacle and propaganda.

In Britain, just one website offers consistently independent media criticism. This is the remarkable Media Lens – remarkable because its founders and editors as well as its only writers, David Edwards and David Cromwell, since 2001 have concentrated their gaze not on the usual suspects, the Tory press, but the paragons of reputable liberal journalism – the BBC, the *Guardian*, Channel 4 News.

Their method is simple. Meticulous in their research, they are respectful and polite when they email a journalist to ask why he or she produced such a one-sided report, or failed to disclose essential facts or promoted discredited myths. The replies they receive are often defensive, at times abusive; some are hysterical, as if they have pushed back a screen on a protected species.

My impression is that they have shattered a silence about corporate journalism. Like Edward Herman and Noam Chomsky in *Manufacturing Consent*, they represent a Fifth Estate, questioning, deconstructing and ultimately demystifying the media's monopoly.

What is especially interesting about them is that neither is a journalist. David Edwards was a teacher, David Cromwell is a former scientist. Yet, their understanding of the morality of real journalism – a term rarely used; let's call it true objectivity – is a bracing quality of their online Media Lens dispatches.

In 2007, they were awarded the Gandhi Foundation International Peace Award. I was asked to contribute to the citation. 'Without Media Lens during the attack on and occupation of Iraq,' I wrote, 'the full gravity of that debacle might have been consigned to oblivion, and to bad history.'

Such is the importance of their work, which I think is heroic. I would place a copy of this book in every journalism school that services the corporate system, as they all do.

How does the system work? Chapter 9, 'Dismantling the National Health Service', describes the critical part played by journalists in the crisis facing Britain's pioneering health service.

The NHS crisis is the product of a political and media construct known as 'austerity', with its weasel language of 'efficiency savings' (the BBC term for the slashing of public expenditure) and 'hard choices' (meaning the wilful destruction of many of the premises of civilised life in Britain).

'Austerity' is a political and media construct, an invention. Britain is a rich country with a debt owed not by its people but by crooked banks. The resources that would comfortably fund the National Health Service are stolen in broad daylight by the few allowed to avoid and evade billions in taxes.

The publicly-funded health service is being deliberately run down by free-market zealots, to justify its selling-off. The Conservative Secretary of State for Health, Jeremy Hunt, is one such zealot.

This is sometimes alluded to in the media, but rarely explained.

Edwards and Cromwell do what journalists should have done: they dissect the 2012 Health and Social Care Act, whose innocuous title belies its dire consequences. Unknown to most of the population, the Act ends the legal obligation of British governments to provide universal free healthcare: the bedrock on which the NHS was set up following the Second World War. Private companies can now take over NHS infrastructure, insinuating their piracy, piece by piece.

Where, ask Edwards and Cromwell, was the BBC while the bill was making its way through Parliament? With a statutory commitment to 'providing a breadth of view' and properly to inform the public of 'matters of public policy', the BBC never spelt out the threat posed to one of the nation's most cherished institutions. BBC News reported, 'Bill which gives power to GPs passes'. This was pure state propaganda.

There is a striking similarity with the BBC's coverage of the build-up to Tony Blair's lawless invasion of Iraq in 2003, which left a million dead and millions more dispossessed. A study by Cardiff University, Wales, found that the BBC reflected the government line 'overwhelmingly' while relegating reports of civilian suffering. A Media Tenor study placed the BBC at the bottom of a league of Western broadcasters in the time they gave to opponents of the invasion. The corporation's much-vaunted 'principle' of impartiality was never a consideration.

One of the most telling chapters describes the smear campaigns mounted by journalists against dissenters, political mavericks and whistle-blowers. The *Guardian*'s campaign against the WikiLeaks founder Julian Assange is the most disturbing. Assange, whose epic WikiLeaks disclosures brought fame, journalism prizes and largesse to the *Guardian*, was abandoned when he was no longer useful, then subjected to a vituperative onslaught. With not a penny going to WikiLeaks, a hyped *Guardian* book led to a lucrative Hollywood movie deal. The book's authors, Luke Harding and David Leigh, gratuitously described Assange as a 'damaged personality' and 'callous'. They also disclosed the secret password he had given the paper in confidence, which was designed to protect a digital file containing the US embassy cables.

With Assange now trapped in the Ecuadorean embassy, Harding, standing among the police outside, gloated on his blog that 'Scotland Yard may get the last laugh.'

His colleague James Ball wrote, 'It's difficult to imagine what Ecuador's London embassy smells like more than five and a half years after Julian Assange moved in.'

Such bile appeared in a newspaper described by its editor, Katharine Viner, as 'thoughtful and progressive'. What is the root of this vindictiveness? Is it jealousy, a perverse recognition that Assange and WikiLeaks have achieved more journalistic firsts than the snipers can claim in a lifetime? Is it that he refuses to be 'one of us' and shames those who have long sold out the independence of their craft?

Journalism students might well study this period to understand that the source of 'fake news' is not only the trollism, or the likes of Fox News, or Donald Trump, but a journalism self-anointed with a false respectability: a 'liberal' journalism that claims to challenge corrupt state power but, in reality, courts and protects it.

'[It is] an age in which people yearn for new ideas and fresh alternatives,' wrote Katharine Viner. Her political writer Jonathan Freedland dismissed the yearning of young people who supported Labour leader Jeremy Corbyn as 'a form of narcissism'.

'How did this man ...' brayed the *Guardian*'s Zoe Williams, 'get on the ballot in the first place?' The paper's choir of precocious windbags joined in, thereafter queuing to fall on their blunt swords when Corbyn came close to winning the 2017 general election in spite of the media.

Complex stories are reduced to a cult-like formula of bias, hearsay and omission: Brexit, Venezuela, Russia, Syria. On Syria, only the investigations of a group of independent journalists have countered this, revealing a sordid network of Anglo-American backing of jihadists in Syria, including those related to ISIS.

Supported by a 'psyops' campaign funded by the British Foreign Office and the US Agency of International Aid, the aim is to hoodwink the public and speed the overthrow of the government in Damascus, regardless of the blood-soaked alternative and the risk of war with Russia.

The Syria campaign, set up by a New York PR agency, Purpose, funds a group known as the White Helmets, who claim to be 'Syria Civil Defence' and are seen uncritically on TV news, apparently rescuing the victims of bombing, which they film and edit themselves, though viewers are unlikely to be told this. A slick film about them won an Oscar; George Clooney is a fan.

The White Helmets are appendages to the jihadists with whom they share addresses. Their media-smart uniforms and equipment are supplied by their Western paymasters and belie their mujihadeen alliances. That their exploits are not questioned by major news organisations is an indication of how deep the influence of state-backed PR now runs in the media.

In what is known as a hatchet job, a *Guardian* reporter based in San Francisco, Olivia Solon, who has never visited Syria, was allowed to smear the substantiated investigative work of journalists Vanessa Beeley and Eva Bartlett on the White Helmets as 'propagated online by a network of anti-imperialist activists, conspiracy theorists and trolls with the support of the Russian government'.

This abuse was published without permitting a single correction, let alone a right-of-reply. Even the *Guardian* Comment page was blocked, as Edwards and Cromwell had previously documented. I saw the list of questions Solon emailed to Beeley; it reads like a McCarthyite charge sheet – 'Have you ever been invited to North Korea?'

Too much of journalism has descended to this level. Subjectivism is all; facts and evidence have no place, slogans and outrage are deemed proof enough. What matters is 'perception'.

When he was US commander in Afghanistan, General David Petraeus described a 'war of perception ... conducted continuously using the news media'. What really mattered was not the facts but the way the story played in the United States. The real enemy was, as always, an informed and sceptical public at home.

In the 1970s, I met Leni Riefenstahl, Hitler's film-maker, whose propaganda mesmerised the German public. She told me the 'messages' of her films were dependent not on 'orders from above', but on the 'submissive void' of the public.

'Did that include the liberal, educated bourgeoisie?' I asked.

'Everyone,' she said. 'Propaganda always wins, *if you allow it*.'

John Pilger
February 2018

Preface
The Devil's Greatest Trick

We are reminded of the line from the 1995 movie, *The Usual Suspects*:

> The greatest trick the Devil ever pulled was convincing the world he didn't exist.[1]

Likewise, the greatest trick corporate media bias ever pulled was convincing the world that corporate media bias doesn't exist. After all, consider the corporate media entities called 'newspapers'. We are to understand that a 'newspaper' humbly channels news, the unadorned facts of what is happening, where and why. And yet everyone can see that the front pages of these papers openly declaim the bias of their billionaire owners and advertisers on a daily basis. Over the last two decades, we have studied in depth how these 'newspapers' – unaccountably described as 'mainstream' – are in fact billionaire *viewspapers* peddling an extreme and extremely biased view of the world.

On every single issue of consequence – from party politics, to the economy, from Iraq, to Libya, to Syria, to Venezuela, to climate change, to the nature of human happiness and the prospects for human survival – corporate media reporting and commentary are systematically filtered to further the interests of the state-corporate elites who own, manage and fund them. It is not that corporate media 'spin', 'hype' or 'sex up' the news – they *fundamentally distort every significant issue they touch*, often rendering them incomprehensible to readers, listeners and viewers.

'Comment is Free, but Facts are Sacred'

Consider the deceptiveness of the very term 'media'. It suggests a neutral utility service, a kind of informational pipe made of inert material such as clay, steel or stone that conveys 'news' without contaminating the contents with opinion or bias. As the *Guardian* proudly insists:

> Comment is free, but facts are sacred.[2]

Journalists are allowed to indulge in commentary in editorials, but we are to believe that it is the sacred duty of reporters to deliver facts in pure, unadulterated form, untainted by personal opinion.

Unfortunately, the idea is itself biased, and in fact trumpeted precisely *because* it serves a structurally corrupt system. Historian Howard Zinn wrote:

> Behind any presented fact ... is a judgement – the judgement that this fact is important to put forward (and, by implication, other facts may be ignored). And any such judgement reflects the beliefs, the values of the historian [or journalist], however he or she pretends to 'objectivity'.[3]

In other words, facts are *not* more 'sacred' than comment, because facts are a *form* of comment. The historian or journalist selects and highlights *this* fact rather than *that* fact.

The suggestion that media employees (journalists) are 'neutral' suppliers of 'sacred' facts, allows media corporations owned and sponsored by billionaires to *claim* that they are merely highlighting the objectively most important facts. In support of the claim, they can point to the fact that other corporate media, all pursuing much the same agenda, highlight and ignore much the same facts.

In reality, some criticism – *fact* – is presented, while other criticism – *also fact* – is not. During the 2017 UK general election, the BBC's Mark Mardell, former North America editor, now presenter of 'The World This Weekend', commented on Labour leader Jeremy Corbyn:

> One cynic told me expectations are so low, if Corbyn turns up and doesn't soil himself, it's a success.[4]

Mardell would not dream of discussing the prospect of Barack Obama, Hillary Clinton or Theresa May soiling themselves. It is simply understood that they are 'respectable', to be treated accordingly, whereas Corbyn is fair game.

Because media corporations tend to highlight the same facts, the bias looks like an informed consensus – it's just that *those facts matter more*. Everyone agrees!

In reality, media corporations function like giant magnifying glasses that roam the world, highlighting facts that benefit corporate-friendly parties, leaders, allied states and voices. They also magnify facts that undermine and harm corporate-unfriendly parties, leaders, groups and voices. They just 'naturally' avoid hovering over facts that might embarrass the 'good guys', just as they never give a boost to the 'bad guys'. Corporate journalists might casually exaggerate the Syrian government's death toll in Syria based on deeply suspect sources, but never the US–UK death toll in Iraq (always massively under-estimated. For more on how the corporate media has systematically underplayed the Iraq death toll, see Chapters 6 and 7 of our previous book, *Newspeak in the 21st Century* (Pluto Press, London, 2009)). Any media magnifying glass that hovers over the 'wrong' people will be accused of 'crusading', 'polemical' journalism by fellow journalists who themselves reflexively speak for the powerful.

Shared Interests

Corporate media are not neutral channels supplying news and views through divinely disinterested journalism. The media 'pipelines' supplying 'news' are filthy with money, bloody with arms-industry gore, lubricated by the fossil-fuel industry that is destabilising the climate.

And the financial engines pumping 'sacred' facts through the system are elite corporate advertisers that support a buying environment promoting their products, which they want sold to an affluent audience. Corporate advertisers have the same worldview as the corporations who both own and *are* media corporations – all want the same kind of media 'pipes' delivering the same kind of 'sacred' facts promoting a society run in the same interests.

A key source of 'facts' piped by the media is governments. Does this offer some kind of check and balance? Six-times presidential candidate Ralph Nader indicated a problem with this view:

> We have a two-party dictatorship in this country. Let's face it. And it is a dictatorship in thraldom to these giant corporations who control every department agency in the federal government.[5]

Numerous government departments – defence, for example – supply a torrent of subsidised, cheap propaganda. These make up a lot of the 'news' items, the 'sacred' facts that fill the corporate media pipeline. This flood of subsidised information *does not flow* to dissident media that resist the idea that society should be run in the interests of corporations and allied elites.

In sum, we find that highly-regarded quality or 'broadsheet' corporate media pipelines pump 'news' that promotes their interests, their corporate advertisers' interests, corporate-friendly parties' and governments' interests to wealthy media consumers who often work for corporations. It is this system that is routinely described as a 'free press'.

So, the very term 'media' is fake. The media *are not conduits for news and views; they are global systems designed and evolved to highlight a certain type of news to impose a certain kind of view.*

And this also gives the lie to the idea that corporate media are 'mainstream'. Why would we consider views generated by profit-maximising hierarchies of authoritarian power 'mainstream'? Are the activities of climate-denying fossil-fuel companies, cancer-denying tobacco companies, and the arms industry, 'mainstream'? These extreme positions are not accidental, not exceptions to the rule, and corporate media do not behave differently.

A Note on Reading This Book

This book is not intended to be a history of various key domestic and international political issues. It is intended to challenge the illusion of 'mainstream' impartiality and to show that the corporate media really is a system of mass thought control.

To make our case for corporate media bias – to expose the bias of even the best of the corporate 'mainstream' – we have to supply numerous quotes from *the most trusted and respected sources.* This is why we focus more heavily on more 'liberal' media like the *Guardian,* the *Independent* and the BBC. We focus on more right-wing media like *The Times* and the *Telegraph* to indicate how the supposed media 'spectrum' in fact imposes the same power-friendly propaganda on key issues.

Although we may often quote journalists saying much the same thing, please bear in mind that you are reading supposedly independent, critical-thinking individuals placed on a supposedly wide journalistic 'spectrum', and yet all travelling in *exactly the same direction.*

While it may occasionally seem we have over-egged the dissident pudding, focusing on numerous examples of this kind leaves the reader with a powerful impression of the true extent of corporate media conformity. These media work hard to suggest that all right-thinking people agree on key issues – awareness that this apparent consensus is manufactured, fake, can become a powerful basis for awakening from the 'mainstream' illusion.

We have no doubt that the 'free press' is a political, cultural and intellectual prison masquerading as a window on the world. It is a prison that keeps us trapped in a state-corporate system that inflicts fantastic, completely unsustainable levels of violence on people and planet. The issue of corporate media bias is tremendously important because it is the issue that determines what the public is able to know and understand about *all other issues.*

Exposing the fraudulence of the 'free press' is therefore highly efficient for positive change – even small gains have immense significance for the creation of a more compassionate, open and less violent society. If there is to be genuine change, it begins here.

1

Anatomy of a Propaganda Blitz

A regular feature of corporate media manipulation involves the launching of what we call a propaganda blitz, attacking and discrediting 'Official Enemies', often preparing the way for 'action' or 'intervention' of some kind.

Propaganda blitzes are fast-moving attacks intended to inflict maximum damage in minimum time. They are:

1. based on allegations of dramatic new evidence
2. communicated with high emotional intensity and moral outrage
3. apparently supported by an informed corporate media/ academic/expert consensus
4. reinforced by damning condemnation of anyone daring even to question the apparent consensus
5. often generated with fortuitous timing
6. characterised by tragicomic moral dissonance.

Dramatic New Evidence

A propaganda blitz is often launched on the back of allegedly dramatic new evidence indicating that an establishment enemy should be viewed as uniquely despicable and actively targeted. The basic theme: *This changes everything!*

Propagandists are well aware that media attention will rapidly move on from claims of dramatic new evidence, so the durability of the claims is not a key concern. Marginalised media websites and rare 'mainstream' articles may eventually expose the hype. But propagandists know that most corporate media will not notice and will not learn the lesson that similar claims should be received with extreme caution in future.

One of the most obvious recent examples of a propaganda blitz was the Blair government's infamous September 2002 dossier on Iraqi weapons of mass destruction (WMD), which included four mentions of a dramatic new claim that Iraq was able to deploy WMD against British citizens within 45 minutes of an order being given.

Senior intelligence officials later revealed that the original 45-minute claim referred to the length of time it might have taken the Iraqis to fuel and fire a Scud missile or rocket launcher. But that original intelligence said exactly *nothing* about whether Iraq possessed the chemical or biological weapons to use in those weapons. The Blair government had transformed a purely hypothetical danger into an immediate and deadly threat.

The fakery surrounding the Iraq War was so extreme that even the 'mainstream' media could not ultimately ignore the collapse of the case for war. But by then the powers that be had got the invasion and occupation they were seeking.

In 1964, in what became known as the Gulf of Tonkin incident, the US government and US corporate media launched a propaganda blitz based on the claim that US destroyers had come under attack from North Vietnamese patrol boats. The goal was to justify a massive escalation of the US assault on Vietnam. Media analyst Daniel Hallin wrote that the episode 'was a classic of Cold War management ... On virtually every important point, the reporting of the two Gulf of Tonkin incidents ... was either misleading or simply false.' Edward Herman and Noam Chomsky noted that the lies were simply 'in accordance with the needs of the US executive at that crucial moment'.[1]

In February 2008, the US Naval Institute reported on the release of nearly 200 declassified documents related to the incident:

> These new documents and tapes reveal what historians could not prove: There was not a second attack on U.S. Navy ships in the Tonkin Gulf in early August 1964. Furthermore, the evidence suggests a disturbing and deliberate attempt by

Secretary of Defense McNamara to distort the evidence and mislead Congress.[2]

As for the first 'attack', US naval aggression had provoked three North Vietnamese patrol boats to pursue the US aggressor in an engagement in which the patrol boats 'were almost entirely destroyed', while the US ship 'may have sustained "one bullet hole"'.[3]

In October 1990, in the aftermath of the Iraqi invasion of Kuwait, as the US worked hard to build a case for war, it was claimed that Iraqi stormtroopers had smashed their way into a Kuwait City hospital, torn hundreds of babies from their incubators and left them on the floor to die. In their book, *Toxic Sludge Is Good For You*, John Stauber and Sheldon Rampton described how the most powerful and heart-rending testimony came from a 15-year-old Kuwaiti girl, initially known only as Nayirah:

> Sobbing, she described what she had seen with her own eyes in a hospital in Kuwait City ... 'I volunteered at the al-Addan hospital', Nayirah said. 'While I was there, I saw the Iraqi soldiers come into the hospital with guns, and go into the room where ... babies were in incubators. They took the babies out of the incubators, took the incubators, and left the babies on the cold floor to die.'[4]

In fact, Nayirah was a member of the Kuwaiti Royal Family. Her father was Saud Nasir al-Sabah, Kuwait's Ambassador to the US. Stauber and Rampton noted that Nayirah had been coached by US PR company Hill & Knowlton's vice-president Lauri Fitz-Pegado 'in what even the Kuwaitis' own investigators later confirmed was false testimony'. The story of the 312 murdered babies was an outright lie. Journalist John MacArthur, author of *The Second Front: Censorship and Propaganda in the 1991 Gulf War*, commented:

> Of all the accusations made against the dictator [Saddam Hussein], none had more impact on American public opinion than the one about Iraqi soldiers removing 312 babies from their incubators and leaving them to die on the cold hospital floors of Kuwait City.[5]

As another war loomed in March 2003, in an article titled, 'See men shredded, then say you don't back war', Labour MP Ann Clwyd claimed that Saddam Hussein's goons were feeding opponents into a machine 'designed for shredding plastic' and dumping their minced remains into 'plastic bags' for use as 'fish food'.[6]

Who, in good conscience, then, could deny the righteousness of a war against Saddam? Alas, as Brendan O'Neil commented in the *Guardian*, Clwyd had based her story on the uncorroborated claims of 'one individual from northern Iraq. Neither Amnesty International nor Human Rights Watch, in their numerous investigations into human rights abuses in Iraq, had ever heard anyone talk of a human-shredding machine'.[7]

The story was baseless nonsense.

In 2011, dramatic claims were made that the Libyan government was planning a massacre in Benghazi, exactly the kind of action that Gaddafi knew could trigger Western 'intervention'. Again, as we will see later in this book (Chapter 5, Libya – 'It is All About Oil'), the claim was eventually exposed as baseless even by a UK parliamentary committee report. But once again, the warmongers had already achieved the regime change and control they desired.

In August 2013, corporate politicians and journalists instantly declared the Syrian government to blame for the use of chemical weapons in the Ghouta area of Damascus. Just one day after the attacks, a *Guardian* leader claimed there was not 'much doubt' who was to blame, and yet, as we will see in Chapter 6, the media's certainty was again utterly bogus.[8]

In May 2016, an excellent example of a propaganda blitz saw Jeremy Corbyn targeted by dramatic new 'evidence': namely, the discovery of a graphic posted by Naz Shah two years earlier, before she had become a Labour MP. The graphic showed a map of the United States with Israel superimposed in the middle, suggesting that a solution to the Israel-Palestine conflict would be to relocate Israel to the US.

Shah's post was highlighted by right-wing blogger Paul Staines, who writes as 'Guido Fawkes':

Naz Shah ... shared a highly inflammatory graphic arguing in favour of the chilling 'transportation' policy two years ago, adding the words 'problem solved'.[9]

Feeding the Naz Shah propaganda blitz in the *Guardian*, Jonathan Freedland, formerly comment editor, argued that leftists view Israel as 'a special case, uniquely deserving of hatred', and that this hatred 'lay behind' Shah's call 'for the "transportation" [of Israel to America] – a word with a chilling resonance for Jews'.[10]

A few days later, in the *Observer*, columnist Andrew Rawnsley echoed the claim that Shah believed 'that Israelis should be put on "transportation" to America, with all the chilling echoes that has for Jews'.[11]

By contrast, Israel-based former *Guardian* journalist Jonathan Cook, who was given a Martha Gellhorn special award for his work on the Middle East, argued that the map 'was clearly intended to be humorous rather than anti-semitic. I would make a further point. It is also obvious that the true target of the post is the US, not Jews or even Israel – making the anti-semitism claim even more ridiculous.'[12]

Norman Finkelstein, Jewish author of *The Holocaust Industry*, and the son of Holocaust survivors, commented that he had originally posted the graphic on his website in 2014:

An email correspondent must have sent it. It was, and still is, funny. Were it not for the current political context, nobody would have noticed Shah's reposting of it either. Otherwise, you'd have to be humourless. These sorts of jokes are a commonplace in the U.S. So, we have this joke: Why doesn't Israel become the 51st state? Answer: Because then, it would only have two senators. As crazy as the discourse on Israel is in America, at least we still have a sense of humour. It's inconceivable that any politician in the U.S. would be crucified for posting such a map.[13]

Finkelstein responded to the idea that Shah's posting of the image was an endorsement of a 'chilling "transportation" policy':

Frankly, I find that obscene. It's doubtful these Holocaust-mongers have a clue what the deportations were, or of the horrors that attended them. I remember my late mother describing her deportation. She was in the Warsaw Ghetto. The survivors of the Ghetto Uprising, about 30,000 Jews, were deported to Maijdanek concentration camp. They were herded into railroad cars. My mother was sitting in the railroad car next to a woman who had her child. And the woman – I know it will shock you – the woman suffocated her infant child to death in front of my mother. She suffocated her child, rather than take her to where they were going. That's what it meant to be deported. To compare that to someone posting a light-hearted, innocuous cartoon making a little joke about how Israel is in thrall to the U.S., or vice versa ... it's sick. What are they doing? Don't they have any respect for the dead? All these desiccated Labour appa-ratchiks, dragging the Nazi holocaust through the mud for the sake of their petty jostling for power and position. Have they no shame?[14]

Emotional Tone and Intensity

A crucial component of the propaganda blitz is the tone of political and corporate commentary, which is always vehement, even hysterical.

As we will see in following chapters, claims of dramatic new evidence of alleged horrors committed by 'Official Enemies' are invariably followed by expressions of deep moral outrage.

The rationale is clear enough: insanity aside, in ordinary life outrage of this kind is usually a sign that someone has *good reason* to be angry. People generally do not get very angry in the presence of significant doubt. So, the message to the public is that there *is* no doubt.

The picture of the world created must be clear-cut. The public must be made to feel there is no reasonable basis for uncertainty – the 'good guys' are basically benevolent and the 'bad guys' are absolutely appalling and must be removed.

This is achieved by relentless repetition of the theme hammered home over days, weeks, months and even years. Numerous individuals and organisations are used to give the impression of an informed consensus – there is no doubt!

Thus the splenetic eruptions demanding that 'something must be done' to 'save' Syria from impending massacre delivered by journalists blithely indifferent to the consequences of their earlier moral outbursts for Iraq and Libya.

Responding to the Naz Shah 'scandal' discussed above, Richard Littlejohn wrote in the *Mail* under the title, 'The fascists at the poisoned heart of Labour':

Naz [Shah] by name, Nazi by nature, was revealed to have backed the transportation of Jews in Israel to the United States.[15]

The *Jewish Chronicle* commented:

Labour now seems to be a party that attracts antisemites like flies to a cesspit. Barely a week goes by without the identification of a racist party member or allegations of racist behaviour by those involved in the party.[16]

As we will see, these claims were pure propaganda.

In 2017, the BBC website propaganda blitz assailed its readers with endless claims that Venezuela under President Nicolas Maduro was a 'dictatorship' with zero freedom of expression:

'The dictatorship is living its last days and Maduro knows it,' former MP Maria Corina Machado told AFP news agency at the women's march.[17]

On 22 May 2017, a BBC report commented: '"Venezuela is now a dictatorship," says Luis Ugalde, a Spanish-born Jesuit priest who during his 60 years living in Venezuela has become one of the South American nation's most well-known political scientists.'[18]

One would hardly guess that Venezuela has a democratically-elected government. In fact, while recognising that the Maduro government certainly merits criticism for mishandling the current situation, 'both economically and politically', political analyst Greg

Wilpert noted that 'none of the arguments against the democratic legitimacy of the Maduro government hold[s] much water'. Moreover, 'polls repeatedly indicate that even though Maduro is fairly unpopular, a majority of Venezuelans want him to finish his term in office, which expires in January 2019.'[19]

On 11 May 2017, the BBC broadcast 'Inside Venezuela's anti-government protests'. The first comment relayed by the BBC:

> There's no freedom of expression here in Venezuela. There's no freedom of any kind.[20]

Media analyst Joe Emersberger described the reality:

> In fact the protests and the leading opposition leaders' take on the protests are being extensively covered on the largest private networks: Venevision, Televen, Globovision. If people abroad sampled Venezuela's TV media directly, as opposed to judging it by what is said about it by the international media and some big NGOs, they'd be shocked to find the opposition constantly denouncing the government and even making very thinly veiled appeals to the military to oust Maduro.[21]

Appearance of Informed 'Consensus'

A key component of a propaganda blitz is the illusion of informed consensus. For maximum public impact, the supposed dramatic new evidence should be asserted with certainty and outrage right across the media 'spectrum'. The 'consensus' generates the impression that *everyone knows* that the claim is truthful. This is why the myth of a media 'spectrum' is so vital – an apparently credible, snowballing consensus puts pressure on dissidents to toe the line.

This is crucial because while a demonising propaganda blitz may arise from rightist politics and media, the propaganda *coup de grace* ending public doubt often comes from the 'left-liberal' journalists at the *Guardian*, the *Independent*, the BBC and Channel 4; and also from non-corporate journalists who crave acceptance by these media. Again, the logic is clear: if *even* celebrity progressive journalists – people famous for their principled stands, and colourful socks and ties – join the denunciations, then there *must* be something to the claims. At this point, it becomes difficult to doubt it.

Thus, in 2002, it was declared 'a given' by the *Guardian* that Iraq still retained WMD that *might* be a threat, despite the fact that both claims were easily and completely refutable.[22]

In 2007, George Monbiot wrote in the *Guardian*: 'I believe that Iran is trying to acquire the bomb.'[23] As even 16 US intelligence agencies confirmed – it wasn't.

In October 2011, Monbiot wrote of NATO's attack on Libya: 'I feel the right thing has been happening for all the wrong reasons.' In fact, illegal bombing in pursuit of regime change was very much the *wrong* thing happening for the wrong reasons.

At a crucial time in August 2013, with a full-on US-UK propaganda blitz preparing for an all-out military attack, Monbiot affirmed: 'Strong evidence that Assad used CWs [chemical weapons] on civilians.'[24]

As we will see in Chapter 6, the claim was as questionable as it was inflammatory.

In February 2011, as NATO 'intervention' clearly loomed in Libya, the *Guardian's* Owen Jones tweeted:

> I hope it's game over for Gaddafi. A savage dictator once tragically embraced by me on left + lately western governments and oil companies.[25]

On 20 March 2011, one day after NATO bombing began, Jones wrote:

> Let's be clear. Other than a few nutters, we all want Gaddafi overthrown, dead or alive.[26]

In 2012, news of the killings of Syrian ministers in a bomb explosion was greeted by Jones with: 'Adios, Assad (I hope).'[27]

Jones tweeted that 'this is a popular uprising, not arriving on the back of western cruise missiles, tanks and bullets'.[28]

As was obvious then and is indisputable now, Jones was badly wrong – the West, directly and via regional allies, had played a *massive* role in the violence. The *New York Times* reported that the US had been embroiled in a dirty war in Syria that constituted 'one of the costliest covert action programs in the history of the C.I.A', running to 'more than $1 billion over the life of the program'.[29] The aim was to support a vast 'rebel' army created and armed by the US, Saudi Arabia, Qatar and Turkey to overthrow the Syrian government.

As though reading from the NATO playbook, Jones added:

> I'm promoting the overthrow of illegitimate and brutal dictatorships by their own people to establish democracies.[30]

As we will see in the next chapter, both Monbiot and Jones publicly dumped Corbyn in early 2017, which again added enormously to the propaganda blitz attempting to see him ousted as Labour leader.

This is why the mythology of the 'liberal-left' *Guardian* and *Independent*, with their handful of noisy, tub-thumping progressives, is so important and why we work so hard to challenge it. It is why expressions of progressive support for the *Guardian* – with occasional articles appearing by Noam Chomsky and others, and with Russell Brand, for example becoming a '*Guardian* partner' – are so important. It is why we focus so intensely on the *Guardian* and its more progressive commentators. The public is not for one moment fooled by a hard-right consensus. Agreement *must* appear to have been reached by 'all right-thinking people', the 'lefties' at the *Guardian* included.

With regards to the propaganda blitz targeting Corbyn over Naz Shah's comments, the propaganda *coup de grace* was again supplied by a *Guardian* leftist. Owen Jones tweeted:

> John McDonnell [Shadow Chancellor of the Exchequer] was right to swiftly force Naz Shah's resignation – but now the party has to suspend her.[31]

One day later, Jones issued a further decree condemning former London mayor Ken Livingstone, who had defended Shah:

Ken Livingstone has to be suspended from the Labour Party. Preferably before I pass out from punching myself in the face.[32]

Ali Abunimah, co-founder of Electronic Intifada, commented:

Didn't always agree with Ken Livingstone but he's been an anti-racist fighter & took on Thatcher before @OwenJones84 was born. Sad to watch.[33]

He added:

To watch @OwenJones84 throw Ken Livingstone under the bus to appease a bunch of hard-right racists is a truly pitiful sight.[34]

Demonising Dissent

To challenge a propaganda blitz is to risk becoming a target of that blitz. Dissidents can be smeared as 'useful idiots', 'apologists', 'genocide deniers'. As Noam Chomsky commented:

One can proceed – that is, if one is interested in truth and justice and immune to shrieks of horror and a deluge of brickbats.[35]

Anyone even questioning the campaigns targeting Julian Assange and Russell Brand, risked also being labelled a 'sexist', a 'misogynist', a 'narcissist', and in the case of Assange, a 'rape apologist'.

Monbiot has consistently added to a snowballing 'consensus' by attacking dissidents with real ferocity. In 2017, he supported a claim that Media Lens was guilty of 'whitewashing mass murder' for daring to ask why expert voices had been excluded from the media discussion of events at Khan Sheikhoun in Syria prior to Trump's attack with 59 cruise missiles.[36]

For two decades, whenever we have challenged media bias, the reflexive accusation has been that we are therefore supporting the target of bias – a very obvious *non sequitur*. Thus, when we suggested that Donald Trump is likely to be the only US president in our lifetimes we will see openly scorned by BBC journalists, former *Guardian* Political Editor, Michael White, tweeted:

A bit desperate for you two to be supporting an authoritarian nationalist? Or am I just late to spot it's always been your illiberal thing?[37]

White's tweet received a single 'like' and no retweets. The 'like' was from BBC reporter Wyre Davies.

In reality, of course, our comment was intended to highlight and undermine the BBC's standard deference to power – our goal was to encourage more dissent, not to defend Trump.

Following the same illogic, Owen Jones tweeted us:

Genuinely think sometimes you're a right-wing front[38]

In another article, Monbiot lumped us in with political commentators Noam Chomsky, Edward Herman, David Peterson and John Pilger who, he claimed, comprised a 'malign intellectual subculture that seeks to excuse savagery by denying the facts' of the genocides in Bosnia and Rwanda.[39]

Monbiot also wrote an article with the title, 'Media Cleanse', on the same theme.[40]

A year later, Monbiot published a piece under the title, 'Lord McAlpine – an abject apology'. Monbiot commented:

I have done a few stupid things in my life, but nothing as stupid as this.[41]

The *Independent* reported that Monbiot had sent tweets 'wrongly naming Lord McAlpine as a paedophile on Twitter'.[42]

In so doing, Monbiot wrote:

I helped to stoke an atmosphere of febrile innuendo around an innocent man, and I am desperately sorry for the harm I have done him.[43]

Monbiot reached a settlement with McAlpine's legal representatives, and agreed to carry out three years of charity work to a value of £25,000. Monbiot's advice to his readers:

Finally, please make sure you check your facts and think before you tweet.[44]

Many of Monbiot's ostensibly liberal-left attacks on us and other progressive writers began life with hard-right commentator Oliver Kamm, one of Rupert Murdoch's columnists at *The Times*. For some time, Kamm has claimed, without an atom of evidence, that we have 'long espoused genocide denial, misogyny & xenophobia'.[45]

Monbiot is either unaware, or unconcerned, that writing for the Mondoweiss website, Theodore Sayeed discussed a leaked memo of a meeting of the Henry Jackson Society:

One of the items on the minutes, listed prominently in fourth place, was to discredit [Noam] Chomsky. Their tack was to allege that he is a 'denier' of the Srebrenica massacre in Bosnia. In the art of controversy, slapping the label 'denier' on someone is meant to evoke the Holocaust. Chomsky, the furtive charge proceeds, is a kind of Nazi.[46]

Sayeed assessed the credibility of the claim:

The only conclusion possible after surveying the material is that the evidence for this 'denial' has all the merits of the evidence for chastity in a brothel.

He noted that the 'task of getting this slur into circulation was delegated to [academic] Marko Attila Hoare and Oliver Kamm'. The memo stated:

Push forward on Chomsky/Srebrenica issue: Approach Guardian, *Johann Hari, Bruce Anderson,* THES, Spectator. *Approach Sacranie and ask what he is to do about it. (Marko: coordinate with Oliver Kamm)...*

It seems clear that Chomsky was not alone in being targeted in this way.

Indeed, like Chomsky, we at Media Lens have been accused of supporting, or apologising for, everyone from Stalin to Milosevic, from the Iranian Ayatollahs to the North Korean dictatorship, Assad, Gaddafi, Saddam, Putin, Trump, and so on. It seems we are so deranged that we support completely contradictory political and religious movements, even enemies who despise each other. This may be a function of our swivel-eyed hatred of the West, or perhaps because we are challenging a deeply cynical corporate media system willing to sink to any depths of dishonesty to smear its critics.

To critique media bias targeting Iraq or North Korea does not mean we ever held candles for Saddam Hussein's thugs or Pyongyang's totalitarian state. If we fail to support the vast number of people denouncing these tyrannies, it's because doing so would achieve nothing beyond minutely adding to the case for war. And yes, we *are* passionately opposed to the West's endless wars of first resort serving corporate greed and state power.

While the moral outrage of a propaganda blitz is often fake, the resulting damage to dissidents' reputations and outreach is very real. When respected writers like Monbiot, Jones and others apply their seal of approval to right-wing propaganda, the public naturally assumes that there must be at least *some* fire behind the smoke – they may well come away with a sense that the target is 'dodgy', almost morally unhygienic. The smear can last for the rest of a person's career and life.

This, of course, is a major concern for anyone protecting, or aspiring to, a career in the corporate media. They may quickly learn to keep their heads down, to steer well clear of challenging propaganda blitzes, especially when an attack is raging at full intensity. In other words, they will say *least* at exactly the time when dissent is needed *most*, exactly as intended. And, of course, they have the option of cementing their reputations with the propaganda blitzers by supporting the blitz and attacking dissent. We are fortunate in that we rely solely on donations from readers who, so far at least, have been able to see the pattern in the smears and have seen through them.

The demonisation works also to silence the wider public. Most people have, or had, little idea about the status of WMD in Iraq, about Gaddafi's intentions and actions in Libya, or what Corbyn thinks about antisemitism. Given this uncertainty, it is hardly surprising that the public is impressed by an explosion of moral outrage from so many political and media 'experts'.

Expressions of intense hatred targeting 'bad guys' and their 'apologists' persuade members of the public to keep any doubts to themselves. They know that even declaring mild scepticism, even requesting clarification, can cause a giant Finger of Blame to be cranked around in their direction. Perhaps they, too, will be declared 'supporters of tyranny', 'apologists for genocide denial', 'sexists', 'racists', 'misogynists'. The possibility of denunciation is highly intimidating and potentially disastrous for anyone dependent on any kind of corporate employment or sponsorship. Corporations, notably advertisers, hate to be linked to any kind of unsavoury 'controversy'. It is notable how 'celebrities' with potentially wide public outreach very often stay silent.

It is easy to imagine that people will often prefer to decide that the issue is not *that* important to them, that they don't know *that* much about it – not enough to risk getting into trouble. And, as discussed, they naturally imagine that professional journalists have access to a wealth of information and expertise – best to just keep quiet. This is the powerful and disastrous chilling effect of an all-out propaganda blitz.

Timing and Fortuitous Coincidences

The 'dramatic new evidence' fuelling a propaganda blitz often seems to surface at the worst possible time for the establishment target. On one level, this might seem absurdly coincidental – why, time after time, would the 'Official Enemy' do *the one thing* most likely to trigger invasion, bombing, electoral disaster, and so on, at *exactly* the wrong time? Why would Saddam Hussein be so idiotic as to coyly keep the West guessing that he *perhaps* retained some WMD, thus inviting attack? Why would Gaddafi commit the one kind of atrocity likely to trigger Western 'intervention' in 2011? Why would Assad use chemical weapons just as chemical weapons inspectors entered the Syrian capital in August 2013? Why would Corbyn quietly lay out a welcome mat for antisemitism in the Labour Party *just* when he is being attacked by all corporate media for everything he says and does, and just when he has a real possibility of gaining power?

But remember, we are talking about 'bad guys' who, as everyone knows from watching James Bond and Austin Powers movies, are famously perverse. It is part of the Dr Evil mind-set to strut provocatively, pinkie inserted in the corner of the mouth, and laugh in the face of certain disaster. Idiotic, blindly self-destructive self-indulgence is what being a 'bad guy' is all about; it's in the job description.

So the implausibly perfect timing may actually help persuade the public to shake its collective head and think: 'This guy really is nuts. He's absolutely *asking* for it!' Much 'mainstream' coverage of Official Enemies is about suggesting they are comically, in fact cartoonishly, foolish in exactly this way. They may be writing about different individuals – Milosevic, bin Laden, Saddam Hussein, Chávez, Gaddafi, Assad, Corbyn – but the public is really being presented with the same Bond villain over and over again.

We have no doubt that, with sufficient resources, media analysts could easily prove that propaganda blitzes consistently arise with impeccable timing just ahead of key votes at the UN, in Parliament and in elections. For example, in November 2002, before the UN vote on Resolution 1441, which 'set the clock ticking' for the 2003 Iraq War, the Blair regime began issuing almost daily warnings of dramatic new evidence of imminent terror threats against UK cross-channel ferries, the London Underground, airports and major public events. In 2003, Blair surrounded Heathrow airport with tanks; an action said to be in response to increased terrorist 'chatter' warning of a 'missile threat', of which nothing more was subsequently heard. Even the *Guardian* editors expressed scepticism about this sudden flood of 'threats':

> It cannot be ruled out that Mr Blair may have political reasons for talking up the sense of unease, in order to help make the case for a war against Iraq that is only backed by one voter in three.[47]

John Pilger cited a former intelligence officer who described the government's terror warnings as 'a softening up process' ahead of the Iraq War and 'a lying game on a huge scale'.[48]

In fact, Blair was perpetrating a form of psychological terrorism on his own people.

Likewise, atrocity claims from Syria clearly peaked as the US drew closer to war in the summer of 2013. After Obama chose not to bomb, it was extraordinary to see the BBC's daily headline atrocity claims simply dry up.

George Eaton, the fiercely anti-Corbyn Political Editor of the hard-right 'centre-left' *New Statesman*, tried hard to coin the term 'Hitlergate' to describe the scandal that engulfed Naz Shah and Ken Livingstone (alas, the Nexis media database finds no other mentions of the term). Eaton cited an anonymous MP arguing that the supposed scandal 'firmly pins responsibility for next week's [local election] results on the hard-left antics'.[49]

As so often, then, the Shah/Livingstone propaganda blitz erupted at just the right time.

Tragicomic Moral Dissonance

Propaganda blitzes are consistently directed at Official Enemies whose actual, alleged and often invented crimes are dwarfed by crimes most certainly committed by Western governments and their allies. This raises a few interesting questions: Why would corporate journalists rage uncontrollably at Gaddafi for allegedly *threatening* a massacre, but not at British and US leaders who killed 500,000 Iraqi children by means of sanctions, and then one million Iraqis as a result of the 2003 invasion and occupation?[50]

Why would they revile the late Venezuelan President Hugo Chávez and yet welcome Tony Blair into the TV studio to chat about everything from Corbyn to Brexit to football? Why are Barack Obama and Hillary Clinton not considered completely beyond the pale for the key role they played in destroying Libya? Why are journalists who praise and interview the likes of Blair never described as 'apologists' and 'genocide deniers'?

In the pages that follow, we will see how Assange, Brand, Corbyn and others are afforded vitriolic treatment that is simply never experienced by UK prime ministers and US presidents who devastate whole countries. (Trump being the exceptional, far-right establishment outsider who proves the rule.) What is the moral calculation that causes corporate journalism to *despise* Russell Brand for his 'misogynism' while, year after year, literally hundreds of soulless, sociopathic UK MPs go completely unnoticed as they line up to sell British weapons to foreign tyrannies like Saudi Arabia and Egypt that use them to oppress, maim and kill? How can journalists rage at Gaddafi and Assad, and yet have nothing much to say about Big Oil executives in the US and UK working hard to cause the literal extinction of the human race, and indeed of most life on earth by feverishly opposing action to protect the climate in the name of short-term profits? (See Chapter 11, 'Climate Chaos: An Inconvenient Emergency' for details.)

Why would high-profile journalists rage at our supposed sins of 'misogyny' and 'denial' at Media Lens – a tiny, two-man website run on donations reaching a few thousand people – when every corporate media entity one can think of is responsible for promoting deceptions that have led to wars that have destroyed *whole countries*? When every media entity is financially dependent on promoting the mindless mass consumption that increasingly looks like killing us all? Why would it be a bigger moral priority to target us rather than them?

It is astonishing but true that, time and again in the pages ahead, you will see corporate journalism judging the mere *words* of the likes of Brand and Corbyn as far more morally despicable than the *actions* of 'mainstream' politicians that result in mass death. How can words that offend be worse than actions that kill? Why are people a million miles from executive power – clearly well-intentioned hippies like Brand, chattering at the margins – deemed *more destructive, more reprehensible* than corporate and state executives with awesome power doing awesome, measurable, provable damage?

And why are the US and UK – authors of truly historic crimes – forever depicted as ethical agencies with a moral 'responsibility to protect' suffering people in other countries? Did Al Capone have a 'responsibility to protect' victims of oppression? What would we have made of Mongolian journalists angrily demanding that it was the 'duty' of Genghis Khan to engage in 'humanitarian intervention', and claiming that his stubborn refusal to intervene militarily abroad was a source of deep shame? Would we think they had lost their minds, their moral compass? Would we call them 'mainstream'? Would we call them 'impartial'?

Propaganda blitzes never make moral sense. The reason is that they are a form of ethical posturing generated by a structurally violent, greed-driven system for immoral ends. The Italian humanist Machiavelli, who would have greatly appreciated the Western enthusiasm for 'humanitarian intervention', commented:

> The experience of our times shows those princes to have done great things who have had little regard for good faith, and have been able by astuteness to confuse men's brains.[51]

A vital aspect of the effort to 'confuse men's brains' involved the use and abuse of five 'good qualities'. Machiavelli summarised:

> It is not essential, then, that a Prince should have all the good qualities which I have enumerated above, but it is most essential that he should *seem* to have them ... Thus, it is well to seem merciful, faithful, humane, religious and upright, and also to be so; but the mind should remain so balanced that were it needful to be so, you should be able and know how to change to the contrary.[52]

What Machiavelli actually meant was that leaders should *appear* merciful and compassionate, but should *be* merciless, inhuman and cruel, as required, because, after all:

> Everyone sees what you seem, but few know what you are.[53]

And this is precisely the philosophy of the propaganda blitz. The truth about any given person or event is often deeply hidden from public view – the important thing is to *seem* to have dramatic new evidence that *seems* to be affirmed by all who are 'merciful, faithful, humane, religious and upright', corporate dissidents included. With the public pacified, the powerful can then do as they please.

2

Killing Corbyn

In 1975, the Trilateral Commission, a thinktank closely linked to the US government, published an influential report titled 'The Crisis of Democracy'. The report's author, Samuel Huntington, noted:

> The effective operation of a democratic political system usually requires some measure of apathy and non-involvement on the part of some individuals and groups.[1]

Thanks to this apathy, President Truman had 'been able to govern the country with the cooperation of a relatively small number of Wall Street lawyers and bankers'.

Unfortunately, the report continued, by the mid-1960s, 'the sources of power in society had diversified tremendously'. This was a result of the fact that 'previously passive or unorganized groups in the population', such as 'blacks, Indians, Chicanos, white ethnic groups, students and women ... became organized and mobilized in new ways to achieve what they considered to be their appropriate share of the action and of the rewards'.

This public mobilisation constituted a 'crisis in democracy'; or, more accurately, an 'excess of democracy'. The solution lay in 'a greater degree of moderation in democracy' and determined efforts 'to restore the prestige and authority of central government institutions'. Demands on government had to be reduced in a way that restored 'a more equitable relationship between government authority and popular control'. The 'effective operation of a democratic political system' requires the promotion of 'apathy and non-involvement'.

The Trilateral Commission report thus gave a rare insight into the mind-set of elite power. Today, a relatively small number of wealthy people who own global media corporations, and the parent companies that own them, work hard to attack literally anyone threatening to create another 'crisis of democracy'.

In Britain in 2015, Jeremy Corbyn threatened the greatest 'crisis of democracy' in a generation. He threatened to reverse Tony Blair's hard-won triumph transforming the Labour Party into a similarly pro-corporate, pro-war version of the Tory Party. In August 2015, journalist Peter Oborne wrote:

> Corbyn is our only current hope of any serious challenge to a failed orthodoxy. Blair and Cameron have both adopted a foreign policy based on subservience rather than partnership with the United States, which has done grave damage to British interests.[2]

A month later, Corbyn was elected leader of the Labour Party with 250,000 votes, 'the largest mandate ever won by a Party Leader'.[3]

Writing a few weeks before the June 2017 general election, Oborne noted of media coverage:

> Needless to say, the British media (and in particular the BBC, which has a constitutional duty to ensure fair play during general elections) has practically ignored Corbyn's foreign policy manifesto.[4]

Oborne wrote that the manifesto was 'radical and morally courageous', and explained that, pre-Corbyn:

> Foreign policy on both sides was literally identical. The leadership of both Labour and the Conservatives backed the wars in Iraq, Libya and Afghanistan, the alliance with Saudi Arabia and the Sunni states in the Gulf.
>
> London did what it was told by Washington. [...] This cross-party consensus has been smashed, thanks to Jeremy Corbyn, the current Labour leader. Whatever one thinks of Corbyn's political views (and I disagree with many of them), British

democracy owes him a colossal debt of gratitude for restoring genuine political debate to Britain.

And of course his extremely brave and radical decision to break with the foreign policy analysis of Blair and his successors explains why he is viewed with such hatred and contempt across so much of the media and within the Westminster political establishment.

But, as Oborne noted, this important change has not been fairly represented in media coverage:

it is deeply upsetting that the BBC has betrayed its own rules of impartiality and ignored Corbyn's brave stand on this issue.

Oborne's comments explained the corporate media reaction to Corbyn in the summer of 2015 and thereafter – it was absolutely vital that his moral virtues be ignored and in fact that his reputation be destroyed, so that voters might be returned to their 'apathy and non-involvement'. The response was a relentless storm of propaganda blitzes intended to trash Corbyn's standing with the British public.

In July 2015, as support for Corbyn grew during the Labour leadership contest, a *Guardian* leader warned that 'Politics moves in cycles and some are more vicious than others.'[5]

And Corbyn it was who was leading a vicious 'spiral into irrelevance after defeat', his politics a defunct throwback:

His ideological positions [in the past] did nothing to accelerate escape from opposition ... his solutions long pre-date the challenges of the 21st century.

Instead:

All candidates must turn their attention to more forward-looking alternatives. The challenge for Mr Corbyn's rivals is to match his crusading passion while leading the debate back to a discussion of the country Labour would aspire to lead in 2020.

On the same day, also in the *Guardian*, Executive Editor Jonathan Freedland wrote:

Tony Blair and others tried to sit the kids down and say: 'Look, you've had your fun. But take it from us, even if Corbyn is right – which he isn't – he is never, ever going to get elected. This crusade is doomed. Come back home.'[6]

A day earlier, senior *Guardian* columnist Polly Toynbee had written:

Suddenly the party that has been a reasonably friendly coalition through the Blair, Brown, Miliband years, begins to feel like the poisonous place it was in the early '80s. That's when it split over toxic Militant entryism unchallenged by Michael Foot, its unelectable leader with a raft of impossibilist policies.[7]

The years spent selling Labour out to the neocons had been 'friendly', while resistance was 'poisonous' 'nastiness' in which people had taken 'leave of their senses'. Who on earth would want to disrupt the status quo and jeopardise the shifting of deck chairs on the Titanic a couple of inches to the left? 'This is summer madness,' Toynbee concluded; Corbyn was 'a 1983 man', 'a relic'.

The *Guardian's* Suzanne Moore described Corbyn as a 'slightly less feral version of Ken Livingstone'.[8]

Moore understood why the less enlightened were attracted to Corbyn's authenticity, 'but Blair is right, surely, to talk of the challenges of the future'.

Moore thus respectfully cited, and sided with, one of the great neocon war criminals of our time. If Corbyn's campaign achieves nothing else, it has already exposed the reality that the deaths of one million human beings in Iraq have done *nothing* to alter the *Guardian* Blairites' view of their idol.

Moore bitterly rejected the self-harming lunacy of supporting Corbyn:

The Labour party can choose to be part of what is happening or it can further cut itself off. Right now they appear to be in the process known to post-Marxists as the 'Nobody loves me. Everybody hates me. I am going down the garden to eat worms' stage.

Martin Kettle, described by John Pilger as 'Blair's most devoted promoter',[9] repeatedly dismissed Corbyn in the *Guardian*, arguing:

> Labour can come back from the brink. But it seems to lack the will to do so.[10]

Kettle added:

> His socialism, though, is more a matter of faith than a viable programme ... Corbyn's position is essentially made up of attitudes and slogans ...

The trend in *Guardian* commentary was very clear, as Craig Murray noted in July 2015:

> The fundamental anti-democracy of the Blairites is plainly exposed, and the panic-driven hysterical hate-fest campaign against Corbyn by the *Guardian* would be unbelievable, if we hadn't just seen exactly the same campaign by the same paper against the rejection of neo-liberalism in Scotland.
>
> I think I am entitled to say I told you so. Many people appear shocked to have discovered the *Guardian* is so anti-left wing. I have been explaining this in detail for years.[11]

The editors of the *Independent* also lamented the loss of Blair. He had 'transformed the fortunes of the Labour Party', although 'his record in office, especially his wars, remains controversial'.[12]

Much as the 9/11 attack on New York 'remains controversial'.

For the *Independent*'s editors, Corbyn was 'not the answer to the Labour Party or the nation's problems'. The piece bowed low to Blair: he had 'won a hat-trick of victories', after all. 'For that alone he earned his right to be listened to.' We wonder if this group of radically right-wing, billionaire-led journalists would say the same, if they were citing Blair, serving life for war crimes, from a prison cell.

The *Evening Standard*, owned by the Russian oligarch, Alexander Lebedev, contemptuously waved Corbyn, and democracy, away:

But given the options available, the most important task is simply to exclude Corbyn ... Labour must have a credible leader, not a fantasist.[13]

A leader in *The Times* commented of Corbyn:

This is a man who five years ago shared with George Galloway the distinction of presenting his own show on Press TV, the English-language propaganda arm of Iran ... He believes Britain has not learnt its lessons from Karl Marx.[14]

The Times' sister paper, the *Sun*, doesn't really do politics in any meaningful sense. But it does do smears. Under the title, 'Marxed man', the editors wrote:

But to Jeremy Corbyn, the man who polls say will be the next Labour leader, Karl Marx is still a hero. He said yesterday: 'We all owe something to him.' Corbyn doesn't want to take Labour back to its Bennite years in the 1980s. He wants to turn the clock back to 1917 and the Russian revolution.[15]

In an article, 'Corbyn's morons have only helped the hard left', Murdoch's *Sunday Times* opined:

The hard left, apparently as extinct for its influence on British politics as the dinosaurs, senses its Jurassic Park moment.[16]

David Aaronovitch asked on Twitter:

What positive debate ... is served by having Corbyn on the ballot?[17]

Spanish versions of Aaronovitch doubtless asked the same of Pablo Iglesias and Podemos. Aaronovitch received an answer, in full, with the general election result on 8 June 2017.

The *Sunday Mirror* guffawed at Corbyn:

He is also a throwback to the party's darkest days when it was as likely to form the government as Elvis was of being found on Pluto.[18]

Rachel Sylvester took the hyperbole to a new level in *The Times* on 1 September:

> Just as the Vikings and the Mayans brought about their own extinction by destroying the environment on which their cultures depended ...[19]

Already the heart has dropped. Is this really leading where we think it's leading?

> ... so the Labour party is threatening its survival by abandoning electoral victory as a definition of success. If Labour chooses Jeremy Corbyn – a man who will never be elected prime minister – as leader next week, its end could be as brutal and sudden as those other once great tribes.

'It's Your Fault, Jeremy'

In June 2016, in common with other corporate news media, the *Guardian* joined a propaganda blitz centred around Corbyn being heckled at Gay Pride:

> Jeremy Corbyn has defended Labour's campaigning in the EU referendum, telling a heckler at London's Pride festival 'I did all I could', after using a defiant speech to insist he would resist attempts to topple him.[20]

'Labour activist' Tom Mauchline, the heckler, who posted a video of the exchange on Twitter, accused Corbyn of failing to get enough traditional Labour voters to polling stations. He said:

> It's your fault, Jeremy. I had a Polish friend in tears because you couldn't get the vote out in Wales, the north and the Midlands.

The incident was also given significant coverage on ITN and Sky News, and even front-page treatment in the *Guardian*.

In fact, as Craig Murray observed, it turned out that Mauchline was a Blairite public relations professional working for Portland Communications,[21] whose 'strategic counsel' was Alastair Campbell, Blair's former media chief, who helped to sell the illegal invasion-occupation of Iraq. Mauchline had previously worked on the campaign for the Labour leadership run by Corbyn's rival, Liz Kendall.

None of this was spelt out in the *Guardian* report by Heather Stewart, the paper's Political Editor. Instead, there was a single cryptic line that concealed more than it delivered:

> Allies of the Labour leader said the confrontation at Pride had been staged by anti-Corbyn activists who were attempting to undermine the leader's position.

There was no further explanation or context. When challenged on Twitter, Stewart responded:

> Story makes clear it was regarded as staged by Corbyn backers; but if part of plot to destabilise him it's news.[22]

This was a facile reply. Craig Murray himself then asked her:

> 1) why does it not make clear that Mauchline is a PR man for Portland Comms? 2) How did you become aware of the story?[23]

The *Guardian's* Political Editor simply ignored these questions.

Meanwhile, BBC News ran a live feed on their home page with the headline, 'Corbyn crisis and Brexit'.[24]

Brexit was almost an afterthought; it certainly seemed to be playing second fiddle to the 'Corbyn crisis'. Anyone seeing this could be forgiven for asking about the BBC News editorial agenda and its setting of priorities. It was as though we were to forget that Prime Minister David Cameron had announced his resignation three days earlier; and that Cameron and the Tory Party had led the country into a referendum that had resulted in the FTSE 100 index falling more than 8 per cent, and the pound falling against the dollar by 10 per cent; and that a number of Tories were scrambling to become the new leader, including the warmongering, climate-denying Boris Johnson. But, true to form, BBC News was happy to hammer on about the 'Corbyn crisis'; this despite the fact that 'Labour persuaded two-thirds of its supporters to vote remain.'[25]

Perhaps the worst example of an anti-Corbyn attack, post-Brexit, was in the *Mail on Sunday* in June 2016. A piece by Dan Hodges was illustrated by a photoshopped image of a malevolent vampiric Corbyn in a coffin with the headline, 'Labour MUST kill vampire Jezza'.[26]

This appeared ten days after Labour MP Jo Cox had been brutally murdered.

When challenged by readers, Hodges responded with the standard cop-out:

Sorry, but I don't write the headlines.[27]

It is true that subeditors write newspaper headlines. But Hodges could still have indicated that he recognised the callousness and irresponsibility of the headline and 'photo'.

One reader fired off this rational follow-up challenge:

But are you condoning the headline? Do you agree with it? Or is [it] just no comment from you?[28]

Hodges did not reply; understandably enough. In March, a tragicomic announcement had noted:

Britain's best political columnist DAN HODGES joins the *Mail on Sunday*.[29]

A lucrative contract for Hodges, to be sure, and one he would be reluctant to jeopardise by criticising his paymasters. 'It's hard to make the sums add up when you are kicking the people who write the cheques,' as the BBC's Andrew Marr once observed.[30]

Laura Kuenssberg: Trophy Hunter

Senior corporate media figures have virtually queued up to smear Corbyn. For a time, journalists acted like trophy hunters eager to break the story that would see his head hung from their living room walls. Thus, it was no great surprise to read in the *Independent*:

Jeremy Corbyn's weapons pledge makes 'nuclear holocaust more likely'.[31]

This was a reference to Corbyn's declaration that he would not 'press the nuclear button' in any circumstance. It gave the state-corporate commentariat their first sniff at what they hoped was their great 'gotcha!'

Rather than celebrating Corbyn as a rare, principled politician sticking to a lifelong, anti-war commitment shared by many reasonable people – in a geopolitical context where Britain faces no remotely credible nuclear threats – he was portrayed as a dangerous loon risking nuclear annihilation.

We could provide any number of examples of media propaganda in response, but a high-profile piece on the BBC's flagship 'News at Ten' programme on 30 September 2015 supplied a truly stand-out performance. Here, BBC Political Editor Laura Kuenssberg starred in an almost comically biased, at times openly scornful, attack on Corbyn's stance on nuclear weapons.[32]

Kuenssberg asked Corbyn:

> Would you ever push the nuclear button if you were Prime Minister?

He replied:

> I'm opposed to nuclear weapons. I'm opposed to the holding and usage of nuclear weapons. They're an ultimate weapon of mass destruction that can only kill millions of civilians if ever used. And I am totally and morally opposed to nuclear weapons. I do not see them as a defence. I do not see them as a credible way to do things ...

> LK [interrupting]: 'So yes or no. You would never push the nuclear button?

> JC: 'I've answered you perfectly clearly. It's immoral to have or use nuclear weapons. I've made that clear all of my life.'

> LK: 'But, Jeremy Corbyn, do you acknowledge there is a risk that it looks to voters like you would put your own principles ahead of the protection of this country?'

The content of the question, together with the obvious emphasis and passion, betrayed Kuenssberg's own view on the matter.

Corbyn responded:

It looks to the voters, I hope, that I'm somebody who's absolutely and totally committed to spreading international law, spreading international human rights, bringing a nuclear-free world nearer ...

LK [interrupting]: 'And that's more important than the protection of this country?'

Kuenssberg, sounding incredulous, appeared to be all but scolding Corbyn. Almost as an afterthought, she added:

Some voters might think that.

This was her token gesture to the BBC's mythical 'impartiality'.

The idea that the possession and threatened use of nuclear weapons might endanger the British public clearly fell outside Kuenssberg's idea of 'neutral' analysis.

Her 'impartiality' took another blow a few months later when she helped to orchestrate the live resignation of Labour Shadow Foreign Minister Stephen Doughty on the BBC2 'Daily Politics' show, presented by Andrew Neil.[33]

Doughty was teed-up by Neil:

Are you considering your position, Mr Doughty?

In fact, this was the prearranged prompt for Doughty to announce his resignation, before going on to accuse Jeremy Corbyn's team of 'unpleasant operations' and 'lies'. This was timed to have maximum political impact, just five minutes before Prime Minister's Questions (PMQs) began in the House of Commons. And, indeed, David Cameron used that information a few minutes later to mock Corbyn.

There was a considerable backlash against the BBC via social media. The BBC's discomfort was highlighted by the fact that a piece written by BBC political producer Andrew Alexander about the live resignation was swiftly deleted. The article, published on the BBC's College of Journalism website for trainees, stated (our emphasis):

Just before 9am we learned from Laura Kuenssberg, who comes on the programme every Wednesday ahead of PMQs, that she was speaking to one junior shadow minister who was considering resigning. *I wonder, mused our presenter Andrew Neil, if they would consider doing it live on the show?*

The question was *put to Laura, who thought it was a great idea ...*

Within the hour we heard that Laura had sealed the deal: the shadow foreign minister Stephen Doughty would resign live in the studio ... we knew his resignation just before PMQs would be a dramatic moment with big political impact ... Our only fear was that he might pull his punches when the moment came.

When it did, with about five minutes to go before PMQs, he was precise, measured and *quietly devastating* – telling Andrew that 'I've just written to Jeremy Corbyn to resign from the front bench' and *accusing Mr Corbyn's team of 'unpleasant operations' and telling 'lies'.*[34]

The corporate press published a handful of articles about the live resignation, uniformly leading with the angle that the BBC was defending itself from attack by the Labour Party and its supporters. The *Guardian* wrote:

The BBC has launched a staunch defence of its journalism.[35]

The Times:

The BBC has defended its handling of Stephen Doughty's resignation on air.[36]

The *Telegraph*:

The BBC has rejected an official complaint from Labour that it 'orchestrated' the resignation of frontbencher Stephen Doughty on live television.[37]

Independent columnist Jane Merrick even suggested that the people who had complained 'didn't understand journalism'. She argued:

This was not news created, but news reported. Stories happen all the time, it is just a question of how to make sure it is your readers or viewers, and not those of your rivals, who get to see it first.[38]

Award-winning journalist Nic Outterside, a former chief investigative reporter at the *Scotsman*, saw it differently. He commented on this passage in the deleted BBC blog:

This was a story where we could make an impact ... We knew his resignation just before PMQs would be a dramatic moment with big political impact ... We took a moment to watch the story ripple out across news outlets and social media. Within minutes we heard David Cameron refer to the resignation during his exchanges with Jeremy Corbyn.[39]

As Outterside observed, the producer's blog: 'admitted that the BBC team were not just reporting the day's news but trying to influence it'. He summed up:

As a fellow journalist I find this admission shocking, but also symptomatic of degraded and biased practice.

As for Stephen Doughty himself, the politician brusquely dismissed public concerns with a bizarre tweet mocking complainants as David Icke-style conspiracy theorists:

Epilogue: twitter goes into meltdown + lizards running the BBC (all members of the Bilderberg group) are exposed in the harsh sunlight ...[40]

In fact, once again the 'Corbyn phenomenon' had 'exposed in the harsh sunlight' the disdain for the public shared by corporate media, neocons and Blairite politicians alike.

'I Told You So You Fucking Fools'

On 8 June 2017 – after two long years of attacks of the kind described above – Jeremy Corbyn surprised and humbled the entire corporate media commentariat.

Without doubt, the outcome of the 2017 general election was one of the most astonishing results in UK political history. Dismissed by all corporate pundits, including the clutch of withered fig leaves at the *Guardian*; reviled by scores of his own Blairite MPs, Corbyn 'increased Labour's share of the vote by more than any other of the party's election leaders since 1945' with 'the biggest swing since ... shortly after the Second World War'.[41] In fact, he won a larger share of the vote than Tony Blair in 2005.

Corbyn achieved this without resorting to angry lefty ranting. His focus was on kindness, compassion, sharing, inclusivity and forgiveness. This approach held up a crystal-clear mirror to the ugly, self-interested cynicism of the Tory Party, transforming the endless brickbats into flowers of praise.

On Twitter, John Prescott disclosed that when Rupert Murdoch saw the exit poll 'he stormed out of the room'.[42]

As ever, while the generals made good their escape, front-line troops were less fortunate. Outfought by Team Corbyn, outthought by social media activists, outnumbered in the polls, many commentators had no option but to fall on their microphones and keyboards. LBC radio presenter Iain Dale led the way:

> Let me be the first to say, I got it wrong, wholly wrong. I should have listened more to my callers who have been phoning into my show day after day, week after week.[43]

The *Guardian*'s Gaby Hinsliff, who had written in January, 'This isn't going to be yet another critique of Corbyn, by the way, because there is no point. The evidence is there for anyone with eyes',[44] tweeted:

> This is why I trust @iaindale's judgement; he admits when it was way off. (As mine was. As god knows how many of ours was.)[45]

Hinsliff promised:

> Like everyone else who didn't foresee the result, I'll be asking myself hard questions & trying to work out what changed ...[46]

Annoying as ever, we asked:

But will you be asking yourself about the structural forces, within and outside *Guardian* and corporate media generally, shaping performance?[47]

And:

Is a corporate journalist free to analyse the influence of owners, profit-orientation, ad-dependence, state-subsidised news? Taboo subjects.[48]

Presumably engrossed in introspection, Hinsliff failed to reply.

Right-winger John Rentoul, who had insisted four weeks earlier in the *Independent* that, 'we are moving towards the end of the Corbynite experiment',[49] appeared to be writing lines on a detention blackboard:

I was wrong about Jeremy Corbyn – the Labour leader did much better in the election than I expected. I need to understand and learn from my mistakes[50]

Channel 4 News presenter and *Telegraph* blogger, Cathy Newman tweeted:

Ok let's be honest, until the last few weeks many of us under-estimated @jeremycorbyn[51]

Translating from the 'newspeak': many corporate journalists waged a relentless campaign over two years *to persuade the public* to 'underestimate' Corbyn, but were wrong about the public's ability to see through the propaganda.

Piers Morgan, who had predicted the Conservatives would win a '90–100 seat majority', wrote:

I think Mr Corbyn has proved a lot of people, including me, completely wrong.[52]

In a typically dramatic flourish, Channel 4's Jon Snow's summation was harsh but, we think, fair:

I know nothing. We the media, the pundits, the experts, know nothing.[53]

Guardian columnist Rafael Behr, who had written in February, 'Jeremy Corbyn is running out of excuses',[54] also ate humble pie:

Fair play to Jeremy Corbyn and his team. They have done a lot of things I confidently thought they – he – could not do. I was wrong.[55]

In March, *Observer* columnist Nick Cohen graphically predicted that 'Corbyn's Labour won't just lose. It'll be slaughtered.'[56] In a furious article entitled, 'Don't tell me you weren't warned about Corbyn', Cohen described the words that would 'be flung' at Corbynites 'by everyone who warned that Corbyn's victory would lead to a historic defeat':

I Told You So You Fucking Fools![57]

Apparently foaming at the mouth, Cohen concluded by advising the 'fools' who read his column that, following the predicted electoral disaster, 'your only honourable response will be to stop being a fucking fool by changing your fucking mind'.

Awkward, then, for Cohen to have to 'apologise to affronted Corbyn supporters ... I was wrong', presumably feeling like a fucking fool, having changed his fucking mind.[58]

Cohen then proceeded to be 'wrong' all over again:

The links between the Corbyn camp and a Putin regime that persecutes genuine radicals. Corbyn's paid propaganda for an Iranian state that hounds gays, subjugates women and tortures prisoners. Corbyn and the wider left's indulgence of real anti-semites (not just critics of Israel). They are all on the record. That Tory newspapers used them against the Labour leadership changes nothing.

The *Guardian*'s senior columnist Jonathan Freedland spent two years writing a series of anti-Corbyn hit pieces.[59] In May 2017, Freedland had written under the title, 'No more excuses: Jeremy Corbyn is to blame for this meltdown', lamenting:

What more evidence do they need? What more proof do the Labour leadership and its supporters require?[60]

Freedland helpfully relayed focus group opinion to the effect that Corbyn was a 'dope', 'living in the past', 'a joke', 'looking as if he knows less about it than I do'.

Freedland also, now, had no choice but to back down:

Credit where it's due. Jeremy Corbyn defied those – including me – who thought he could not win seats for Lab. I was wrong.[61]

Like Freedland, senior *Guardian* columnist Polly Toynbee had relentlessly attacked Corbyn. On 19 April, she wrote of how Corbyn was 'rushing to embrace Labour's annihilation':

Wrong, wrong and wrong again. Was ever there a more crassly inept politician than Jeremy Corbyn, whose every impulse is to make the wrong call on everything?[62]

After Corbyn's success, Toynbee's tune changed:

Nothing succeeds like success. Jeremy Corbyn looks like a new man, beaming with confidence, benevolence and forgiveness to erstwhile doubters ...[63]

Apparently channelling David Brent of the TV series, 'The Office', Toynbee added:

When I met him on Sunday he clasped my hand and, with a twinkle and a wink, thanked me for things I had written.

With zero self-awareness, Toynbee noted that the *Mail* and *Sun* had helped Corbyn: 'by dredging up every accusation against him yet failing to frighten voters away, they have demolished their own power'.

Former *Guardian* Political Editor Michael White, yet another regular anti-Corbyn commentator, admitted:

I was badly wrong. JC had much wider voter appeal than I realised[64]

Former *Guardian* journalist, Jonathan Cook, replied:

Problem is you *all* got it wrong. That fact alone exposes structural flaw of corporate media. You don't represent us, you represent power[65]

White responded with his usual perspicacity:

You're not still banging on, are you Jonathan. You do talk some bollocks[66]

Guardian, Telegraph, Independent and *New Statesman* contributor Abi Wilkinson tweeted:

Don't think some of people making demands about who Corbyn puts in shadow cabinet have particularly earned the right to be listened to ...[67]

On Twitter, we paired this comment with another by Wilkinson from June 2016:

Any hope I once held about Corbyn's ability to steer the party in a more positive direction has been well and truly extinguished[68]

Wilkinson replied: 'oh fuck off', before concluding that we are 'two misogynistic cranks in a basement', and 'just some dickheads who aren't actually fit' to hold the media to account. After numerous complaints, Wilkinson later deleted her abusive tweets and the 'right to be listened to' tweet.

When a tweeter suggested that Corbyn's result was 'brilliant',[69] *New Statesman* Editor Jason Cowley replied: 'Yes, I agree.'[70] Just three days earlier, Cowley had written beneath this ominous title:

The Labour reckoning – Corbyn has fought a spirited campaign but is he leading the party to worst defeat since 1935?[71]

In March, Cowley had opined:

The stench of decay and failure coming from the Labour Party is now overwhelming – Speak to any Conservative MP and they will say that there is no opposition. Period.[72]

Like everyone else at the *Guardian*, columnist Owen Jones' initial instinct was to tweet away from his own viewspaper's ferocious anti-Corbyn campaign:

> The British right wing press led a vicious campaign of lies, smears, hatred and bigotry. And millions told them where to stick it[73]

But in fact, as with so many propaganda blitzes, it was the handful of corporate dissidents, including Jones himself, who had attempted to supply the *coup de grace*. In July 2016, Jones had written:

> As Jeremy Corbyn is surrounded by cheering crowds, Labour generally, and the left specifically, are teetering on the edge of looming calamity.[74]

In November 2016, Jones then offered this damning assessment:

> Jeremy Corbyn, a person who will never win a British general election ... I know him personally and I know he never wanted to be leader; it was presented as a sense of obligation. He never anticipated this result and now leads the party without having any experience.[75]

In February 2017:

> The Left has failed badly. I'd find it hard to vote for Corbyn ... They have made lots of bad mistakes. There's been a lack of strategy, communication, vision.[76]

In March 2017:

> My passionate and sincere view is Jeremy Corbyn should stand down as soon as possible in exchange for another left-wing MP being allowed to stand for leadership in his place: all to stop both Labour and the left imploding, which is what is currently on the cards.[77]

Jones added:

> Corbyn's acceptance speech – his first attempt to address the country – lacked coherence and had no core message to connect to people outside of the left's bubble.

In April 2017, less than two months before the election, Jones used his *Guardian* column to depict Corbyn as an utterly pathetic figure:

> A man who stood only out of a sense of duty, to put policies on the agenda, and who certainly had no ambition to be leader, will now take Labour into a general election, against all his original expectations. My suggestion that Corbyn stand down in favour of another candidate was driven by a desire to save his policies ...[78]

Having consistently traduced the Labour leader's reputation in this way, Jones found himself in a fine pickle in the aftermath of the election. He wrote under the title: 'Jeremy Corbyn has caused a sensation – he would make a fine prime minister':

> I owe Corbyn, John McDonnell, Seumas Milne, his policy chief Andrew Fisher, and others, an unreserved, and heartfelt apology ...
>
> I wasn't a bit wrong, or slightly wrong, or mostly wrong, but totally wrong. Having one foot in the Labour movement and one in the mainstream media undoubtedly left me more susceptible to their groupthink. Never again.[79]

To his credit, Jones managed to criticise his own employer (something he had previously told us was an unthinkable and absurd idea):

> Now that I've said I'm wrong ... so the rest of the mainstream commentariat, including in this newspaper, must confess they were wrong, too.

Despite the blizzard of *mea culpas* from colleagues, George Monbiot also initially pointed well away from his employer:

> The biggest losers today are the billionaires who own the *Mail*, *Sun*, *Times* and *Telegraph*. And thought they owned the nation.[80]

Monbiot mocked Corbyn's tabloid detractors:

> It was the *Sun* wot got properly Cor-Binned.[81]

The mogul-owned press – that is, *not* the *Guardian* – were also to blame:

> By throwing every brick in the house at Corbyn, and still failing to knock him over, the billionaire press lost much of its power.[82]

After receiving criticism, and having, of course, seen Jones' *mea culpa*, Monbiot subsequently admitted that anti-Corbyn bias was found 'even in the media that's not owned by billionaires':

> This problem also affects the *Guardian* ... Only the *Guardian* and the *Mirror* enthusiastically supported both Labour and Corbyn in election editorials.
> But the scales still didn't balance.[83]

This was a change from Monbiot's declared position of three years earlier, when he rejected the idea that the *Guardian* was part of the problem.[84] He now recalled his own dumping of Corbyn in a tweet from January: 'I have now lost all faith.' In fact, the full tweet read:

> I was thrilled when Jeremy Corbyn became leader of the Labour Party, but it has been one fiasco after another. I have now lost all faith.[85]

He had also tweeted:

> I hoped Corbyn would be effective in fighting the government and articulating a positive alternative vision. Neither hope has materialised.[86]

Curiously, in his *Guardian mea culpa*, Monbiot blamed media bias on the way journalists are selected – 'We should actively recruit people from poorer backgrounds' – and wrote, 'the biggest problem, I believe, is that we spend too much time in each other's company.'

We suggested to Monbiot that this was not at all 'the biggest problem' with 'mainstream' media, and pointed instead to elite ownership, profit-orientation, advertiser dependence and use of state-subsidised 'news', as discussed by Edward Herman and Noam Chomsky in their 'propaganda model'.[87]

Jonathan Cook responded to Monbiot, describing the limits of free speech with searing honesty:

> This blindness even by a 'radical' like Monbiot to structural problems in the media is not accidental either. Realistically, the furthest he can go is where he went today in his column: suggesting organisational flaws in the corporate media, ones that can be fixed, rather than structural ones that cannot without rethinking entirely how the media functions. Monbiot will not – and cannot – use the pages of the *Guardian* to argue that his employer is structurally incapable of providing diverse and representative coverage.
>
> Nor can he admit that his own paper polices its pages to limit what can be said on the left, to demarcate whole areas of reasonable thought as off-limits. To do so would be to end his *Guardian* career and consign him to the outer reaches of social media.[88]

The same, of course, applies to Jones, who made no attempt at all to account for corporate media bias.

Media grandee Will Hutton, former Editor-in-Chief of the *Observer*, now Principal of Hertford College, Oxford, had fun writing 'How the rightwing tabloids got it wrong – It was the *Sun* wot hung it.' [89]

We hated to spoil the party, but on Twitter reminded Hutton of his own article, one month earlier:

> Er, excuse us ...! Will Hutton, May 7: 'Never before in my adult life has the future seemed so bleak for progressives.'[90]

Tragicomically, given the awesome extent of his employer's anti-Corbyn bias, John Cody Fidler-Simpson CBE, BBC World Affairs Editor, tweeted:

> I suspect we've seen the end of the tabloids as arbiters of UK politics. *Sun*, *Mail* & *Express* threw all they had into backing May, & failed.[91]

We replied:

Likewise the 'quality' press and the BBC, which has been so biased even a former chair of the BBC Trust spoke out[92]

A year earlier, Sir Michael Lyons, who chaired the BBC Trust from 2007 to 2011, had commented on the BBC's 'quite extraordinary attacks on the elected leader of the Labour party':

I can understand why people are worried about whether some of the most senior editorial voices in the BBC have lost their impartiality on this.[93]

3

Smearing Assange, Brand and Chávez

Julian Assange: 'Turd', 'Weirdo', 'Narcissist'

On 19 June 2012, in a final bid to avoid extradition to Sweden, WikiLeaks founder Julian Assange requested asylum in the Ecuadorian embassy in London.

Credible commentators recognised that Assange had good reason to fear extradition to the United States from Sweden. Ray McGovern, who was a CIA analyst for 30 years, commented:

> Not only is Julian Assange within his rights to seek asylum, he is also in his right mind. Consider this: he was about to be sent to faux-neutral Sweden, which has a recent history of bowing to U.S. demands in dealing with those that Washington says are some kind of threat to U.S. security.[1]

Pulitzer-prize winning journalist and former US constitutional and civil rights lawyer, Glenn Greenwald, supplied some detail:

> The evidence that the US seeks to prosecute and extradite Assange is substantial. There is no question that the Obama justice department has convened an active grand jury to investigate whether WikiLeaks violated the draconian Espionage Act of 1917. Key senators from President Obama's party, including Senate intelligence committee chairwoman Dianne Feinstein, have publicly called for his prosecution under that statute. A leaked email from the security firm Stratfor – hardly a dispositive source, but still probative – indicated that a sealed indictment has already been obtained against him. Prominent American figures

in both parties have demanded Assange's lifelong imprisonment, called him a terrorist, and even advocated his assassination.[2]

Journalist Daniel Ellsberg, who leaked the Pentagon Papers, stated:

Political asylum was made for cases like this. Freedom for Julian in Ecuador would serve the cause of freedom of speech and of the press worldwide. It would be good for us all; and it would be cause to honor, respect and thank Ecuador.[3]

The evidence, then, that Assange had plenty to fear was overwhelming. But not for the great and the good of liberal journalism, who launched a massive propaganda blitz. The *Guardian*'s Suzanne Moore set the tone on Twitter on June 19, 2012:

Seems like Assange's supporters did not expect him to skip bail? Really? Who has this guy not let down?[4]

She added: 'I bet Assange is stuffing himself full of flattened guinea pigs. He really is the most massive turd.'[5]

Moore later complained that, after writing articles about Assange, she had suffered 'vile abuse'. We wrote to her:

That's a real shame, sorry to hear that. But how would you describe calling someone 'the most massive turd'? Vile abuse? [6]

Moore replied: 'no I wouldnt call that vile abuse. I mean nasty threats etc.'[7] She added: 'also I would advise you to stop sounding so bloody patronising.'[8]

Despite his dire plight, and despite his courageous work exposing US crimes of state, journalists found Assange's predicament endlessly amusing. The *Guardian*'s Luke Harding commented:

Assange's plight seems reminiscent of the scene in Monty Python where the knights think to storm the castle using a giant badger[9]

Christina Patterson of the *Independent* wrote:

Quite a feat to move from Messiah to Monty Python, but good old Julian Assange seems to have managed it. Next Timbuktu?[10]

The *Guardian*'s Technology Editor Charles Arthur tweeted:

It is absolutely not true that Julian Assange got twitter to fall over so that he could sneak out of the Ecuadorean embassy for a latte.[11]

David Aaronovitch of *The Times* wrote:

When the embassy stunt fails expect Assange, slung over the shoulders of muscular friend, to be swung into St Paul's shouting 'thanctuary!'[12]

Twitter provides a marvellous insight into the way corporate journalists move as an intellectual herd. Like wildebeest fording the Zambezi, there is a sense that one is witnessing an awesome natural phenomenon.

Charlie Beckett, *Guardian* contributor and director of Polis at the London School of Economics, wrote:

Fly Me To Cuba! (Or Ecaudaor) [sic] Julian Assange hijacks WikiLeaks[13]

The Deputy Editor of the *Guardian* US, Stuart Millar, tittered:

I like to think that Assange chose the Ecuadorean embassy because it's so convenient for Harrods[14]

The *Independent's* Joan Smith wrote a piece under the title: 'Why do we buy Julian Assange's one-man psychodrama?':

The news that the increasingly eccentric founder of WikiLeaks had sought political asylum in Knightsbridge, of all places, was greeted with equal measures of disbelief and hilarity. The London embassy of Ecuador is convenient for Harrods, although I don't imagine that was a major consideration when Assange walked into the building on Tuesday afternoon.[15]

Indeed not – Harrods was, of course, a total irrelevance. In the *Guardian*, Tim Dowling offered 'five escape routes from the Ecuadorean embassy', including:

Ascend to embassy roof. Fire cable-loaded crossbow (all embassies have these; ask at reception) across the street to

Harrod's [sic] roof. Secure and tighten the cable, then slide across, flying-fox style, using your belt as a handle. Make your way to the Harrod's helipad.[16]

BBC World Affairs correspondent, Caroline Hawley, enjoyed Dowling's piece, sending the link to her followers on Twitter:

Advice for #Assange escape: order a pizza and escape as delivery boy via @Guardian Guardian.co.uk/media/2012/jun ...[17]

Aaronovitch tweeted:

Don't you think that many Assange supporters are misogynistic?[18]

On the Reuters website, John Lloyd, a contributing editor to the *Financial Times*, took the prize for crazed comparisons:

When we talk of fallen angels, we invoke the original fallen angel, Satan or Lucifer, once beloved of God, the highest in his closest council, whose pride impelled him to challenge for heaven's rule – and came before his fall to Hell. Assange was an angel of a sort, at least to many.[19]

On and on, the journalistic scorn poured. The *Guardian*'s Deborah Orr tweeted: 'I think we can safely say that Julian Assange's bid to run the world has faltered. A bit.'[20] She added: 'It's hard to believe that, until fairly recently, Julian Assange was hailed not just as a radical thinker, but as a radical achiever, too.'[21]

The subheading above Orr's article read: 'Of course Assange should face the charges brought against him in Sweden.'

We, and others, asked her: 'What "charges"?'[22]

Orr took a short break from guffawing with the rest of her profession to apologise:

I've informed the *Guardian*'s readers' editor of the Assange inaccuracy. They'll follow it up. Thanks to all who pointed it out, and sorry.[23]

The gaffe was corrected.[24]

Ian Dunt, editor of politics.co.uk. wrote:

Julian Assange, Chris Brown and Mike Tyson are party [sic] of the same depressing tapestry of hatred towards women bit.ly/LjSKZI[25]

Chris Brown and Mike Tyson had both been convicted of serious criminal violence against women – assault and rape, respectively. Assange had not been charged with *any* crime. After the Swedish prosecutor dropped the case against Assange, John Pilger commented:

> Julian Assange has been vindicated because the Swedish case against him was corrupt. The prosecutor, Marianne Ny, obstructed justice and should be prosecuted. Her obsession with Assange not only embarrassed her colleagues and the judiciary but exposed the Swedish state's collusion with the United States in its crimes of war and 'rendition'.[26]

Pilger added on the media campaign:

> For almost seven years, this epic miscarriage of justice has been drowned in a vituperative campaign against the WikiLeaks founder. There are few precedents. Deeply personal, petty, vicious and inhuman attacks have been aimed at a man not charged with any crime yet subjected to treatment not even meted out to a defendant facing extradition on a charge of murdering his wife. That the US threat to Assange was a threat to all journalists, and to the principle of free speech, was lost in the sordid and the ambitious. I would call it anti-journalism.

Intermission: 'Dubya' – Everyone's Favourite Grandpa

At this point, it might be helpful to take a step back and return to the kind of questions raised in the first chapter:

Why did corporate journalists across the 'spectrum' so passionately revile Assange, someone who had risked his personal safety and freedom to expose crimes of state, and who was now in such a terrible situation?

And how do the same media respond to other political actors responsible for truly awesome crimes?

Consider George W. Bush, 43rd president of the United States, who bears responsibility for the destruction of an entire country, the killing of one million Iraqis, the wounding and displacement of countless millions more. Before 'Dubya', there had never been a suicide bomb attack in Iraq – the car bombs, the mass executions, the bombs in London and Madrid, the rise of Islamic State, and everything else that resulted from the 2003 invasion of Iraq began with 'Dubya'.

About this war criminal, Britain's leading 'left-liberal' newspaper wrote in February 2017 under the title: 'The *Guardian* view on George W Bush: a welcome return.'[27] A lead article in the paper commented:

> Mr Bush can be seen now as a paragon of virtue. He sounds a lot better out of office than in it. And so the 43rd US president should be applauded.

The fact that the paper was using Bush to attack Donald Trump did not justify this assertion, however tongue-in-cheek. The *Guardian* said not one word about Bush's millions of victims.

In an article titled, 'How George W Bush went from "war criminal" to the internet's favourite grandpa', the *New Statesman* opined:

> It sounds flippant to say that compared to Trump, Bush is starting to look good, and this sentiment has become a popular online joke within itself. Nonetheless, the claim is grounded in some reality.[28]

In similar vein, the *Guardian* gave space for hard-right, former *Spectator* editor Matthew d'Ancona to explain that 'Blair has a far bigger vision than saving us from Brexit', rooted in the fact that he 'profoundly believes in the power of human agency', which inspires 'a sense of responsibility'.[29]

The rehabilitation of Bush and Blair followed the deeper rehabilitation of the US brand under Obama. After the Iraq disaster

– drenched in too much blood and too many lies for even the propaganda system to whitewash – Obama's task was to reassert the myth of US benevolence. Corporate media adulation duly followed. Two *Guardian* headlines from 2016 give an idea:

Listening to Obama makes me want to be American for a day[30]

And:

Barack Obama: He has such power ... yet such humility[31]

This moral makeover played a vital role in reassuring the public that, with Obama at the helm, the US was under new, compassionate management.

As we read the smears of Assange above and other dissident voices below, we spend our time well when we reflect that Obama's destruction of Libya (see Chapter 5: Libya – 'It is All About Oil') was essentially never discussed during the 2016 US presidential election. Plunging an entire country of 6 million people into despair was not deemed a significant issue in discussing either Obama's or Hillary Clinton's record.

Russell Brand: 'Poseur', 'Charlatan', 'Jesus Clown'

Unlike Bush and Blair, comedian and activist Russell Brand is another good example of someone attempting to defy the 'apathy and non-involvement' identified by the Trilateral Commission as vital for a smooth-running kleptocracy.

On 23 October 2013, Brand appeared to crash past the gatekeepers protecting the public from dissident opinion. His 10-minute interview with Jeremy Paxman on the BBC's 'Newsnight' programme in October 2013 had attracted 11.6 million views – a major achievement defying the propaganda system.[32]

Spurred on by the rapturous public response, Brand then wrote and published a book of political, personal and spiritual analysis, *Revolution*. Unlike some reviewers, we read the book – it contains powerful, important arguments delivered with Brand's trademark sincerity. He wrote:

Oxfam say a bus with the eighty-five richest people in the world on it would contain more wealth than the collective assets of half the earth's population – that's three-and-a-half billion people.[33]

He added:

The same interests that benefit from this ... need, in order to maintain it, to deplete the earth's resources so rapidly, violently and irresponsibly that our planet's ability to support human life is being threatened.[34]

We are therefore at a crossroads:

Today humanity faces a stark choice: save the planet and ditch capitalism, or save capitalism and ditch the planet.[35]

Openly threatening a 'crisis of democracy', Brand wrote:

We are living in a zoo, or more accurately a farm, our collective consciousness, our individual consciousness, has been hijacked by a power structure that needs us to remain atomised and disconnected.[36]

What kind of problem might an elite-owned, advertiser-dependent, profit-maximising corporate media system have with this kind of message reaching millions of people?

Once again, the *Guardian* gatekeepers led the way. Once again, the clever take was to pour scorn: in this case, to turn Brand the comedian into Brand the fool. Suzanne Moore lampooned 'the winklepickered Jesus Clown who preaches revolution'. She repeated the 'Jesus Clown' jibe four times, noting:

A lot of what he says is sub-Chomskyian [sic] woo.[37]

An earlier version of Moore's article had been even more damning: 'A lot of what he says is ghostwritten sub-Chomskyian woo.' This was 'corrected' by the *Guardian* after Moore received a letter from Brand's lawyers.

Anyone who dares to mention Chomsky is automatically denigrated as 'sub-Chomsky' in the 'mainstream'. In 2008, *The Times'* smear artist-in-chief, Oliver Kamm, wrote of Media Lens:

ML is a sub-Chomskyite grouping that purports to 'correct for the distorted vision of the corporate media'.[38]

Sarah Ditum sneered from the *New Statesman*:

Russell Brand, clown that he is, is taken seriously by an awful lot of young men who see any criticism of the cartoon messiah's misogyny as a derail from 'the real issues' (whatever they are).[39]

The *Guardian*'s Hadley Freeman imperiously dismissed Brand's perfectly rational analysis of corporate psychopathy:

I'm not entirely sure where he thinks he's going to go with this revolution idea because [SPOILER!] revolution is not going to happen. But all credit to the man for making politics seem sexy to teenagers. What he lacks, though – aside from specifics and an ability to listen to people other than himself – is judgment.[40]

In the *Independent*, Yasmin Alibhai-Brown's patronising judgement was clear:

Russell Brand might seem like a sexy revolutionary worth getting behind, but he will only fail his fans – Politics needs to be cleaned up, not thrown into disarray by irresponsible populists.[41]

Writing in the *Independent*, Howard Jacobson won the prize for unabashed intellectual snobbery:

When Russell Brand uses the word 'hegemony' something dies in my soul.[42]

As with Corbyn and Assange, we must surely stand aghast at this level of invective directed at a lone voice challenging Britain's crass, moribund political system, openly dominated by elite interests. But the list goes on ...

Boris Johnson wrote in the *Telegraph*:

Of course his manifesto is nonsense – as I am sure he would be only too happy, in private, to admit ... Yes, it is bilge; but that is not the point. Who cares what he really means or what he really thinks?[43]

Again, another busy individual who may not have troubled to read the book.

From the moral summit of Murdoch's equivalent of Mount Doom, David Aaronovitch of *The Times* declared Brand's book 'uniquely worthless both as an exercise in writing and as a manifesto for social change – I feel able to dismiss Brand's new self-ascriptions, both as self-taught man and revolutionary.'[44]

This was simply false. In fact, in identifying the fundamental disaster of a corporate system subordinating people and planet to profit, Brand's analysis has great merit – he is simply right about the most important crisis of our time.

Tanya Gold commented in the *Guardian*:

His narcissism is not strange: he is a comic by trade, and is used to drooling rooms of strangers.[45]

Also in the *Guardian*, Martin Kettle dismissed 'the juvenile culture of Russell Brand's narcissistic anti-politics'.[46]

Hard-right 'leftist' warmonger Nick Cohen of the 'left-of-centre' hard-right *Observer* was naturally appalled:

Brand is a religious narcissist, and if the British left falls for him, it will show itself to be beyond saving.[47]

Similarly, Cohen took the cheap shot of casually lampooning Brand's 'cranky' focus on meditation:

Comrades, I am sure I do not need to tell you that no figure in the history of the left has seen Buddhism as a force for human emancipation.

We tweeted in reply:

@NickCohen4 'no figure in the history of the left has seen Buddhism as a force for human emancipation'. Erich Fromm, for one.[48]

Cohen was so unimpressed by this response that he instantly blocked us on Twitter.

As with Assange, snorts of derisive laughter were heard across the 'spectrum'. For Peter Hitchens in the *Daily Mail*, Brand was a 'Pied piper who peddles poison' – the poison of concern for gross inequality, for the destruction of the environment, for the benefits of meditation and other vile toxins.[49]

In the same paper, Stephen Glover performed the party trick of snorting as he guffawed:

Why does anyone take this clown of a poseur seriously? ... Russell Brand is a ludicrous charlatan, a 'narcissistic hero'.[50]

Another *Daily Mail* altruist, Max Hastings, also perceived gross egotism at play:

Mr Brand is a strutting narcissist, who, despite having no idea what he is talking about ...[51]

In the *Sunday Times*, Katie Glass described Brand as 'an exhibitionistic narcissist obsessed with celebrity'.[52]

Joan Smith of the *Independent* wrote of Brand under the title, 'Spare us the vacuous talk and go back to Hollywood':

I don't think you would have to be a passionate feminist to conclude that this guy is (a) a sexist idiot and (b) a narcissist ....[53]

We have provided many examples (and there are many more!) to emphasise just how intense corporate media opposition was right across the media 'spectrum'. In a world being observably trashed by unconstrained corporate greed, the 'free press' directed a tsunami of scorn at a rational, clearly well-intentioned and completely non-violent voice trying to draw attention to the facts. This indicates the staggering toxicity and irrationality of the 'mainstream' press. As with Assange and Corbyn, the aim was to portray Brand as so ridiculous, so pitiable, that the public would feel ashamed to be associated with his name and cause in any way.

Mark Steel made the point in a rare defence of Brand in the *Independent*:

This week, by law, I have to deride Russell Brand as a self-obsessed, annoying idiot. No article or comment on Twitter can legally be written now unless it does this ...[54]

Intermission: Who Are You Calling a Narcissist?

Above all, Brand, like Julian Assange, is reviled as an insufferable 'narcissist'. Interestingly, by happy coincidence, it turns out that *anyone* who challenges the status quo is a 'narcissist'. *Bloomberg Businessweek* featured an article entitled, 'The unbearable narcissism of Edward Snowden'.[55] In the *New Yorker*, Jeffrey Toobin condemned Snowden as 'a grandiose narcissist'.[56] And in the *Guardian*, Harold Evans also condemned 'the narcissistic Edward Snowden'.[57]

As we have already seen, Jeremy Corbyn is afflicted by a range of personality disorders. In 2016, Labour MP Chris Evans noted Corbyn's 'self-indulgence, egotism, arrogance and narcissism'.[58] Corbyn naturally acts as a magnet to fellow-sufferers. In 2015, Jonathan Freedland noted in the *Guardian* 'that support for Corbynism, especially among the young, is a form of narcissism'.[59] In the *Daily Mail*, Dominic Sandbrook wrote of Corbyn's press spokesman, Seumas Milne, formerly of the *Guardian*:

> In his malignancy, mendacity and hypocrisy, in his narcissism and anti-patriotism, he is betraying not only the history of the Labour Party but the basic values of this country...[60]

Janice Turner noted of Corbyn in *The Times*:

> He's beloved of narcissists and conspiracists, such as Julian Assange, George Galloway, John Pilger and Ken Livingstone ...[61]

Readers will not be surprised to learn of the motive behind our own political activism. The *Guardian's* (then) Associate Editor, Michael White, noted that Media Lens 'betrays the narcissism of small difference that is so destructive on the left'.[62]

Dear reader, given that you are reading this book, you might like to take a long, hard (not too self-admiring!) look in the mirror. For as Gavin Esler, (then) BBC 'Newsnight' presenter, commented:

The reason no one takes media lens seriously is not the substance of your complaints. It is the robotic, identikit, narcissistic manner in which they are expressed.[63]

In 2016, the BBC's New York correspondent, Nick Bryant, commented on the US presidential election:

I have tried to learn more about narcissistic personality disorder. Many commentators from both sides believe having a basic grasp of the condition was important in making sense of the behaviour of Donald Trump.[64]

Okay, we agree, here the BBC had a point! But the comment served to indicate just how completely Trump is judged to be beyond the corporate media's pale of 'respectability'. The charge could be made of any number of previous US and UK leaders – think Clinton, Bush, Blair – but would ordinarily be deemed an unforgivable, unprofessional slur.

Hugo Chávez:
'Dictator', 'Showman', Purveyor of 'Narcissistic Populism'

Following the death of Venezuelan president Hugo Chávez on 5 March 2013, Craig Murray, former British Ambassador to Uzbekistan, commented:

He applied the huge increase in revenues to massively successful poverty alleviation via social programmes, housing and education.

The western states of course do everything to stop developing countries doing this, on behalf of the multinationals who control the politicians. They threaten (and I am an eye-witness) aid cancellation, disinvestment and trade sanctions. They work to make you a political pariah (just watch the media on Chávez today). They secretly sponsor, bankroll and train your opponents. The death of such 'dangerous' leaders is a good outcome for them, as in Allende or Lumumba.

Chávez faced them down. There are millions of people in Venezuela whose hard lives are a bit better and have hope for the future because of Chávez. There are billionaires in London and New York who have a few hundred million less each because of Chávez. Nobody can deny the truth of both those statements.[65]

American economist Mark Weisbrot observed that:

... once [Chávez] got control of the oil industry, his government reduced poverty by half and extreme poverty by 70 per cent.

Millions of people also got access to health care for the first time, and access to education also increased sharply, with college enrolment doubling and free tuition for many. Eligibility for public pensions tripled.

He kept his campaign promise to share the country's oil wealth with Venezuela's majority, and that will be part of his legacy.[66]

By contrast, *Guardian* Assistant Editor, Martin Kettle – who, as we have seen, cannot stand narcissists like Corbyn or Brand – wrote: 'it is a mistake to concentrate on Chávez's strutting and narcissistic populism to the exclusion of all the other aspects of his presidency. And it is even wrong to judge him solely as an abuser of human rights, a hoarder of power, an intimidator of opponents and a rejecter of international covenants and critics.'[67]

Compare the tone and content with the *Guardian*'s obituary of the tyrant Saudi Crown Prince Sultan bin Abdul-Aziz from 2011:

Sultan had a reputation for a fierce temper but his habit of working deep into the night won him the nickname of 'bulbul' – nightingale. He was both a conservative and political moderate. 'Sultan,' wrote Holden, 'whose vigour on the couch [he had 32 children by 10 wives] was a cause for even more concern and respect, had proved a stern, tough and headstrong character.'[68]

Without irony, the BBC's John Sweeney commented of Venezuela:

The country should be a Saudi Arabia by the sea; instead the oil money has been pissed away by foolish adventurism and unchecked corruption.[69]

In other words, the country should be a barbaric, head-chopping, warmongering, mysogynistic tyranny by the sea. As ever, 'our' allies can be forgiven their sins by 'independent' journalists.

In the *Guardian*, Simon Tisdall wrote under the gracious title: 'Death of Hugo Chávez brings chance of fresh start for US and Latin America.'[70] Apparently with a straight face, Tisdall lamented 'Washington's historical neglect of Latin America'. The *Independent* reported: 'The death of one of Latin America's most egotistical, bombastic and polarising leaders.'[71]

Was Chávez, with all his 'strutting and narcissistic populism', more 'egotistical' and 'polarising' than Bush, Blair, Obama, Cameron, or indeed Sultan bin Abdul-Aziz? Are the West's 'good guys' ever described this way in news reports? Did Chávez invade and destroy whole countries like Iraq and Libya on false pretexts?

The BBC spoke of 'Venezuela's charismatic and controversial president'.[72] Although Bush, Blair, Cameron *et al.* are no strangers to controversy, it is impossible to imagine the BBC writing of 'America's controversial president, Barack Obama'. For the BBC, it simply does not register as in any way controversial that Obama bombed seven Muslim countries. That's just what US presidents do.

For the *Telegraph*, Chávez was 'one of the region's most popular, yet divisive leaders'.[73] For the *Guardian*, he was 'the much-loved, but also divisive, leader'.[74] For the *Independent's* David Usborne, he was 'divisive in his political life'.[75]

An *Independent* leader noted that 'one of the world's more colourful, charismatic and divisive political leaders passes into history'.[76] The *Independent* editorial's headline read: 'Hugo Chávez – an era of grand political illusion comes to an end.' It opined:

> Mr Chávez was no run-of-the-mill dictator. His offences were far from the excesses of a Colonel Gaddafi, say. What he was, more than anything, was an illusionist – a showman who used his prodigious powers of persuasion to present a corrupt autocracy

fuelled by petrodollars as a socialist utopia in the making. The show now over, he leaves a hollowed-out country crippled by poverty, violence and crime. So much for the revolution.

For the Russian oligarch-owned, advert-dependent *Independent*, then, Chávez – who won 15 democratic elections,[77] including four presidential elections – *was* a 'dictator'.

For *The Economist*, Chávez was 'as reckless with his health as with his country's economy and its democracy ... A majority of Venezuelans may eventually come to see that Mr Chávez squandered an extraordinary opportunity for his country.'[78]

Perhaps the millions of people who mourned his death will one day see the sense in the corporate propaganda issuing out of London and Washington.

4

Israel and Palestine: 'We Wait in Fear for the Phone Call from the Israelis'

If you don't understand media coverage of Israel and Palestine, it's for a reason: the truth is so horrific, so embarrassing to Britain and the US – and indeed to Israel, a key ally – that it has to be obfuscated, hidden, buried out of sight. Ignorance, after all, is strength.

In 2009, we challenged the BBC's Middle East Editor Jeremy Bowen about the BBC's long record of biased reporting on these issues. He responded: 'we have reported the facts about Israel's occupation many times, and we will do so again.'[1]

But they haven't; this is simply untrue. Unknown to most of the British public, huge numbers of Palestinians were massacred and forced from their land when the state of Israel was established in 1948. The Israeli historian Ilan Pappé described the reality in a superb and shocking book, *The Ethnic Cleansing of Palestine*.[2] By contrast, BBC viewers and listeners have never heard Bowen or the BBC report on Israel's 'ethnic cleansing of Palestine' in the process of setting up its state. But the facts are clear enough.

Pappé noted that more than half of Palestine's native population, close to 800,000 people, were uprooted, with 531 villages destroyed. This was conducted by the military forces of what was to become Israel in an operation called 'Plan Dalet'. The aim was to ethnically cleanse a large part of Palestine of hostile 'Arab elements'. Numerous terrible massacres occurred in Deir Yassin, Ayn Al-Zaytun, Tantura and elsewhere.

In 1948, David Ben-Gurion, Israel's first prime minister, asserted:

> We must use terror, assassination, intimidation, land confisca-
> tion, and the cutting of all social services to rid the Galilee of its
> Arab population.[3]

Avi Shlaim, another Israeli historian who has thoroughly investigated this period, writes:

> The novelty and audacity of the plan lay in the orders to capture
> Arab villages and cities, something [Jewish forces] had never
> attempted before ... Palestinian society disintegrated under
> the impact of the Jewish military offensive that got underway
> in April, and the exodus of the Palestinians was set in motion
> ... by ordering the capture of Arab cities and the destruction of
> villages, it both permitted and justified the forcible expulsion of
> Arab civilians.[4]

The Palestinians were forced to live as refugees in Lebanon,
Syria, Jordan, on the West Bank of the Jordan River, and the Gaza
Strip. A series of conflicts and, at times, outright war followed
between Israel and its Arab neighbours. During the 1967 Six-Day
War, Israel occupied the West Bank and East Jerusalem (previously
under Jordanian control), the Gaza Strip and the Sinai peninsula
(Egypt), and the Golan Heights (Syria). This occupation brought
many Palestinian refugees under Israeli military control. Jerusalem, a religious centre for Muslims, Jews and Christians, became
a major centre of conflict. The Israelis also built illegal settlements in the newly occupied areas of Gaza and the West Bank,
and exploited natural resources, in particular taking control of vital
water resources.

Shlaim observes that these settlements were part of a systematic
policy intended to exert strategic and military control, which in
this case involved 'surrounding the huge Greater Jerusalem area
with two concentric circles of settlements with access roads and
military positions'.[5]

If much of the above is news to you, it is because it has *not* been
news for the 'mainstream' media, which have kept the public in
ignorance about such central facts – as the Glasgow University
Media Group (GUMG) has documented repeatedly. In their 2004

book, *Bad News From Israel*, Greg Philo and Mike Berry of GUMG summarised their audience study, which investigated public understanding of media reporting on the Middle East:

> The lack of historical knowledge made it very difficult for people to understand key elements of the conflict. For example, some [television viewers] had written that 'land' was an issue but there was a great deal of confusion over what this meant. Another participant described how his understanding included no sense of the Palestinian case that land had been taken from them.[6]

In 2011, Philo and Berry published an updated and even more extensive book, *More Bad News From Israel*.[7] In the largest study of its kind ever undertaken, the authors illustrated major biases in the way Palestinians and Israelis are represented in the media, including how casualties, and the motives and rationale of the different parties involved, are depicted.

In follow-up interviews with viewers and listeners, the book also revealed the extraordinary differences in levels of public knowledge and understanding of the issues. It was significant that the opinions of those interviewed, and their gaps in understanding, often reflected the propaganda generated by Israel and its supporters in the West. Indeed, the book exposed the 'success of the Israelis in establishing key elements of their perspective and the effect of these being relayed uncritically in media accounts'.

'The most striking feature of the news texts', wrote Philo and Berry, 'is the dominance of the Israeli perspective, in relation to the causes of the conflict.'[8] Specifically, they noted that the constantly repeated Israeli stress on 'ending the rockets' (fired from the Gaza Strip by Hamas into neighbouring Israel), the 'need for [Israel's] security' and the claimed objective of 'stopping the smuggling of weapons' (by Hamas into Gaza) were given prominence by the BBC. Other Israeli propaganda messages, such as the need to 'hit Hamas', and that 'Hamas and terrorists are to blame' for the conflict, were likewise promoted by BBC News.[9]

As for the BBC's 'explanations' of the Palestinian perspective, they lacked substance, according to Philo and Berry: 'the bulk of the Palestinian accounts do not explain their case beyond saying that they will resist.' What was almost non-existent were crucial facts that are utterly central to the Palestinian viewpoint: about 'how the continuing existence of the [Israeli] blockade [of Gaza] affects the rationale for Palestinian action and how they see their struggle against Israel and its continuing military occupation'.[10]

In classic academic understatement, Philo and Berry concluded:

> It is difficult in the face of this to see how the BBC can sustain a claim to be offering balanced reporting.[11]

Tim Llewellyn, a former BBC Middle East correspondent, backed up Philo and Berry's careful analysis, arguing that BBC coverage of Israel and Palestine 'is replete with imbalance and distortion'. He pointed to his ex-employer's

> continuing inability to describe in a just and contextualised way the conflict between military occupier and militarily occupied. There is no attempt to properly convey cause and effect, to report the misery, violence and pillage that demean and deny freedom to the Palestinians and provoke their (limited) actions.[12]

Why is pro-Israel media bias so prevalent? The beginnings of an explanation lie in the words of one senior BBC editor who told Philo:[13]

> We wait in fear for the phone call from the Israelis.

The taboo fact is that intense pressure is brought to bear on the media by the powerful pro-Israel lobby. This helps to keep British politics, including media coverage, within 'acceptable' bounds. In 2009, Channel 4 broadcast a documentary entitled 'Inside Britain's Israel Lobby' by the political journalist Peter Oborne, who observed:[14]

> Despite wielding great influence among the highest realms of British politics and media, little is known about the individuals and groups which collectively are known as the pro-Israel lobby.

In a pamphlet accompanying the documentary, Oborne and film-maker James Jones noted that:[15]

> Making criticisms of Israel can give rise to accusations of anti-semitism – a charge which any decent or reasonable person would assiduously seek to avoid. Furthermore most British newspaper groups – for example News International, *Telegraph* newspapers and the Express Group – have tended to take a pro-Israel line and have not always been an hospitable environment for those taking a critical look at Israeli foreign policy and influence. Finally, media critics of Israeli foreign policy – as we will vividly demonstrate in this pamphlet – can open themselves up to coordinated campaigns and denunciation.

Whether as a result of these pressures or for some other reason, 'mainstream' political publishing in Britain tends simply to ignore Israeli influence. Andrew Marr's *Ruling Britannia: The Failure and Future of British Democracy* contains not a single mention of either Israel or the Israel lobby. Nor does Alan Clark's *The Tories*, or Robert Blake's *The Conservative Party from Peel to Major*.

The fake 'impartiality' of BBC News is summed up by the example of James Harding, Director of News and Current Affairs at the BBC from 2013–17. As editor of *The Times* under Rupert Murdoch, he had candidly declared: 'I am pro-Israel.' He added that in reporting on the Middle East, 'I haven't found it too hard' because '*The Times* has been pro-Israel for a long time.'[16]

'The Key Feature of the Occupation Has Always Been Humiliation'

One of the central, but missing, facts of the Israel-Palestine 'conflict' is that the Palestinians are seen as an obstacle by Israel's leaders; an irritant to be subjugated. Noam Chomsky observes:

> Traditionally over the years, Israel has sought to crush any resistance to its programs of takeover of the parts of Palestine it regards as valuable, while eliminating any hope for the indigenous population to have a decent existence enjoying national rights.[17]

Moreover:

> The key feature of the occupation has always been humilia-
> tion: they [the Palestinians] must not be allowed to raise their
> heads. The basic principle, often openly expressed, is that the
> 'Araboushim' – a term that belongs with 'nigger' or 'kike' – must
> understand who rules this land and who walks in it with head
> lowered and eyes averted.[18]

Hamas has repeatedly declared its readiness to negotiate a
long-term ceasefire with the Jewish state within its pre-1967
borders. Indeed, as we were writing this chapter, Hamas leader
Hassan Yousif reiterated the offer.[19] But Israel has repeatedly
rejected the offer, just as it rejected a peace plan proposed by the
Arab League in 2002; and just as it has always rejected the international consensus for a peaceful solution in the Middle East. Why?
Because the threat of such 'peace offensives' would involve unac-
ceptable concessions and compromises. The well-known Israeli
writer Amos Elon has written of the 'panic and unease among our
political leadership' caused by Arab peace proposals.[20]

Thus, the hidden backstory, ignored by the Western media, is
that Israel is trying to terrorise the Palestinians into accepting a
process of ethnic cleansing as their land and resources are stolen.
This Israeli grab for land and resources cannot be conducted under
conditions of peace. It requires perpetual war; a phoney, one-sided
'war' dominated by Israel's perennial trump card: high-tech
military power supplied by that eternal 'peace broker', the United
States.

Chomsky spelt it out in a January 2009 article, 'Exterminate all
the Brutes', as Israel pulverised Gaza in a huge military operation
it called 'Operation Cast Lead'. Chomsky commented on Israel's
attack:

> The planning had two components: military and propaganda.
> It was based on the lessons of Israel's 2006 invasion of Lebanon,
> which was considered to be poorly planned and badly advertised.
> We may, therefore, be fairly confident that most of what has been
> done and said was pre-planned and intended.[21]

He continued:

> That surely includes the timing of the assault: shortly before noon, when children were returning from school and crowds were milling in the streets of densely populated Gaza City. It took only a few minutes to kill over 225 people and wound 700, an auspicious opening to the mass slaughter of defenseless civilians trapped in a tiny cage with nowhere to flee.

Chomsky was suggesting that Israeli leaders had actually *intended* to kill large numbers of Palestinian civilians for reasons which, from their perspective, were entirely rational. In support of this claim, Chomsky quoted an article by the *New York Times* correspondent Ethan Bronner, 'Parsing gains of Gaza War'. Bronner argued that Israel calculated that it would be advantageous to appear to 'go crazy', by causing massive destruction:

> The Israeli theory of what it tried to do here is summed up in a Hebrew phrase heard across Israel and throughout the military in the past weeks: '*baal habayit hishtageya*', or 'the boss has lost it.' It evokes the image of a madman who cannot be controlled.[22]

The tactic of 'going crazy' appears to have been successful, Bronner concluded, with 'limited indications that the people of Gaza felt such pain from this war that they will seek to rein in Hamas'.

This is the 'mad man' theory of international relations in action. In a key document from 1995, the US Strategic Command (STRATCOM) advised that American planners should not portray themselves 'as too fully rational and cool-headed'. Instead, the impression that the US 'may become irrational and vindictive if its vital interests are attacked should be a part of the national persona we project'. It is 'beneficial' for our strategic posture if 'some elements may appear to be potentially "out of control"'.[23]

Similarly, Chomsky has argued that the 1982 Israeli attack on Lebanon had nothing to do with responding to 'intolerable acts of terror', as claimed at the time. Instead, it had to do with 'intolerable acts: of diplomacy'. Shortly after Israel's invasion of Lebanon began, Yehoshua Porath, Israel's leading academic specialist on the

Palestinians, wrote that PLO leader Yasser Arafat's success in maintaining a ceasefire represented 'a veritable catastrophe in the eyes of the Israeli government', since it opened the way to a political settlement. The government hoped that the PLO would resort to terrorism, undermining the threat that it would be 'a legitimate negotiating partner for future political accommodations'.[24]

Israel's then Prime Minister Yitzhak Shamir stated that Israel went to war because there was 'a terrible danger ... Not so much a military one as a political one.' Israeli historian Benny Morris recognised that the PLO had observed the ceasefire, and explained that 'the war's inevitability rested on the PLO as a political threat to Israel and to Israel's hold on the occupied territories.'[25]

Likewise, Chomsky noted that when Israel broke a four-month ceasefire in November 2008, killing six Palestinians, it came at a significant time. The attack came shortly before a key meeting in Cairo when Hamas and its political rival Fatah were to hold talks on 'reconciling their differences and creating a single, unified government', reported the *Guardian*. It would have been the first meeting at such a high level since the near Palestinian civil war of 2007.[26]

The meeting, Chomsky said, 'would have been a significant step towards advancing diplomatic efforts. There is a long history of Israel provocations to deter the threat of diplomacy, some already mentioned. This may have been another one.'[27]

The attack also came on the day of the 2008 US presidential election, won by Barack Obama. Israeli leaders knew the world would be focusing elsewhere. This would help obscure the fact that Israel, not Hamas, had broken the ceasefire. It would also help provide a rationale for the slaughter planned for later in the month and clearly timed to end just before Obama's inauguration.

Chomsky summarised the appalling truth:

The effort to delay political accommodation has always made perfect sense ... It is hard to think of another way to take over land where you are not wanted.

The reality underpinning Israeli policy is summed up by the title of former *Guardian* journalist Jonathan Cook's book, *Disappearing*

Palestine: Israel's Experiments in Human Despair. Behind 'a mask of false legitimacy', Israel 'has carried out the destruction of Palestinian identity and living space and the theft of resources'.[28]

Cook argues that Israel's real intention is to replicate the apartheid model of South Africa; to transform Palestinian cities into Bantustans in a sea of Israeli-dominated territory, leaving Israeli settlers in possession of the arable land and vital water resources. He warns:

> The apartheid model is unlikely to be the end of the story, however ... Another solution – transfer – will be needed. The Israeli public is already being softened up, with government ministers openly subscribing to it. Palestinians will have to be encouraged, or made, to leave their homes and land.[29]

This is, in essence, the continuation of Plan Dalet's ethnic cleansing from the 1948 founding of Israel. In 1998, Ariel Sharon, who became Israel's prime minister in 2001, stated bluntly:

> It is the duty of Israeli leaders to explain to public opinion, clearly and courageously, a certain number of facts that are forgotten with time. The first of these is that there is no Zionism, colonization or Jewish state without the eviction of the Arabs and the expropriation of their lands.[30]

On 24 May 2006, Israeli Prime Minister Ehud Olmert told a joint session of congress that 'I believed and to this day still believe, in our people's eternal and historic right to this entire land'.[31]

Disturbingly, up to 60 per cent of Israeli Jews support schemes to encourage or force Arabs to leave both the occupied territories and Israel.[32]

Virtually all of the above is buried or omitted by BBC News and the rest of the corporate media. This is the truth that contradicts Jeremy Bowen's assertion that 'we have reported the facts about Israel's occupation many times, and we will do so again.'

No 'Responsibility to Protect' When Israel Attacks Palestinians

The brutality of Israel's treatment of Palestinians was evident once again during the eight-day 'Operation Pillar of Defence' in

November 2012. The Israeli Deputy Prime Minister Eli Yishai apparently promised a massacre:

> We must blow Gaza back to the Middle Ages destroying all the infrastructure including roads and water.[33]

A prominent front-page article in the *Jerusalem Post* by Gilad Sharon, son of the former Israeli Prime Minister, Ariel Sharon, openly advocated mass killing:

> We need to flatten entire neighborhoods in Gaza. Flatten all of Gaza. The Americans didn't stop with Hiroshima – the Japanese weren't surrendering fast enough, so they hit Nagasaki, too.
>
> There should be no electricity in Gaza, no gasoline or moving vehicles, nothing. Then they'd really call for a ceasefire.[34]

One week into Israel's military operation, on a day when 13 Palestinians were killed – with more than 136 people in Gaza killed by that point in 1,500 attacks since the operation began on 14 November – 28 people were injured in a Tel Aviv bomb attack.[35] ITV News International Editor Bill Neely ran the headlines: 'Tel Aviv bus bomb is first terror attack there in 6 years.'[36] And: 'Israeli Police confirm terror attack.'[37]

We wrote to Neely: 'Bill, are the attacks on Gaza "terror attacks"? Have you described them as such?'[38]

Neely replied: 'Media Lens; Love what U try 2 do – keep us all honest – but pedantry & refusing 2 C balance hs always bn ure weakness.'[39]

He wrote to us again in another tweet: 'U & Media Lens R absolutely right. Language is v. important. But a bomb on a bus, like a missile, is terror weapon.'[40]

Neely clearly agreed that missiles were also weapons of terror. So we asked him: 'Bill, agreed. Given that's the case have you ever referred to Israel's "terror attacks" in a TV news report?'[41]

The ITV News journalist responded: 'Just to be clear, do you think British bombs on Afghanistan are terrorism? Or on Berlin in 44?'[42]

We answered: 'Very obviously. Winston Churchill thought so, too.'[43]

We sent[44] Neely a note written by Churchill to Arthur Harris, Commander-in-Chief of RAF's Bomber Command in 1945:

It seems to me that the moment has come that the bombing of German cities simply for the sake of increasing the terror, though under other pretexts, should be reviewed.[45]

Neely wrote back: 'States use terror – the UK has in war, but groups do 2 & we shd say so.'[46]

We tried again: 'Bill, you're not answering. You've described Hamas attacks as "terror" on TV. How about Israeli, US, UK attacks?'[47]

Neely wouldn't answer our question. But how could he? The truth, of course, is that ITV News, like BBC News, would never refer to these as 'terror attacks'. Words like 'terror', 'terrorism', 'militant', 'regime', 'secretive', 'hermit' and 'controversial' are used to describe the governments of official enemies, not the UK government and its leading allies.

Consider, too, the media's reporting of the next massive Israeli attack on Gaza, billed by Israel as 'Operation Protective Edge', which began less than two years later, in 2014. The Israeli pretext for this was the kidnapping and brutal killing of three Israeli teenagers in the occupied West Bank. Israeli leader Benjamin Netanyahu accused Hamas of the murders – a charge they denied – and vowed a tough response.[48]

On 8 July 2014, Israeli armed forces began bombarding the trapped civilian population of Gaza with airstrikes, drone strikes and naval shelling. Remarkably, as the massive Israeli assault intensified, the World section of the BBC News website had this as its headline:

Israel under renewed Hamas attack.[49]

By 18 July 2014, around 300 people had been killed in Gaza, 80 per cent of them civilians. The Israeli-Palestinian conflict is, of course, a key political issue of our time, one that was clearly developing rapidly after 8 July. And yet at no point had the BBC set up a live feed with rolling news.

That finally changed on 20 July 2014, after many days in which so many Palestinians had been killed. Why 20 July? The answer was apparently to be found in the fourth entry of the live feed under the title 'Breaking News':

> Some 13 Israeli soldiers were killed overnight in Gaza, news agencies, quoting Israeli military sources, say. Israeli Prime Minister Benjamin Netanyahu is expected to address the nation shortly.[50]

Despite this small number of military deaths compared to the Palestinian toll, it seems that *the killing of the Israeli troops* triggered the BBC live feed. It focused intensely on these deaths, with entries of this kind:

> Ben White, writer tweets: Israel has lost more soldiers in a 3 day old ground offensive than it did during Cast Lead & Pillar of Defense combined.

And:

> View to the Mid East, a writer in Ashdod, Israel tweets: One of the soldiers who was killed in Gaza tonight prays at the same synagogue I go to. Grew up in the same neighbourhood.

The feed incorporated five photographs from two funerals of the Israeli soldiers, but none from the far more numerous Palestinian funerals (one picture showed Palestinian relatives collecting a body from a morgue), with these captions:

> Friends and relatives of Israeli Sergeant Adar Barsano mourn during his funeral at the military cemetery in the northern Israeli city of Nahariya.

And:

> Sagit Greenberg, the wife of Israeli soldier Maj Amotz Greenberg, mourns during his funeral in the central town of Hod Hasharon.

Obviously, Israeli suffering merits compassion. But these military deaths were overshadowed by a far higher loss of Palestinian lives, most of them civilian men, women and children.[51]

For some time on the morning of 21 July 2014, the sole Gaza content on the BBC News home page was 'Breaking News' of an 'Israeli soldier missing in Gaza'.[52]

The level of BBC bias was emphasised by a headline that placed inverted commas around the siege in Gaza, as if it were a matter for debate: 'Palestinian PM says lift Gaza "siege" as part of ceasefire'.[53] The BBC subsequently changed the title, but a tweet promoting the article with the original wording remained and is still visible.[54]

The BBC also implied that 'Rockets fired from Gaza' are comparable to 'Gaza targets hit by Israel'.[55] Readers were to understand that attempted attacks by unguided, low-tech rockets were comparable to attacks by state-of-the-art bombs, missiles and shells. The BBC's source? 'Israel Defence Forces.'

On 21 July 2014, BBC 'News at Ten' presenter Huw Edwards asked a colleague live on air:

> ... the Israelis saying they'll carry on as long as necessary to stop the Hamas rocket attacks. Do you detect any signs at all that there's a hope of a coming together in the next few days or weeks, or not?

In other words, BBC News presented Hamas rocket attacks as the stumbling block to peace, exactly conforming to Israeli state propaganda.

BBC bias was also typified by its downplaying, or complete blanking, of large-scale demonstrations in several UK cities protesting BBC coverage. As activist Jonathon Shafi noted of the BBC's lack of interest:

> It is misinformation of the worst sort, and it is an insult to journalism.[56]

After four Palestinian boys, all cousins aged between 9 and 11, were killed by an Israeli bombardment of the beach in Gaza, the *New York Times* headline on 16 July 2014 read:

Boys Drawn to Gaza Beach, and Into Center of Mideast Strife.[57]

This worked well to obscure the truth that the boys had been killed by Israeli forces while playing football on a beach.

Even indisputable evidence that Israel had fired on hospitals in Gaza – major war crimes – brought little outrage from politicians and media.[58] Jonathan Whittall, Head of Humanitarian Analysis at Médecins Sans Frontières/Doctors Without Borders (MSF), reminded the world:

> Our role is to provide medical care to war casualties and sick detainees, not to repeatedly treat the same patients between torture sessions.[59]

Despite the unequal battle and high civilian death toll, no high-profile advocates of the West's 'responsibility to protect' ('R2P') civilians in Iraq, Libya and Syria called for 'intervention'.[60]

We asked passionate 'R2Pers' like David Aaronovitch,[61] Jonathan Freedland[62] and Menzies Campbell[63] if they felt 'we must do something'. They did not reply. Freedland commented in a BBC interview that the death toll was 'very lopsided';[64] a polite euphemism for a massacre that, according to Unicef, claimed 10 children per day.[65]

'Grievous Censorship' by the Guardian

One of the most stunning examples of capitulation to the fear of offending Israeli sensibilities came in 2014 when the *Guardian* dropped respected journalist Nafeez Ahmed from its roster of regular contributors.

In July 2014, as Israel's brutal massacre of Palestinians in Gaza was underway, Ahmed examined claims that Israel was seeking to create a 'political climate' conducive to the exploitation of Gaza's considerable offshore gas reserves – 1.4 trillion cubic feet of natural gas, valued at $4 billion – which had been discovered off the Gaza coast in 2000.[66]

Ahmed quoted Israeli Defence Minister, Moshe Ya'alon, to the effect that military efforts to 'uproot Hamas' were in part driven by Israel's determination to prevent Palestinians from developing their own energy resources. Ahmed also cited Anais Antreasyan who argued, in the highly-respected University of California's *Journal of Palestine Studies*, that this was part of a wider strategy of:

> separating the Palestinians from their land and natural resources in order to exploit them, and, as a consequence, blocking Palestinian economic development. Despite all formal agreements to the contrary, Israel continues to manage all the natural resources nominally under the jurisdiction of the PA [Palestinian Authority], from land and water to maritime and hydrocarbon resources.

By the end of 2014, Ahmed's piece had received a massive 68,000 social media shares and it was far and away the most popular online *Guardian* article on the Gaza conflict. In the event, however, it was the last article published by him in the *Guardian*. The following day, his valuable *Earth Insight* blog, covering environmental, energy and economic crises, was killed off.

The *Earth Insight* series had accrued around three million views and was the most popular *Guardian* environment blog. Ironically, given that the *Guardian* had just dropped him, Ahmed won a 2015 Project Censored Award for Outstanding Investigative Journalism for a *Guardian* article on Ukraine.[67] He also won a 2014 Project Censored award for his first *Guardian* article, published in 2013, which was about food riots as 'the new normal'.[68] In 2014, Ahmed was included as one of the *Evening Standard*'s 'Power 1000' most globally influential Londoners, in the 'Campaigners: Ecowarriors' section.[69]

Jonathan Cook commented:

> Ahmed is that rare breed of journalist who finds stories everyone else either misses or chooses to overlook; he regularly joins up the dots in a global system of corporate pillage. If the news business were really driven by news rather than a corporate-friendly business agenda, publications would be beating a path to his door.[70]

High praise indeed. At first sight, then, the *Guardian*'s ditching of Nafeez Ahmed was odd, to say the least. Ahmed later published the 'inside story' of how he had been subjected to 'grievous censorship' by the *Guardian*.[71] As a regular and trusted online blogger since April 2013, he had approval to post his pieces direct to the *Guardian* website. Ahmed describes what happened after he uploaded his Gaza piece in July 2014:

> The day after posting it, I received a phone call from James Randerson, assistant national news editor. He sounded riled and rushed. Without beating around the bush, James told me point blank that my *Guardian* blog was to be immediately discontinued. Not because my article was incorrect, factually flawed, or outrageously defamatory. Not because I'd somehow breached journalistic ethics, or violated my contract. No. The Gaza gas piece, he said, was 'not an environment story', and therefore was an 'inappropriate post' for the *Guardian*'s environment website.

Ahmed was 'shocked' and 'more than a little baffled' by this 'over-reaction'. Any concerns could surely be resolved amicably? But Randerson 'refused point blank, instead telling me that my "interests are increasingly about issues that we don't think are a good fit for what we want to see published on the environment site"'.

This was curious indeed because the agreed remit was for Ahmed's column to address 'the geopolitics of environmental, energy and economic crises'. Indeed, when he had first applied to blog for the newspaper, he had submitted a portfolio that included an earlier piece on the link between Israeli military operations and Gaza's gas. However, Ahmed's polite protests fell on deaf ears. Within an hour, he had received an email from the *Guardian* rights manager telling him that his contract had been terminated. And yet, according to Ahmed, he had committed no breach of his contractual obligations with the *Guardian*:

> On the contrary, the *Guardian* had breached its contractual obligation to me regarding my freedom to determine the contents of my blog, simply because it didn't like what I wrote. This is censorship.

This censorship was all the more blatant given the *Guardian*'s publication of Ahmed's June 2014 piece: 'Iraq blowback: Isis rise manufactured by insatiable oil addiction – West's co-optation of Gulf states' jihadists created the neocon's best friend: an Islamist Frankenstein.'[72] Adam Vaughan, the editor of the *Guardian*'s environment website, had approved the piece, telling Ahmed, 'yes – I think it's fine'.

As Ahmed notes ironically:

So an article about ISIS and oil addiction is 'fine', but a piece about Israel, Gaza and conflict over gas resources is not. Really? Are offshore gas resources not part of the environment? Apparently, for the *Guardian*, not in Palestine, where Gaza's environment has been bombed to smithereens by the IDF.

Cook commented on the link between Israeli policy and Gaza's resources:

This story should be at the centre of the coverage of Gaza, and of criticism of the west's interference, including by the UK's own war criminal Tony Blair, who has conspired in the west's plot to deny the people of Gaza their rightful bounty. But the *Guardian*, like other media, have ignored the story.[73]

Cook was scathing about the reasons given by the *Guardian* for Ahmed's dismissal:

the *idea* that an environment blogger for the liberal media should not be examining the connection between control over mineral resources, which are deeply implicated in climate change, and wars, which lead to human deaths and ecological degradation, is preposterous beyond belief.

He concluded:

It is not that Ahmed strayed too far from his environment remit, it is that he strayed too much on to territory – that of the Israel-Palestine conflict – that the *Guardian* rigorously reserves for a few trusted reporters and commentators. Without knowing it, he went where only the carefully vetted are allowed to tread.

5

Libya: 'It is All About Oil'

With the Iraq War, propaganda really came of age. Assisted by corporate media, state propagandists were able to ensure that the entire debate revolved around a central, fake news focus: that Iraq possessed 'weapons of mass destruction', or 'WMD', that might pose a genuine threat to the West.

As intended, the acronym 'WMD' triggered mental (and media) images of mushroom clouds looming over devastated Western cities, although Iraq had never developed nuclear weapons and had only ever had battlefield chemical and biological weapons fired by artillery.

In truth, after 13 years of 'genocidal' sanctions, war, bombing and yet more bombing, Iraq presented as much of a threat to Britain and the US as Iceland. Saddam Hussein had no connections with his sworn enemy, al-Qaeda, had played no part in the 11 September 2001 attacks, and had not used chemical or biological weapons even when his army was being massacred during the 1991 Gulf War. According to Scott Ritter, the UN's chief Weapons Inspector in Iraq between 1991-8, the Iraqi government had allowed UN inspectors to 'fundamentally disarm' the country of '90-95%' of its 'weapons of mass destruction', with any remaining weapons long since reduced to the status of 'useless sludge'.[1]

Any number of UN weapons inspectors and documents could have testified to these facts, but corporate media were not interested. In 2002-3, the Iraqi government gave permission for yet more UN weapons inspections, even though the CIA had infiltrated earlier inspections in an attempt to target and kill Saddam Hussein.

The idea that Iraq offered some kind of threat to the US and Britain, bristling with superpower military hardware, including thousands of nuclear warheads, was an audacious lie. But the 'mainstream' media took it seriously; they made it the framework for discussion.

Anyone reading credible sources beyond the 'mainstream' press could see that the Iraqi leader was trying hard to avoid a war that he knew would very likely end in his own death, with the West desperate to find any excuse to invade and occupy the country. As the Downing Street memo revealed, Bush and Blair were using the UN to create a facade of diplomacy, while privately hoping Saddam would be provoked, would obstruct the UN, and thus provide a *casus belli* for war. Any excuse would do.

The real motive for the war was explained by economist Alan Greenspan, former Chairman of the US Board of Governors of the Federal Reserve, who wrote in his memoir:

I am saddened that it is politically inconvenient to acknowledge what everyone knows: the Iraq war is largely about oil.[2]

Greenspan quickly back-pedalled under a barrage of flak. But the truth of what he said was confirmed even by business reports of this kind from 2010:

More Than 1,000 New Wells at West Qurna 1.

The Exxon-Shell contract to develop the 8.7-billion-barrel West Qurna Phase One project was one of a series that Iraq has signed with international oil companies to develop its vast reserves.

If the projects all turn out as planned, Iraq could quadruple its oil output capacity to Saudi levels of 12 million barrels per day, potentially giving it the billions of cash it needs to rebuild after decades of war, sanctions and neglect.[3]

In December 2016, BP Middle East in Iraq announced: 'Rumaila oilfield achieves 3 billion barrel production landmark'.[4] Achievements include:

Production increased by more than 40% since BP joined partnership to redevelop Rumaila oilfield in 2010

Oil production rate highest in 27 years

Around $200 billion generated for the Iraqi economy.

The results were impressive. As Boris Johnson would say, 'all they have to do is clear the dead bodies away'.[5]

Profits are a common, hidden theme in Western wars. Historian Howard Zinn noted of the Vietnam War:

When I read the hundreds of pages of the Pentagon Papers entrusted to me by [military analyst] Daniel Ellsberg, what jumped out at me were the secret memos from the National Security Council. Explaining the U.S. interest in Southeast Asia, they spoke bluntly of the country's motives as a quest for 'tin, rubber, oil'.[6]

In his memoir, *Collision Course*, John Norris – director of communications for deputy Secretary of State Strobe Talbott during NATO's air assault on Serbia in 1999 – wrote: 'it was Yugoslavia's resistance to the broader trends of political and economic reform – not the plight of Kosovar Albanians – that best explains NATO's war'.[7]

Of course, some of the truth of the Iraq deception – the invented crisis and fraudulent 'diplomacy' – *was* exposed by corporate media. But this filtered truth emerged long after it really mattered, after the powers that be had got the war and 'regime change' they wanted. This made the propaganda campaign on Libya that followed just eight years later, if anything, even more shocking and grotesque.

Libya: From Mythical Mercenaries to Mythical Mass Rape

If the lie at the heart of the Iraq War was 'WMD', the lie at the heart of the Libyan conflict was the threat of a 'massacre' demanding preventative 'humanitarian intervention' by the same powers that had destroyed Iraq.

On 23 February 2011, just days into the Libyan uprising, Amnesty International sparked a propaganda blitz when it began condemning Libyan government actions, noting 'persistent reports of mercenaries being brought in from African countries by the Libyan leader to violently suppress the protests against him.'[8]

A few days later, Human Rights Watch reported that they had 'seen no evidence of mercenaries being used in eastern Libya. This contradicts widespread earlier reports in the international media that African soldiers had been flown in to fight rebels in the region as Muammar Gaddafi sought to keep control.'[9]

Genevieve Garrigos, President of Amnesty International France, later commented:

> Today we have to admit that we have no evidence that Gaddafi employed mercenary forces ... we have no sign nor evidence to corroborate these rumours.[10]

Garrigos repeated that Amnesty's investigators found no 'mercenaries', agreeing that their existence was a 'legend' spread by the mass media.

In his excellent book, *Slouching Towards Sirte*, Maximilian Forte of Concordia University, Montreal, describes 'the revolving door between Amnesty International-USA and the US State [D]epartment'.[11] In November 2011, Amnesty International-USA appointed Suzanne Nossel as its executive director. From August 2009 to November 2011, Nossel had been the US State Department's Deputy Assistant Secretary for the Bureau of International Organization Affairs.

Luis Moreno-Ocampo, Chief Prosecutor of the International Criminal Court, caused more media outrage when he told the world's media that there was 'evidence' that Gaddafi had distributed Viagra to his troops in order 'to enhance the possibility to rape', and that Gaddafi had ordered mass rape. Moreno-Ocampo insisted:

> We are getting information that Qaddafi himself decided to rape ... we have information that there was a policy to rape in Libya those who were against the government.[12]

US Ambassador Susan Rice also asserted that Gaddafi was supplying his troops with Viagra to fuel a campaign of mass rape. No evidence was supplied.

US military and intelligence sources quickly contradicted Rice, telling NBC News that 'there is no evidence that Libyan military forces are being given Viagra and engaging in systematic rape against women in rebel areas.'[13]

Cherif Bassiouni, who led a UN human rights inquiry into the situation in Libya, suggested that the Viagra and mass rape claim was the product of 'massive hysteria'. Bassiouni's team 'uncovered only four alleged cases' of rape and sexual abuse.[14]

The propaganda culminated on 28 March 2011, with President Obama's justification for the 'intervention' that had begun on 19 March:

> If we waited one more day, Benghazi ... could suffer a massacre that would have reverberated across the region and stained the conscience of the world.[15]

As the documentary film-maker Michael Moore had tweeted a week earlier:

> Let's hear from the 'liberals' who say this is a just war because we're protecting innocent Libyans – like that's what we do![16]

Plenty certainly *was* heard from the 'liberals'. At a critical time in February and March 2011, the *Guardian* published a long list of news reports boosting government propaganda and comment pieces advocating 'intervention' on the basis of the West's supposed 'responsibility to protect'. *Guardian* columnist, later Comment Editor (2014–16), Jonathan Freedland, wrote an article entitled: 'Though the risks are very real, the case for intervention remains strong.'[17]

Brian Whitaker, the *Guardian*'s former Middle East Editor, wrote: 'the scale and nature of the Gaddafi regime's actions have impelled the UN's "responsibility to protect". Entitled, 'The difference with Libya', the article contrasted events in Libya with crises in Bahrain and Yemen. The catastrophe in Iraq, that had been created just eight years earlier, was not mentioned.[18]

Under the title, 'Our duty to protect the Libyan people', Menzies Campbell, former leader of the Liberal Democrats, and Philippe Sands, Professor of Law at University College London, wrote in the *Guardian*:

> International law does not require the world to stand by and do nothing as civilians are massacred on the orders of Colonel Gaddafi ...[19]

An *Observer* leader agreed: 'The west can't let Gaddafi destroy his people.' And thus: 'this particular tyranny will not be allowed to stand.'[20]

With tongue no doubt firmly in Wodehousian cheek, as ever, Boris Johnson wrote in the *Telegraph*:

> The cause is noble and right, and we are surely bound by our common humanity to help the people of Benghazi.[21]

David Aaronovitch, haunted[22] by his warmongering on Iraq, wrote an article for *The Times* entitled: 'Go for a no-fly zone over Libya or regret it.' He declaimed:

> If Colonel Gaddafi is permitted to murder hundreds or thousands of his citizens from the air, and we stand by and let it happen, then our inaction will return to haunt us ....[23]

The *New York Times* backed the war: military intervention 'must be used sparingly', an editorial opined, but 'Libya is a specific case.' If Gaddafi was allowed 'to crush the opposition, it would chill pro-democracy movements across the Arab world'.[24]

Vindication: 'A Sort of Moral Glow'

NATO's 'Final Mission Stats' reported that, deploying 260 aircraft and 21 ships, the coalition launched 26,500 sorties destroying 'over 5,900 military targets including over 400 artillery or rocket launchers and over 600 tanks or armored vehicles'.[25]

Recall, this was supposed to be a 'no-fly zone'.

The 'mainstream' press was quick to perceive a famous victory. A *Guardian* leader quietly celebrated:

> But it can now reasonably be said that in narrow military terms it worked, and that politically there was some retrospective justification for its advocates as the crowds poured into the streets of Tripoli to welcome the rebel convoys earlier this week.[26]

As though concluding what was indeed a fairy-tale version of events, Simon Tisdall commented in the *Guardian*:

> The risky western intervention had worked. And Libya was liberated at last.[27]

With touching naivety, an *Observer* editorial entitled, 'An honourable intervention. A hopeful future', commented:

> The motives of Cameron and Sarkozy, as they first ordered their planes into action, seemed more humanitarian and emotional than cynically calculated. There was no urgent reason in realpolitik to oust Gaddafi as winter passed ... No: what sent British jets across the Mediterranean was a perceived need to save lives.[28]

In an article that lauded the 'liberation' of Libya and mocked the sceptics, Chief Political Commentator and Associate Editor, Andrew Rawnsley, wrote in the *Observer*:

> We were told that it would be impossible to get a UN resolution – and one was secured. We were told that Arab support would not stay solid – and, by and large, it did. We were told, as recently as 10 days ago, that the campaign was stuck in a stalemate which exposed the folly of David Cameron and Nicolas Sarkozy in pursuing the enterprise. So much for the wisdom of the conventional.[29]

This was a 'relief' for all 'who hold that democracies sometimes have both the right and the obligation to take up arms against dictators'. And after all, the price had been impressively low:

The number of civilian casualties inflicted by the airstrikes seems to have been mercifully light ... You might call it intervention-lite.'

You might indeed. But then you might also say of Iraq, as Rawnsley did in April 2003:

The war in Iraq would undo Tony Blair, they cried. It would be his Suez on the Tigris, they said. Wrong. It would be Vietnam crossed with Stalingrad. Wrong. To win the war, the Anglo-American forces could only prevail by inflicting casualties numbered in their hundreds of thousands. The more extravagantly doom-laden predictions had the deaths in millions. Wrong.[30]

By August 2011, even Rawnsley had to acknowledge the 'searing experiences of Afghanistan and Iraq', above all the 'horrors of Iraq' with its 'slide into bloody anarchy'. Alas, this revised opinion appeared in the article cited above lauding the 'intervention-lite' 'liberation' of Libya.

Needless to say, Rawnsley has paid no price at all for being wrong in mocking others for misreporting these issues of life and mass death.

The BBC's then Political Editor Nick Robinson observed that Downing Street 'will see this, I'm sure, as a triumphant end'.[31] He waxed Churchillian:

Libya was David Cameron's first war. Col. Gaddafi his first foe. Today, his first real taste of military victory.

The jingoistic bias was bad enough; worse was the presumption that war is a kind of prime-ministerial rite of initiation – they *all* have to face and defeat their first foe and, hopefully, sup from the cup of 'military victory'. Is it really 'mainstream', indeed sane, to present war as *just something prime ministers do*?

The BBC's then Chief Political Correspondent, Norman Smith, declared that Cameron 'must surely feel vindicated'.[32] Translating from the newspeak: 'Cameron surely *has* been vindicated.'

Likewise, the BBC's Ian Pannell, who surmised from Washington that Obama 'is feeling that his foreign policy strategy has been vindicated – that his critics have been proven wrong'.[33] This echoed the infamous comment made by BBC Political Editor Andrew Marr, as Baghdad 'fell' to US tanks on 9 April 2003:

Mr Blair is well aware that all his critics out there in the party and beyond aren't going to thank him – because they're only human – for being right when they've been wrong.[34]

John Humphrys asked from the heart of the impartial, objective BBC:

What, apart from a sort of moral glow ... have we got out of it?[35]

'We' won! Who cared that the whole thing was illegal, that thousands died, that the country had been plunged into chaos? As Harold Pinter said so well in an interview with one of us:

When they said, 'We had to do something', I said: 'Who is this "we" exactly that you're talking about? First of all: *Who is the "we"*? Under what heading do "we" act, under what law? And also, the notion that this "we" has the right to act,' I said, 'presupposes a moral authority of which this "we" possesses not a jot! It doesn't exist!'[36]

Andrew Grice, Political Editor of the *Independent*, declared that Cameron had 'proved the doubters wrong'. Grice added: 'By calling Libya right, Mr Cameron invites a neat contrast with Tony Blair.'[37]

An editorial in the *Telegraph* argued that Gaddafi's death 'vindicates the swift action of David Cameron and Nicolas Sarkozy in halting the attack on Benghazi'.[38]

Telegraph columnist and former editor of the *Spectator* magazine, Matthew d'Ancona (now writing for the *Guardian*), agreed:

It is surely a matter for quiet national pride that an Arab Srebrenica was prevented by a coalition in which Britain played an important part ...[39]

Bitterly ironic now, but also then, d'Ancona's article was headlined: 'Libya is Cameron's chance to exorcise the ghost of Iraq.' As if the blood of one million Iraqi dead could so easily be pacified. In the event, Libya added many more ghosts.

An *Independent* leader observed:

Concern was real enough that a Srebrenica-style massacre could unfold in Benghazi, and the UK Government was right to insist that we would not allow this.[40]

A leader in *The Times* joined the corporate herd in affirming that without 'intervention', there 'would have been a massacre in Benghazi on the scale of Srebrenica'.[41]

The *Guardian* was understanding:

Obama, who made reform and democratisation in the Arab world a key plank of his foreign policy [sic] when he spoke in Cairo in 2009, could not stand by and watch as Gaddafi crushed the uprising.[42]

Another leader in *The Times* hailed 'the West's role as wetnurse to democracy in Libya', as the country slipped ever further into a chaos that, at the time of writing, has continued for seven years. The West, 'having dipped its toe into Libya's affairs' – that is, 26,500 sorties destroying over 5,900 military targets – was ready 'to steer Libya towards stability, democracy, legal freedoms and engagement with the world'.[43]

In reality, the results were summed up by the single fact that, by 2014, 'about 1.8 million Libyans – nearly a third of the country's population' had fled to Tunisia.[44] Civilians were 'driven away by random shelling and shooting, as well as shortages of cash, electricity and fuel', with conditions 'only worsening', the *New York Times* reported.

NATO's 'intervention' had left as many as 1,700 armed gangs fighting over a country in which at least five governments had tried and failed to restore basic order. Djiby Diop, a 20-year-old from Senegal who spent three months amidst the chaos, explained:

Everyone in Libya is armed now. Every guy of my age has a gun. If you don't work for them, they shoot you. If you don't give them all your money, they shoot you. Or they shoot you just for fun. Or they will throw you in prison and you have to pay 400 dinars [£200] to get released.[45]

Or in the words of Flavio Di Giacomo, a spokesman for the International Organisation for Migration:

It's complete anarchy in Libya and it has become very, very dangerous for migrants.[46]

Libyans' annual income had decreased from $12,250 in 2010 to $7,820.28. The United Nations ranked Libya as the world's 94th most advanced country in its 2015 index of human development, down from 53rd place in 2010. In 2016, the UN Office for the Coordination of Humanitarian Affairs estimated that out of a total Libyan population of 6.3 million, 2.4 million people required protection and some form of humanitarian assistance.[47]

One consequence is that thousands of Libyan refugees have risked their lives in rough winter seas trying to reach Italy. The bad weather and small vessels mean the journey, frequently forced at gunpoint, was and is like a death sentence.

This, then, was the corporate media 'spectrum' on the cynical abuse of a UN resolution in the cause of illegally overthrowing the government of an oil-rich state that ended in complete disaster for Libya.

Alas, voices to the left of this 'mainstream' also got Libya badly wrong; most embarrassingly, Professor Juan Cole, who wrote:

The Libya intervention is legal and was necessary to prevent further massacres ... If NATO needs me, I'm there.[48]

Robert Fisk commented in the *Independent* that, had 'Messrs Cameron, Sarkozy and Obama stopped short after they saved Benghazi', disaster could have been avoided.[49]

Ironically, in an article ostensibly challenging the warmongers' hysterical claims, Mehdi Hasan wrote in the *New Statesman*:

The innocent people of Benghazi deserve protection from Gaddafi's murderous wrath.[50]

In May 2017, former BBC and Channel 4 News journalist, Paul Mason, who has reinvented himself as a leftist 'man of the people', wrote in the *Guardian*:

David Cameron was right to take military action to stop Gaddafi massacring his own people during the Libyan uprising of 2011: the action was sanctioned by the UN, proportionate, had no chance of escalating into an occupation. And Cameron and Nicolas Sarkozy had a stabilisation plan.[51]

Even Noam Chomsky has repeatedly claimed:

The no-fly zone prevented a likely massacre ...[52]

As we have already noted in Chapter 1, Sheriff Owen Jones of the *Guardian* repeatedly wished for the removal of Gaddafi, 'dead or alive', as war clouds were gathering and thereafter.[53]

To his credit, John Pilger rubbished the entire case for war, including the claim that Gaddafi was plotting 'genocide' against his people. In May 2011, Pilger declared: 'There is no evidence of this.'[54]

Then *Guardian* columnist Seumas Milne (later Corbyn's director of communications and strategy) also managed to stand against the propaganda blitz. He wrote in October 2011:

But there is in fact no evidence – including from other rebel-held towns Gaddafi re-captured – to suggest he had either the capability or even the intention to carry out such an atrocity against an armed city of 700,000.[55]

As ever, we at Media Lens were damned as 'useful idiots' for challenging media bias in these and other atrocity claims. We were reflexively taking Gaddafi's side based on some primitive sense that 'My enemy's enemy is my friend.'[56] The fact that we held no candle whatever for Gaddafi, and had never expressed a scintilla of support for him, mattered not at all.

'Not Supported by the Available Evidence':
Demolishing the Case for War

The propaganda nature of the *casus belli* for war was thoroughly exposed by a 9 September 2016 report on the war from the Foreign Affairs Committee of the House of Commons:

The evidence base: our assessment:

> Despite his rhetoric, the proposition that Muammar Gaddafi would have ordered the massacre of civilians in Benghazi *was not supported by the available evidence* ... Gaddafi regime forces targeted male combatants in a civil war and did not indiscriminately attack civilians. More widely, Muammar Gaddafi's 40-year record of appalling human rights abuses *did not include large-scale attacks on Libyan civilians* [our emphasis].[57]

And:

> Professor Joffé [Visiting Professor at King's College London] told us that 'the rhetoric that was used was quite blood-curdling, but again there were past examples of the way in which Gaddafi would actually behave ... The evidence is that he was well aware of the insecurity of parts of the country and of the unlikelihood that he could control them through sheer violence. Therefore, he would have been very careful in the actual response ... the fear of the massacre of civilians was vastly overstated.[58]

Analyst and author Alison Pargeter agreed with Professor Joffé, concluding that there was no 'real evidence at that time that Gaddafi was preparing to launch a massacre against his own civilians'. Related claims, that Gaddafi used African mercenaries, launched air strikes on civilians in Benghazi, and employed Viagra-fuelled mass rape as a weapon of war, were also invented.

These were remarkable findings. But according to the ProQuest media database, neither Professor Joffé nor Pargeter was quoted by name in any UK press article covering the report, with only the *Express* and *Independent* noting that 'available evidence' had shown Gaddafi had no record of massacres: a different, less damning, point.[59]

As disturbingly, the report noted:

> We have seen no evidence that the UK Government carried out a proper analysis of the nature of the rebellion in Libya ... It could not verify the actual threat to civilians posed by the Gaddafi regime ....[60]

Professor Alan J. Kuperman, Professor of Public Affairs at the University of Texas, wrote in the *Boston Globe*:

> The best evidence that Khadafy did not plan genocide in Benghazi is that he did not perpetrate it in the other cities he had recaptured either fully or partially – including Zawiya, Misurata, and Ajdabiya, which together have a population greater than Benghazi.
>
> Libyan forces did kill hundreds as they regained control of cities. Collateral damage is inevitable in counter-insurgency. And strict laws of war may have been exceeded.
>
> But Khadafy's acts were a far cry from Rwanda, Darfur, Congo, Bosnia, and other killing fields. Libya's air force, prior to imposition of a UN-authorized no-fly zone, targeted rebel positions, not civilian concentrations. Despite ubiquitous cellphones equipped with cameras and video, there is no graphic evidence of deliberate massacre. Images abound of victims killed or wounded in crossfire – each one a tragedy – but that is urban warfare, not genocide.
>
> Nor did Khadafy ever threaten civilian massacre in Benghazi, as Obama alleged. The 'no mercy' warning, of March 17 [2011], targeted rebels only, as reported by *The New York Times*, which noted that Libya's leader promised amnesty for those 'who throw their weapons away'. Khadafy even offered the rebels an escape route and open border to Egypt, to avoid a fight 'to the bitter end'.[61]

On the other hand, it is clear that NATO's war to overthrow Gaddafi was a war crime. Lord Richards (Baron Richards of Herstmonceux), Chief of the Defence Staff at the time of the conflict, told the BBC that Cameron asked him 'how long it might take to depose, regime change, get rid of Gaddafi'.[62]

British historian Mark Curtis made the obvious point:

> Three weeks after Cameron assured Parliament in March 2011 that the object of the intervention was not regime change, he signed a joint letter with President Obama and French President Sarkozy committing to 'a future without Gaddafi'.

That these policies were illegal is confirmed by Cameron himself. He told Parliament on 21 March 2011 that the UN resolution 'explicitly does not provide legal authority for action to bring about Gaddafi's removal from power by military means'.

'They Ain't Reading WikiLeaks': Oil!

Despite everything they had seen in Iraq, 'mainstream' media *still* preferred to take US-UK claims of 'humanitarian' concern at face value on oil-rich Libya. The *Washington Post*, however, noted in 2011:

Libya has some of the biggest and most proven oil reserves – 43.6 billion barrels – outside Saudi Arabia, and some of the best drilling prospects.[63]

Johann Hari wrote in the *Independent*:

Bill Richardson, the former US energy secretary who served as US ambassador to the UN, is probably right when he says: 'There's another interest, and that's energy ... Libya is among the 10 top oil producers in the world. You can almost say that the gas prices in the US going up have probably happened because of a stoppage of Libyan oil production ... So this is not an insignificant country, and I think our involvement is justified.'[64]

WikiLeaks published a cable sent from the US embassy in Tripoli in November 2007 communicating US concerns about the direction being taken by Libya's leadership:

But those who dominate Libya's political and economic leadership are pursuing increasingly nationalistic policies in the energy sector that could jeopardize efficient exploitation of Libya's extensive oil and gas reserves. Effective U.S. engagement on this issue should take the form of demonstrating the clear downsides to the GOL [government of Libya] of pursuing this approach ...[65]

US journalist Glenn Greenwald asked:

Is there anyone – anywhere – who actually believes that these aren't the driving considerations in why we're waging this war in Libya? After almost three months of fighting and bombing – when we're so far from the original justifications and commitments that they're barely a distant memory – is there anyone who still believes that humanitarian concerns are what brought us and other western powers to the war in Libya? Is there anything more obvious – as the world's oil supplies rapidly diminish – than the fact that our prime objective is to remove Gaddafi and install a regime that is a far more reliable servant to western oil interests, and that protecting civilians was the justifying pretext for this war, not the purpose? [66]

The MPs' report discussed above also made a nonsense of the alleged humanitarian motive, noting:

On 2 April 2011, Sidney Blumenthal, adviser and unofficial intelligence analyst to the then United States Secretary of State Hillary Clinton, reported this conversation with French intelligence officers to the Secretary of State:

'According to these individuals Sarkozy's plans are driven by the following issues:

a. A desire to gain a greater share of Libya oil production,

b. Increase French influence in North Africa,

c. Improve his internal political situation in France,

d. Provide the French military with an opportunity to reassert its position in the world,

e. Address the concern of his advisors over Qaddafi's long term plans to supplant France as the dominant power in Francophone Africa.'[67]

Paul Jay of *Real News* interviewed Kevin G. Hall, the national economics correspondent for McClatchy Newspapers, who had studied the WikiLeaked material on Libya. Hall emphasised 'the degree to which oil is kind of the back story to so much that happens'. He explained:

As a matter of fact, we went through 251,000 [leaked] documents – or we have 250,000 documents that we've been poring through. Of those, a full 10 percent of them, a full 10 percent of those documents, reference in some way, shape, or form oil. And I think that tells you how much part of, you know, the global security question, stability, prosperity – you know, take your choice, *oil is fundamental* [our emphasis].[68]

Jay replied with a wry smile:

And we'll do more of this. But those who had said it's not all about oil, they ain't reading WikiLeaks.

Hall replied: 'It is all about oil.'

In January 2018, *Bloomberg Businessweek* reported:

In another sign the sector is stabilizing, Royal Dutch Shell Plc and BP Plc have agreed to annual deals to buy Libyan crude.

Newly reopened fields would 'increase the North African country's crude output by 57,000 barrels a day', although production remained well below the mouth-watering level of 1.6 million barrels a day reached before NATO's war to oust Gaddafi.[69]

Clinton and Libya; 'Hillary's War'

After Hillary Clinton won the Democratic presidential nomination in June 2016, senior *Guardian* columnist Polly Toynbee commented:

This is a time to celebrate. At last, a woman leads a major US party to fight for the presidency.[70]

Moreover, Clinton 'is a feminist with a long track record of standing up for the right causes'.

So why wasn't everyone as cock-a-hoop as Toynbee herself? The columnist advised readers to check for traces of hidden gender bias:

If you are naturally left of centre, especially if you are a woman, yet you find you instinctively dislike her, ask yourself why.

In the real world, there were plenty of reasons to dislike Clinton that had nothing at all to with gender. Mark Landler noted in the *New York Times* magazine:

> For all their bluster about bombing the Islamic State into oblivion, neither Donald J. Trump nor Senator Ted Cruz of Texas has demonstrated anywhere near the appetite for military engagement abroad that Clinton has.[71]

David Sirota wrote:

> Under Clinton's leadership, the State Department approved $165 billion worth of commercial arms sales to 20 nations whose governments have given money to the Clinton Foundation.[72]

US economist Jeffrey Sachs added:

> There's no doubt that Hillary is the candidate of Wall Street. Even more dangerous, though, is that she is the candidate of the military-industrial complex ... Hillary was ... a staunch supporter of the Iraq War ...[73]

Investigative reporter Gareth Porter wrote of the 'active effort' made 'by the US military to mitigate Obama administration regime change policies'. Notably, in 2011, the Joint Chiefs of Staff 'had been strongly opposed to the effort to depose the Muammar Gaddafi regime in Libya *led by then secretary of state Hillary Clinton*' (our emphasis).[74]

Clinton, then, was *more* hawkish even than the US military on Libya.

Writing in the *Sunday Times*, James Rubin, who was Assistant Secretary of State under Bill Clinton, reminded readers how former Defense Secretary Bob Gates had written that it was Clinton's '"considerable clout" that tipped the balance in favour of action' in Libya.[75]

Mary Riddell noted in the *Telegraph*:

> More hawkish than Mr Obama or the dovelike vice president, Joe Biden, she backed the invasion of Afghanistan, while US action in Libya has been described as 'Hillary's War'.[76]

But this is not all. Sachs added:

> Perhaps the crowning disaster of this long list of disasters has been Hillary's relentless promotion of CIA-led regime change in Syria. Once again Hillary bought into the CIA propaganda that regime change to remove Bashir al-Assad would be quick, costless, and surely successful. In August 2011, Hillary led the US into disaster with her declaration Assad must 'get out of the way', backed by secret CIA operations.
>
> Perhaps more than any other person, Hillary can lay claim to having stoked the violence that stretches from West Africa to Central Asia and that threatens US security.[77]

Despite all of this, and much more besides, author Frank Morgan noted in the *Guardian* that, during the 2016 presidential campaign, pretty much the entire media system depicted Clinton as 'a peerless leader clad in saintly white, a super-lawyer, a caring benefactor of women and children, a warrior for social justice'.[78]

Morgan added:

> With the same arguments repeated over and over, two or three times a day, with nuance and contrary views all deleted, the act of opening the newspaper started to feel like tuning in to a Cold War propaganda station.

No one mentioned how, as US Secretary of State, Clinton had let the mask slip in October 2011, after it emerged that Gaddafi had been beaten, sodomised with a knife and murdered. Moments after receiving the news, Clinton laughed, commenting: 'We came, we saw, he died.'[79]

Professor Maximilian Forte of Canada's Concordia University, observed:

> Ghoulish, chilling, and perverse was this utterly remorseless display of how bloodthirsty US power can be.[80]

In October 2017, *Guardian* columnist Zoe Williams wrote an article entitled, without irony, 'Why does nobody mention that Hillary Clinton is perfectly nice?'[81]

In all the coverage of Clinton's presidential bid recorded in the Lexis newspaper database, we found almost no mention of the destruction of Libya among her 'controversies'.

When we asked *Guardian* commentator Hadley Freeman why, in comparing Trump and Clinton, she mentioned Clinton's email server scandal but not her war crimes, she interpreted this as an endorsement of Trump (the reflexive assumption, as discussed in Chapter 1):

> You're right: the racist, war-endorsing misogynist multiply accused of sexual assault was the better option. Thanks for clarity.[82]

Telegraph columnist Helena Horton dismissed our attempts to discuss Clinton's devastating wars as 'whataboutery':

> your whataboutery is detracting from the fact there is a far-right misogynist racist in the White House.[83]

She added:

> im shocked idiot men who pushed a fascist into power because HRC not perfect enough haven't shut up ...[84] and gosh they're foul aren't they[85]

Comedian Robert Webb of 'Peep Show' fame agreed with Horton, describing us as 'pricks' that he was proud to block on Twitter (although we had never written to him).[86]

Guardian journalists Marina Hyde and Hadley Freeman lampooned[87] us as conspiracy theorists for challenging media bias.[88]

To the evident dismay of both journalists, Pulitzer Prize-winning US journalist Glenn Greenwald entered the fray:

> @medialens Mocking you as conspiracists is how UK journalists demonstrate their in-group coolness to one another: adolescent herd behavior.[89]

Greenwald then offered this damning judgement on the UK press:

@medialens I've never encountered any group more driven by group-think and rank-closing cohesion than British journalists.[90]

He also wrote directly to Hyde:

@MarinaHyde @medialens Why not just engage them? They actually make substantive media critiques few others make, even when they're wrong.[91]

It is difficult to establish when Greenwald thinks we've been 'wrong' in identifying media bias – he never shares, tweets or comments on our media alerts – but even this caveated support was appreciated. (By the way, Greenwald's hands-off approach towards us is interesting given that, in 2012, he wrote to us: 'You are really deeper in the heads of the British establishment-serving commentariat than anyone else – congrats.'[92])

Times columnist David Aaronovitch responded to Greenwald's expression of support for us, reminding him we were 'Kooks', before adding his perception of the likely consequences for Greenwald's reputation: 'Your funeral.'[93] In conclusion, Aaronovitch advised Greenwald: 'One last piece of information. You have signed up alongside the stupidest and most extreme section of the British left. Enjoy.'[94]

But, someone asked, surely Greenwald was aware that Media Lens 'deny Serbian atrocities' (we do not).[95] Did he not agree that these accusations were accurate? Greenwald replied: 'I didn't follow their views on that at the time, but from what I've seen since: false.'[96]

Former *Guardian* journalist, Jonathan Cook, commented:

David Aaronovitch's Twitter comment 'Your funeral' to Glenn Greenwald was exceptionally revealing, didn't you think? Among other things, it suggested not only that he sees the UK liberal media as an exclusive old boys' club – and he's not wrong about that, it seems – but that he regards himself as the president of it. Would that make [the *Observer*'s] Nick Cohen the treasurer, and [the *Observer*'s] Peter Beaumont the receptionist?[97]

6

Syria: Instant Certainty Promoting War

NATO's great war crime in Libya was so disturbing because it came so soon after the war crime in Iraq. And yet, despite that earlier experience – despite everything we knew about how Bush and Blair lied, tricked and hyped their way to war – corporate media were actually *less* willing to challenge Obama and Cameron on Libya. It was as if, with many lessons learned, the corporate media doubled-down on its efforts to do *even worse* next time!

Then came Syria. Media performance was again made even less excusable by the fact that it came *after* Libya and Iraq. Despite these earlier deceptions, in the autumn of 2011, 'mainstream' journalists expressed outrage that a Russian and Chinese veto at the UN had thwarted Western efforts to do yet more 'good' in Syria. Russia and China had rejected the latest draft of a UN Security Council resolution condemning the Syrian government and preparing the way for international sanctions. In the *Guardian*, Middle East Editor Ian Black moved into 'responsibility to protect' mode:

> Bashar al-Assad can certainly feel satisfied that powerful allies have stood by him and prevented international action that might – just – have given him pause for thought as he pursues his vicious crackdown on Syria's protest movement.[1]

This was the standard take across the media 'spectrum' – the Syrian government was responsible for a ruthless repression of peaceful protestors very much on the lines of Egypt, Tunisia, Bahrain and Yemen. There was no doubt, no complexity, nothing to discuss – it just was so. When absolute certainty is declared favouring the agenda of the powerful in this way, we are almost always entering the realm of propaganda.

And yet, Stephen Gowans, author of *Washington's Long War on Syria*, assessed US media coverage on the outbreak of Syria's war:

> A review of press reports in the weeks immediately preceding and following the mid-March 2011 outbreak of riots in Daraa – usually recognized as the beginning of the uprising – offers no indication that Syria was in the grips of a revolutionary distemper, whether anti-neo-liberal or otherwise. On the contrary, reporters representing Time magazine and the *New York Times* referred to the government as having broad support, of critics conceding that Assad was popular, and of Syrians exhibiting little interest in protest. At the same time, they described the unrest as a series of riots involving hundreds, and not thousands or tens of thousands of people, guided by a largely Islamist agenda and exhibiting a violent character.[2]

In 2016, former ABC News Chief Middle East Correspondent, Charles Glass, noted that 'most ostensible experts' on Syria 'are *partis pris*, ill-informed, or both'. Writing for The Intercept website, Glass commented on the historical struggle between the US and Russia for domination in Syria:

> In 2011, the struggle became a war. The U.S. and Russia, as well as local hegemons, backed opposite sides, ensuring a balance of terror that has devastated the country and defies resolution.
>
> The Russians, having lost Aden, Egypt, and Libya years earlier, backed their only client regime in the Arab world when it came under threat. The U.S. gave rhetorical and logistical support to rebels, raising false hopes – as it had done among the Hungarian patriots it left in the lurch in 1956 – that it would intervene with force to help them. Regional allies, namely Saudi Arabia, Qatar, and Turkey, were left to dispatch arms, money, and men, while disagreeing on objectives and strategy.[3]

By contrast, for the *Guardian*'s Ian Black, commenting on the UN veto, the story was far more black and white:

This is bad news for protesters in Syria, where at least 2,700 have been killed since March, and bad news for those who yearn for a UN that can prove effective, if not in tackling all the world's ills at once, then at least in responding to one of its most glaring and urgent injustices.

The chorus of condemnation from western capitals sounded genuine.[4]

After the lies of Serbia, Afghanistan, Iraq and Libya, we were to believe that *this time* the 'humanitarian' concern issuing forth from 'western capitals' was 'genuine'. Below, we will examine three great expressions of Western 'humanitarian' concern in response to three atrocities that took place in Syria, in Houla, Ghouta and Idlib.

Instant Blame: The 2012 Houla Massacre

On 27 May 2012, the massacre of 108 people, including 49 children, two days earlier, in Houla, Syria, dominated the *Independent on Sunday*'s front cover. The banner headline read:

SYRIA: THE WORLD LOOKS THE OTHER WAY. WILL YOU?

The text beneath read:

> There is, of course, supposed to be a ceasefire, which the brutal Assad regime simply ignores. And the international community? It just averts its gaze. Will you do the same? Or will the sickening fate of these innocent children make you very, very angry?[5]

This was the corporate press in classic propaganda blitz mode – dramatic new evidence was eliciting fierce moral outrage that must surely be accepted at face value. This is the kind of response we have most certainly *not* seen in response to UK-backed crimes in Yemen (see Chapter 7), Egypt, Gaza and elsewhere.

Readers, then, knew exactly where to direct their anger – the 'brutal' Syrian 'regime' was immediately declared responsible with great certainty.

Also in the *Independent on Sunday*, David Randall wrote:

> He is the President; she is the First Lady; they are dead children. He governs but doesn't protect; she shops and doesn't care ...

And one hopes that those on the United Nations Security Council, when it reconvenes, will look into the staring eyes of these dead children and remember the hollow words of Assad's wife when she simpered that she 'comforts the families' of her country's victims.[6]

On the 'News at Ten', James Robbins, the BBC's Diplomatic Correspondent, claimed:

The UN now says most victims, including many children, were murdered inside their homes by President Assad's militias.[7]

This is what UN peacekeeping chief Herve Ladsous had actually said that day:

Part of the victims had been killed by artillery shells, now that points ever so clearly to the responsibility of the government. Only the government has heavy weapons, has tanks, has howitzers. But there are also victims from individual weapons, victims from knife wounds and *that of course is less clear* but *probably points the way* to the (pro-Assad) shabbihas, the local militia [our emphasis].[8]

This gave the lie to Robbins' emphatic claim on the BBC's highest profile news programme. We emailed him asking for alternative sources but received no reply.

According to the BBC, even the Russians agreed with the Western view that the Syrian government was wholly to blame. The BBC's Washington correspondent, Jonny Dymond, commented on a UN meeting in response to the massacre:

Going into the meeting, Syria's big-power ally, Russia, made it clear that it needed to be convinced of the Syrian government's culpability for what had happened at Houla. It appears to have been persuaded.[9]

And yet, the *Guardian* reported:

Russia said it is unlikely government forces would have killed civilians at point-blank range and suggested there was a third force – terrorists or external agents – seeking to trigger outside intervention.[10]

A week later, the BBC's World News Editor, Jon Williams, back-pedalled from the BBC's initial reporting. His 7 June blog emphasised 'the complexity of the situation on the ground in Syria, and the need to try to separate fact from fiction'. Williams continued:

> In the aftermath of the massacre at Houla last month, initial reports said some of the 49 children and 34 women killed had their throats cut. In Damascus, western officials told me the subsequent investigation revealed none of those found dead had been killed in such a brutal manner. Moreover, while Syrian forces had shelled the area shortly before the massacre, *the details of exactly who carried out the attacks, how and why were still unclear* … In Houla, and now in Qubair, the finger has been pointed at the shabiha, pro-government militia. But tragic death toll aside, *the facts are few: it's not clear who ordered the killings – or why* [our emphasis].[11]

Williams added: 'stories are never black and white – often shades of grey. Those opposed to President Assad have an agenda. One senior western official went as far as to describe their YouTube communications strategy as "brilliant". But he also likened it to so-called "psy-ops", brainwashing techniques used by the US and other military to convince people of things that may not necessarily be true. A healthy scepticism is one of the essential qualities of any journalist – never more so than in reporting conflict. The stakes are high – all may not always be as it seems.'

This promotion of 'healthy scepticism' was in stark contrast to the media's strident propaganda blitz on Houla.

Williams' comments were reinforced on the same day in a further 'shades of grey' paragraph published by the BBC's reporter Paul Danahar on the BBC website:

> There is a sense in Damascus shared by many diplomats, international officials and those opposed to President Assad that

his regime may no longer have complete and direct day-to-day command and control of some of the militia groups being blamed for massacring civilians. The world has looked at the Syrian conflict in very black and white terms over the past 15 months. It now needs to acknowledge the shades of grey that are emerging.[12]

A report in Germany's leading daily, the *Frankfurter Allgemeine Zeitung* (FAZ), claimed that the Houla massacre had in fact been committed by anti-Assad Sunni militants.[13]

Compare Williams and Danahar with Martin Rowson, who just hours after the massacre, depicted Assad in a cartoon in the *Guardian* with his mouth and face smeared with blood.[14] In the *Independent*, Assad was similarly shown sitting in a bath filled with blood.

We challenged Rowson on Twitter: 'On what actual evidence about the massacre in Houla is your cartoon based?'[15] We were asking what sources Rowson could offer indicating that Syrian forces were responsible, indeed that Assad was himself personally responsible. Rowson replied:

I have no more evidence than media & UN reports, like anyone else. Also used cartoonist's hunch – are you saying I'm wrong?[16]

We asked: 'Would you rely on a "hunch" in depicting Obama and Cameron with mouths smeared with the blood of massacred children?'[17]

Rowson responded: 'Or are you saying I need New Yorker levels of verification for every story I cover? I'm a cartoonist, for fuck's sake ...'[18]

Media Lens: 'But shouldn't a cartoon also be based on fundamentally rational analysis, on credible evidence?'[19]

We repeatedly and politely asked Rowson to supply some of the evidence (links to articles, quotes) that had informed his thinking. We received numerous and varied responses but no mention of evidence. Instead, Rowson erupted:

[Media Lens] has succeeded in riling me. Well done. If I'm proved worng [sic] I'll apologise. Meanwhile, fuck off & annoy someone else.[20]

And: 'No time for this anymore. Sorry. I stand convicted as a cunt. End of ...'[21]

The point we were trying to make to Rowson was that two days after his cartoon appeared, the BBC reported the head of the UN Supervision Mission in Syria, Major General Robert Mood, as saying: 'the circumstances that led to these tragic killings are still unclear.'[22]

Mood commented: 'Whatever I learned on the ground in Syria ... is that I should not jump to conclusions.'[23]

But that is *exactly* what Rowson had done, together with virtually the entire corporate media system. And this, we have to stress again, *after* numerous false massacre claims in Iraq and Libya had been used to fuel warmongering *that resulted in catastrophic 'humanitarian' wars devastating two entire countries.*

On 27 June, a UN Commission of Inquiry delivered its report on the massacre. In considering responsibility, the UN described the three most likely possibilities:

> First, that the perpetrators were Shabbiha or other local militia from neighbouring villages, possibly operating together with, or with the acquiescence of, the Government security forces; second, that the perpetrators were anti-Government forces seeking to escalate the conflict while punishing those that failed to support – or who actively opposed – the rebellion; or third, foreign groups with unknown affiliation.[24]

The report's assessment:

> With the available evidence, the CoI [Commission of Inquiry] could not rule out any of these possibilities.

The UN summarised:

> The CoI is unable to determine the identity of the perpetrators at this time; nevertheless the CoI considers that forces loyal to

the Government may have been responsible for many of the deaths. The investigation will continue until the end of the CoI mandate.

Our search of the LexisNexis media database found just six articles mentioning the UN report in UK national newspapers and their websites, with only five of these mentioning Houla. This was an astonishingly low level of coverage given the massive media attention that had preceded it: LexisNexis recorded 1,017 print and online articles mentioning Houla in all UK newspapers since the massacre on 25 May.[25]

In August of the same year, UN investigators released a further report which stated that it was likely that Syrian troops and shabiha militia were responsible for the massacre, concluding that:

On the basis of available evidence, the commission has *a reasonable basis to believe* that the perpetrators of the deliberate killing of civilians, at both the Abdulrazzak and Al-Sayed family locations, were aligned to the Government [our emphasis].[26]

So, while a UN report in June 'could not rule out' any one of three likely possibilities, and a UN report in August said there was 'a reasonable basis to believe' the massacre was committed by Syrian troops and pro-Assad militia, the UK corporate media *had already declared absolute certainty in May*, just two days after the massacre, that Assad was personally responsible for ordering an atrocity that journalists knew was being used to justify direct Western 'intervention'. This is our point – that corporate media rushed to judgement demonising an 'official enemy' in a way that they would never dream of doing in response to claims against 'us' and 'our' allies.

Note that we are *not* arguing that pro-Assad forces were innocent of the Houla massacre – we are not pro-Assad, or 'apologising' for Assad, or 'whitewashing' Assad, or any of the other charges levelled at us. Our point is that, after the catastrophes of Iraq and Libya, the corporate media's instant certainty reeked of warmongering deference to power. In other words, this performance once again points to the deeply power-friendly bias of supposedly independent, impartial media.

Trashcan Flightpath: The 2013 Ghouta Chemical Weapons Attacks

If the political and media focus on Houla, and a long series of atrocity claims, suggested the West was looking to attack Syria, the return to the infamous 'weapons of mass destruction' theme surely left no reasonable observer in any doubt. In December 2012, US broadcaster NBC commented:

> U.S. officials tell us that the Syrian military is poised tonight to use chemical weapons against its own people. And all it would take is the final order from Syrian President Assad.[27]

This sounded ominously familiar. The US media watchdog, Fairness and Accuracy in Reporting (FAIR), asked:

> So where did all of this new information come from?' The familiar, answer: 'Anonymous government officials talking to outlets like the *New York Times*.' This, for example, from the *New York Times*:
>
> > Western intelligence officials say they are picking up new signs of activity at sites in Syria that are used to store chemical weapons. The officials are uncertain whether Syrian forces might be preparing to use the weapons in a last-ditch effort to save the government, or simply sending a warning to the West about the implications of providing more help to the Syrian rebels.[28]

FAIR commented:

> Absent any further details, that would seem to be a strange standard for confirmation ... But the theatrics – satellite images, anonymous sources speaking about weapons of mass destruction and so on – are obviously reminiscent of the lead up to the Iraq War.

They were indeed. A 5 December leading article in *The Times* read: 'Assad's Arsenal'. The first line of the editorial:

> The embattled Syrian regime may be preparing to use chemical weapons. That would be a catastrophe; it must be averted, whatever it takes.[29]

As ever, Rupert Murdoch's editors – and, no doubt, the boss, standing just over their shoulders – regretfully declared that Western military 'intervention' might turn out to be the only answer: 'we must also hope that the US and its allies would take any action that was deemed necessary to prevent the human and moral disaster that would be caused by the Syrian regime attempting its final exit in a cloud of mustard gas.' Again, straight out of the Iraq and Libya regime-change playbook.

In the *Guardian*, Matt Williams and Martin Chulov reported claims 'that the [Syrian] regime is considering unleashing chemical weapons on opposition forces.' The article cited CNN, which in turn cited 'an unnamed US official as the source of its report'. Williams and Chulov expressed not a word of scepticism in their piece, adding a two-sentence denial from the much-demonised Syrian 'regime' as 'balance'.[30]

To his credit, the BBC's Jonathan Marcus managed some scepticism:

Was there an element of political spin here to accompany NATO's decision to deploy patriot missiles in Turkey?

Sources contacted by the BBC say that there are indications of activity at certain chemical weapons storage sites.

However it is of course impossible to determine if this is a pre-liminary to the weapons' use or, as some analysts believe, much more likely, the movement of munitions to ensure their security. Indeed such movement has been noted in the past.[31]

Despite the caution, Marcus promoted the idea that Syrian WMD might fall into the 'wrong' hands and that the US might need to intervene to prevent that happening.

In the *Independent*, Robert Fisk poured scorn on these claims:

The bigger the lie the more people will believe it. We all know who said that – but it still works ... over the past week, all the usual pseudo-experts who couldn't find Syria on a map have been warning us again of the mustard gas, chemical agents, biological agents that Syria might possess – and might use. And the sources? The same fantasy specialists who didn't warn us about 9/11 but insisted that Saddam had weapons of mass destruction in 2003: 'unnamed military intelligence sources' ... And yes, Bashar probably does have some chemicals in rusting bins somewhere in Syria.[32]

In a piece entitled: 'Syria, a weapon of mass deception?', Alex Thomson of Channel 4 News wrote:

Without wishing to delve too far into The Who's back catalogue ... we need to remind ourselves in the UK that we won't get fooled again.[33]

Thomson offered a rare 'mainstream' example of sceptical thinking on the issue:

But just to be old fashioned: what's the evidence of any threat? What's the basis for all this? What, in short, are they all talking about? Yes, by all accounts Syria has nerve and chemical agents. But possession does not mean threat of use. Israel is not credibly threatening to use nuclear weapons against Iran, despite possessing them.

Thomson noted that 'the story built upon nothing [has been] accepted as global fact when it's nothing of the kind'. In other words: fake news.

A few months later, the same corporate system again instantly decided that the current Official Enemy was responsible for the 21 August 2013 attacks in Ghouta, Damascus, long before the UN published the evidence in its report on 'the alleged use of chemical weapons in the Ghouta area' on 16 September.[34]

Just one day after the attacks, a *Guardian* leader claimed there was not 'much doubt' who was to blame, as it simultaneously assailed its readers with commentary on the West's 'responsibility to protect', exactly as it had on Libya in 2011.[35]

An *Independent* front-page headline one week later read like a sigh of relief: 'Syria: air attacks loom as West finally acts'.[36]

The rapid media conclusion on Ghouta was particularly striking because the issues are complex – rocket science, literally – and evidence had again been gathered under live fire in the middle of a notoriously ferocious civil, proxy and propaganda war. As discussed, earlier claims had been adjudged 'a load of old cobblers' by Robert Fisk.[37]

It was also clear that instantly declaring Assad's guilt a 'slam-dunk' fed directly into a rapidly escalating US-UK propaganda blitz intended to justify a massive attack on Syria without UN approval, and therefore illegal.

With Qatar reportedly supplying 'rebels' to the tune of $3 billion between 2011–13 alone,[38] and Saudi Arabia $1 billion by 2013,[39] with the US supplying 15,000 high-tech, anti-tank missiles to 'rebels' via Saudi Arabia,[40] with the CIA spending $1 billion a year,[41] and with Russia supplying the Syrian government with $1 billion in weapons by 2013,[42] the stakes were obviously high. The fog of war obstructs and falsifies the facts at every turn. Who to trust? How can we know the lengths to which different agencies might be willing to go to secure outcomes of vast geopolitical significance?

After the chemical weapons attack in Ghouta, Obama unequivocally pinned the blame on Syrian President Assad, a propaganda claim that was eagerly disseminated around the world by corporate media.[43]

Following Obama's earlier warnings that any use of chemical weapons would cross a 'red line', he then declared on US television on 10 September 2013:

> Assad's government gassed to death over a thousand people ...We know the Assad regime was responsible ... And that is why, after careful deliberation, I determined that it is in the national security interests of the United States to respond to the Assad regime's use of chemical weapons through a targeted military strike.[44]

Based on interviews with US intelligence and military insiders, investigative journalist Seymour Hersh accused Obama of deception in making this case for war. According to Hersh, the US president 'did not tell the whole story':

> In some instances, he omitted important intelligence, and in others he presented assumptions as facts. Most significant, he

failed to acknowledge something known to the US intelligence community: that the Syrian army is not the only party in the country's civil war with access to sarin, the nerve agent that a UN study concluded – without assessing responsibility – had been used in the rocket attack.[45]

Obama did not reveal that American intelligence agencies knew that the al-Nusra Front, a jihadi group affiliated with al-Qaeda, had the capability to manufacture considerable quantities of sarin. When the attack on Ghouta took place, Hersh wrote, 'al-Nusra should have been a suspect, but the administration cherry-picked intelligence to justify a strike against Assad.' Indeed, the 'cherry-picking was similar to the process used to justify the Iraq war'.

Hersh noted that when he interviewed intelligence and military personnel:

I found intense concern, and on occasion anger, over what was repeatedly seen as the deliberate manipulation of intelligence. One high-level intelligence officer, in an email to a colleague, called the administration's assurances of Assad's responsibility a 'ruse'.

He continued:

A former senior intelligence official told me that the Obama administration had altered the available information – in terms of its timing and sequence – to enable the president and his advisers to make intelligence retrieved days after the attack look as if it had been picked up and analysed in real time, as the attack was happening.

The former official said that this 'distortion' of the facts by the Obama administration 'reminded him of the 1964 Gulf of Tonkin incident, when the Johnson administration reversed the sequence of National Security Agency intercepts to justify one of the early bombings of North Vietnam'.

On 21 August 2013, a report on the gas attacks was published by Richard Lloyd and Theodore Postol. Lloyd, who has since died, was a former United Nations Weapons Inspector who in two decades at

Raytheon, a top military contractor, wrote two books on warhead design. In March 2013, the *New York Times* wrote that Lloyd 'has the credentials for a critique'.[46] Postol is a professor and national security expert in MIT's Program in Science, Technology and Society. He has a proven track record in, for example, debunking Pentagon claims on the success of its Patriot missile system.[47] In September 2013, the *New York Times* described Lloyd and Postol as 'leading weapons experts'.[48]

Their 14 January 2014 report, 'Possible Implications of Faulty U.S. Technical Intelligence', examined US government claims regarding the 21 August chemical weapons attacks in Ghouta. The report found that the range of the rocket that delivered sarin in the largest attack that night was too short for the device to have been fired from Syrian government positions, as claimed by the Obama administration. Using mathematical projections about the likely force of the rocket – variously described as 'a trash can on a stick' and 'a soup can' – Lloyd and Postol concluded that the device likely had a maximum range of 2 kilometres, or just more than 1.2 miles. That meant that the 'trash can' had not been capable of flying the 6 miles from the centre of the Syrian-government-controlled part of Damascus to the point of impact in the suburbs, as claimed by the US government, nor even the 3.6 miles from the edges of government-controlled territory. Lloyd and Postol commented in their report:

> This indicates that these munitions could not possibly have been fired at east Ghouta from the 'heart' or the eastern edge of the Syrian Government controlled area depicted in the intelligence map published by the White House on August 30, 2013.
>
> This faulty intelligence could have led to an unjustified US military action based on false intelligence.
>
> A proper vetting of the fact that the munition was of such short range would have led to a completely different assessment of the situation from the gathered data.[49]

Postol added:

I honestly have no idea what happened. My view when I started this process was that it couldn't be anything but the Syrian government behind the attack. But now I'm not sure of anything. The administration narrative was not even close to reality. Our intelligence cannot possibly be correct.[50]

Lloyd, who had carefully studied weapons capabilities in the Syrian conflict, rejected the claim that rebels were less capable of making these rockets than the Syrian military:

The Syrian rebels most definitely have the ability to make these weapons. I think they might have more ability than the Syrian government.[51]

Lloyd and Postol made clear that they were *not* arguing that the rebels were behind the attack, but instead pointing to the flawed assessments behind US claims. Once again, the corporate media were far more certain, far sooner, than credible experts.

Trump's Tomahawks: Khan Sheikhoun

The Ghouta debacle was repeated, almost exactly, in April 2017 when the US-UK press unanimously supported new US President Donald Trump's firing of 59 Tomahawk cruise missiles in response to the Syrian government's alleged use of chemical weapons in Khan Sheikhoun, Idlib, Syria on 4 April. Roy Greenslade reported in the *Guardian* on the media reaction:

There was an identifiable theme in almost every leading article and commentary: 'Well done Donald, but ...' The 'buts' amounted to eloquent judgments on the president's character, conveying explicit messages of disquiet and distrust.[52]

In other words, almost every leading article and commentary in every UK newspaper supported Trump's attack. This being the same Donald Trump who, just a few months earlier, had been declared a grave, indeed Hitlerian threat to democracy and freedom by almost all corporate media.

In the United States, FAIR found that of 46 major editorials, only one, in the *Houston Chronicle*, opposed the attack. Adam Johnson reported:

83% of major editorial boards supported Trump's Syria strikes, 15% were ambiguous and 2% – or one publication – opposed.[53]

The support for Trump's attack was of course based, yet again, on the certainty that Assad had deployed chemical weapons in Idlib. Barely two days after the alleged attacks, a leader in *The Times* commented:

Assad's latest atrocity, the dropping of several hundred kilograms of toxic sarin gas on civilians, including children, is a breach of international law ...[54]

An *Independent* leader one day later titled, 'The US strike against Assad was justified', explained:

The use of chemical weapons is a special crime. It is prohibited by international law. It follows that the sarin gas attack in Idlib, Syria, on Tuesday, ought to have consequences.[55]

The apparent consensus supporting the propaganda blitz, crucially, was reinforced by the *Guardian*'s corporate leftists. Owen Jones wrote of 'the gassing of little kids who suffered unbearable torture as they were murdered by the Assad regime'.[56] Jones's dissident colleague at the *Guardian*, George Monbiot, tweeted:

We can be 99% sure the chemical weapons attack came from Syrian govt.[57]

As noted in Chapter 1, when we asked why 'mainstream' media were ignoring the credible experts challenging the US government account of the attacks (see below), Monbiot tweeted that we were 'whitewashing mass murder'.

Senior *Guardian* columnist and former Comment Editor Jonathan Freedland wrote:

And we almost certainly know who did it. Every sign points to the regime of Bashar al-Assad.[58]

Vanishingly rare dissent challenging this view did appear, and on one occasion quickly disappeared. The BBC published[59] and then deleted[60] the view of Jerry Smith, the official who had led the UN-backed operation to remove Syria's chemical weapons in 2013–14. Smith told Channel 4 News that the Russian version of events *could not* be discounted:

> If it is Sarin that was stored there and conventional munitions were used, there is every possibility that some of those [chemical] munitions were not consumed and that the Sarin liquid was ejected and could well have affected the population.[61]

Professor Ted Postol once again challenged his government's narrative, pouring scorn on a White House report on the Idlib event. He wrote:

> The only source the document cites as evidence that the attack was by the Syrian government [air force] is the crater it claims to have identified on a road in the North of Khan Shaykhun.[62]

But Postol noted that the White House's photographic evidence 'clearly indicates that the munition was almost certainly placed on the ground with an external detonating explosive on top of it that crushed the container so as to disperse the alleged load of sarin'. He added:

> I have reviewed the document carefully, and I believe it can be shown, without doubt, that the document does not provide any evidence whatsoever that the US government has concrete knowledge that the government of Syria was the source of the chemical attack in Khan Shaykhun, Syria at roughly 6 to 7 a.m. on April 4, 2017.
>
> No competent analyst would assume that the crater cited as the source of the sarin attack was unambiguously an indication that the munition came from an aircraft. No competent analyst would assume that the photograph of the carcass of the sarin canister was in fact a sarin canister. Any competent analyst would have had questions about whether the debris in the crater was staged or real. No competent analyst would miss the

fact that the alleged sarin canister was forcefully crushed from above, rather than exploded by a munition within it. All of these highly amateurish mistakes indicate that this White House report ... was not properly vetted by the intelligence community as claimed.

Postol's conclusion could hardly have been more damning:

I have worked with the intelligence community in the past, and I have grave concerns about the politicization of intelligence that seems to be occurring with more frequency in recent times – but I know that the intelligence community has highly capable analysts in it. And if those analysts were properly consulted about the claims in the White House document they would have not approved the document going forward.

We again have a situation where the White House has issued an obviously false, misleading and amateurish intelligence report.

Noam Chomsky commented:

Well, there are some interesting questions there – you can understand why Assad would have been pretty crazy [to provoke a US intervention] because they're winning the war. The worst thing for him is to bring the United States in. So why would he turn to a chemical weapons attack? You can imagine that a dictator with just local interests might do it, maybe if he thought he had a green light. But why would the Russians allow it? It doesn't make any sense. And in fact, there are some questions about what happened, but there are some pretty credible people – not conspiracy types – people with solid intelligence credentials – [who] say it didn't happen.

Lawrence Wilkerson said that the US intelligence picked up a plane and followed that it probably hit an al-Qaeda warehouse which had some sort of chemical weapon stored in it and they spread. I don't know. But it certainly calls for at least an investigation. And those are not insignificant people [challenging the official narrative].[63]

Chomsky pointed to comments made by Wilkerson, former Chief of Staff to General Colin Powell, in a recent interview on the *Real News* Network:

> I personally think the provocation was a Tonkin Gulf incident .... Most of my sources are telling me, including members of the team that monitors global chemical weapons – including people in Syria, including people in the US Intelligence Community – that what most likely happened ... was that they hit a warehouse that they had intended to hit ... and this warehouse was alleged to have to [sic] ISIS supplies in it, and ... some of those supplies were precursors for chemicals .... conventional bombs hit the warehouse, and due to a strong wind, and the explosive power of the bombs, they dispersed these ingredients and killed some people.[64]

There was also the collective judgement of 20 former members of the US Intelligence Community, the Steering Group of the Veteran Intelligence Professionals for Sanity:

> Our U.S. Army contacts in the area have told us this is not what happened. There was no Syrian 'chemical weapons attack'. Instead, a Syrian aircraft bombed an al-Qaeda-in-Syria ammunition depot that turned out to be full of noxious chemicals and a strong wind blew the chemical-laden cloud over a nearby village where many consequently died ... This is what the Russians and Syrians have been saying and – more important – what they appear to believe happened.[65]

Hans Blix, former head of the International Atomic Energy Agency, who served as the head of the UN Monitoring, Verification and Inspection Commission in Iraq, commented:

> I don't know whether in Washington they presented any evidence, but I did not see that in the Security Council. Merely pictures of victims that were held up, that the whole world can see with horror, such pictures are not necessarily evidence of who did it.[66]

Blix said it was natural to jump to the conclusion that the regime was far more likely than the rebels to have the means to carry out an attack of such a magnitude, but that it was far from proven that it did so:

> If you had a murder and you strongly suspect one fellow, do you go to judgment and execution straight away? Three days after the murder?

Former chief UN Weapons Inspector, Scott Ritter, who, as we have seen, defied a false political and media consensus by accurately claiming Iraq had been disarmed of 90–95 per cent of its WMD by December 1998, wrote:

> Mainstream American media outlets have willingly and openly embraced a narrative provided by Al Qaeda affiliates whose record of using chemical weapons in Syria and distorting and manufacturing 'evidence' to promote anti-Assad policies in the west, including regime change, is well documented.
>
> History will show that Donald Trump, his advisors and the American media were little more than willing dupes for Al Qaeda and its affiliates, whose manipulation of the Syrian narrative resulted in a major policy shift that furthers their objectives.[67]

Philip Giraldi was a CIA counterterrorism official from 1976 to 1992. Giraldi has an extremely impressive track record in exposing fake government claims, including the bogus allegations that Iraq had shown interest in purchasing uranium from Niger and that Iran had developed a 'nuclear trigger'.[68] Giraldi commented on Khan Sheikhoun:

> I am hearing from sources on the ground, in the Middle East, the people who are intimately familiar with the intelligence available are saying that the essential narrative we are all hearing about the Syrian government or the Russians using chemical weapons on innocent civilians is a sham. The intelligence confirms pretty much the account the Russians have been giving since last night which is that they hit a warehouse where al Qaida rebels

were storing chemicals of their own and it basically caused an explosion that resulted in the casualties.

Apparently the intelligence on this is very clear, and people both in the Agency and in the military who are aware of the intelligence are freaking out about this because essentially Trump completely misrepresented what he should already have known – but maybe didn't – and they're afraid this is moving towards a situation that could easily turn into an armed conflict.[69]

Giraldi added:

These are essentially sources that are right on top of the issue right in the Middle East. They're people who are stationed there with the military and the Intelligence agencies that are aware and have seen the intelligence. And, as I say, they are coming back to contacts over here in the US essentially that they astonished at how this is being played by the administration and by the media and in some cases people are considering going public to stop it. They [are] concerned about it … upset by what's going on.

Former *Guardian* journalist Jonathan Steele told *Democracy Now!*:

Well, I think the people who've benefited from this terrible gas incident in Khan Sheikhoun last week were certainly not Assad, certainly not the Russian government. The people who've benefited are, as you suggested in the question, the people who were defending themselves against the allegation that Trump is somehow a puppet of Moscow. It was the military-industrial complex in Washington, what we would now – it's Eisenhower's phrase, but what we would now call the deep state, you know, the kind of alliance between the top military brass in Washington, the arms manufacturers and the intelligence agencies, who were really worried that Trump was somehow getting out of control and opening up good relations with Russia, and they wanted to get him back on the traditional track of confrontation with Russia.[70]

Steele discussed the evidence and concluded: 'it seems so unlikely that the Syrians would have used chemical weapons.'

Our search of the Lexis press database (May 2017) found no mentions of Blix, Giraldi or Ritter in any UK newspaper since the alleged attack in Syria.

Obama: The Myth of Non-Intervention

On 20 August 2016, the BBC website featured a Radio 4 'Today' programme discussion hosted by former Political Editor Nick Robinson interviewing BBC World Affairs Editor John Simpson and Dr Karin von Hippel, a former State Department official dealing with US strategy against Islamic State.[71]

On the BBC website, the discussion was introduced with the following written text, which was repeated in slightly altered form in Robinson's spoken introduction:

Exactly five years ago President Obama called on the Syrian President Bashir-Al-Assad to step down but today he is still in power.

The prominence and repetition of the observation of course conferred great significance. After all, if the President of Paraguay had made the same 'call', the BBC's observation would seem simply absurd. The implication, clearly, was that, for the BBC, Obama was not just one more leader; he was a kind of World President with the authority to call on other leaders to 'step down'. In reality, Obama made his demand, not in the name of the United Nations, or of the Syrian people, but because, as President George H.W. Bush once declared: 'what we say goes'.[72]

In his introduction, Robinson described a disturbing image that 'has gone viral on social media' of a Syrian child allegedly injured by Russian or Syrian bombing. The child, five-year-old Omran Daqneesh, was depicted sitting between Obama and Putin. Robinson noted that one of these images carried the sarcastic caption: 'Thank you for keeping me safe.' We found the image although not that caption.

One reasonable interpretation of Robinson's introduction, then: five years earlier, out of humanitarian concern, Obama had called on Assad to go, but had 'failed' to follow through in making that happen – 'little Omran', and numerous other Syrian civilians, were continuing to suffer as a result. As Adam Johnson wrote, the viral picture of Daqneesh had 'amped up calls for direct US intervention against the Syrian government' made by numerous 'laptop bombardiers' 'jumping from one outrage in urgent need of US bombs to the next'.[73]

The BBC's 'Today' discussion can be understood as a further example of this media herd behaviour.

John Simpson agreed with Robinson that Obama had been keen to avoid 'the kind of dreadful errors' – he meant crimes – that George W. Bush had committed in Iraq, and so had 'wanted to stay out of things'. According to Simpson, Obama's failure to intervene in Syria had been a 'disaster'. After all, Russia had recently 'managed to attack Syria with its planes from the airfields of Iran'.

As we note below, investigative journalist Gareth Porter commented that the Syrian government had in fact *invited* Russian military support, so Russia could hardly be described as launching an 'attack' on Syria. Simpson, by contrast, argued that Russo-Iranian cooperation was 'a link up which would have caused absolute consternation in the United States, and worldwide, just a few years ago'. In other words, the world's sole superpower had proven powerless to stop the kind of military cooperation it practises the world over all the time.

Simpson's imperial sympathies had been aired before on the BBC, notably in October 2014:

> The world (well, most of it) wants an active, effective America to act as its policeman, sorting out the problems smaller countries can't face alone.[74]

In a classic example of BBC 'balance', Dr von Hippel then supported both Robinson's and Simpson's interpretation of the cause of the Syria disaster, noting of Obama that, 'as John Simpson was saying, he didn't believe that America interfering in a big way would help ... he was never convinced that force, or greater use of force, would make a difference. Now, I personally disagree with that ...'

Dr von Hippel went so far as to assert that 'there were many things you could do between sending 100,000 troops in and nothing'. The comment was ambiguous but, in the context of the discussion, invited listeners to conclude that Obama had indeed done nothing in Syria. And yet, von Hippel herself noted that US special forces were working with anti-Assad groups in Syria and Turkey, and that this and other support 'has made a difference'.

In fact, this is only the tip of the iceberg. In June 2015, the *Washington Post* reported of the US:

> At $1 billion, Syria-related operations account for about $1 of every $15 in the CIA's overall budget ... US officials said the CIA has trained and equipped nearly 10,000 fighters sent into Syria over the past several years – meaning that the agency is spending roughly $100,000 per year for every anti-Assad rebel who has gone through the program.[75]

FAIR added some context:

> In addition to this, the Obama administration has engaged in crippling sanctions against the Assad government, provided air support for those looking to depose him, incidentally funneled arms to ISIS, and not incidentally aligned the CIA-backed Free Syrian Army with Al Qaeda. Regardless of one's position on Syria – or whether they think the US is somehow secretly in alliance with Assad, as some advance – one thing cannot be said: that the US has 'done nothing in Syria'. This is historically false.[76]

As noted above, the US also supplied 15,000 anti-tank missiles to Syrian 'rebels' via Saudi Arabia. Western liberal commentators have ceaselessly raged at claims that the Syrian government has used chemical weapons and indiscriminate 'barrel bombs'. We are unaware of any who have dared imagine how the US government would respond to thousands of foreign troops fighting on the

US mainland using 15,000 TOW anti-tank missiles supplied by a foreign superpower to kill thousands of US troops, seriously threatening to overthrow the government. In 1945, Hiroshima and Nagasaki were vapourised without US national survival ever being at stake.

In March 2017, it was reported that Raytheon, which makes the TOW missile, had seen its shares triple in value since 2012.[77] InvestorPlace commented:

> As the world's largest missile maker, Raytheon experienced healthy demand for its products, particularly from foreign customers. Notably, rising demand from MENA or the Middle East and North Africa region will likely be the company's key revenue driver, going ahead.[78]

None of this evidence registers with 'mainstream' journalists. Instead, Nick Robinson observed that, 'there were a series of occasions' in which David Cameron 'tried to persuade Obama – others were doing it, too – to take some form of military action, and at each stage he didn't want to do it'. 'Yes', Simpson replied, 'I think that David Cameron was really frustrated towards the end ...'

Obama, we were to believe, then, repeatedly refused 'to take some form of military action' and was even guilty of 'silence, almost' on Syria. Robinson then summarised the whole narrative:

> So, in other words ... this is a disaster, not just for the people of Syria, but a strategic disaster for the United States – makes them look weak.

If there was any doubt what 'strong' means to Robinson, it was removed when he concluded the discussion by asking Simpson to respond to potential listener criticism:

> Just address those people who we know are listening at home who'll go: 'Haven't they learned anything? We know that military intervention in the Middle East always produces a worse disaster than the one that we started with.'

In a Rumsfeldian reply, Simpson acknowledged that the conflict is 'fiendishly complicated, Nick, really, as you know', adding:

Whatever you do is going to have tremendous downsides. But that doesn't mean to say that everything you do, or don't do, um, is, is, is ... simply going to be the worst thing you can possibly do. There are some things that are worse than others.

Perhaps it takes a World Affairs Editor to join the big picture dots with such insight. Simpson continued:

And I think, sitting on your hands watching Putin running away with the whole thing is the worst possible thing that Obama could have done, and I think it's going to be a stain on his reputation permanently.

This reminded us of the many cold-blooded comments that viewed the deaths of hundreds of thousands of people in Iraq as primarily a problem for the American brand, with tragic implications for the reputations of George W. Bush and Tony Blair.

We asked Gareth Porter, one of the most knowledgeable and honest reporters on Syria, to comment on the BBC's discussion. He said:

The BBC interview is so one-sided and distorts the most basic realities of the issue in Syria that it is a caricature of the media propagandizing for war. It has offered the public two flavors of essentially neoconservative thinking – one perhaps closer to Bush administration thinking, the other closer to the views of Hillary Clinton.[79]

With this comment, Porter nutshelled perfectly the truth of the supposed corporate media 'spectrum'.

In March 2014, we challenged Paul Mason (formerly of BBC's 'Newsnight', later Economics Editor of Channel 4 News) to explain why he believed the failure of the US to bomb Syria in August 2013 had been a 'Disaster!'[80] Mason invited us to email him, which we did. He failed to reply. After repeated nudges, he promised to reply when he had the time. More than two months later, journalist Ian

Sinclair reminded Mason that he had still not responded. Mason replied:

Believe it or not, I still have more important things to do[81]

We answered:

Well, Chomsky – famously, the world's busiest human – typically replies within 24 hours with detailed comments[82]

Mason's sage response:

yeah but I deal in fact, not ideology[83]

We replied again:

Time allowing, you should read @ggreenwald's new book, No Place To Hide – it might relieve you of that conceit.[84]

This is one of the passages in Glenn Greenwald's book that we had in mind:

As we are told endlessly, journalists do not express opinions; they simply report the facts.

This is an obvious pretense, a conceit of the profession. The perceptions and pronouncements of human beings are inherently subjective. Every news article is the product of all sorts of highly subjective cultural, nationalistic, and political assumptions. And all journalism serves one faction's interests or another.[85]

Greenwald concludes of the US press:

'Objectivity' means nothing more than reflecting the biases and serving the interests of entrenched Washington. Opinions are problematic only when they deviate from the acceptable range of Washington orthodoxy.[86]

Mason's one-word reply to our suggestion that he might read Greenwald's book:

nope[87]

7

Yemen: Feeding the Famine

At first sight, compassion appears to loom large in 'mainstream' politics and media. When the US and British governments target countries – Serbia, Afghanistan, Iraq, Libya, Syria, among others – 'compassion' is always at or near the top of the agenda. Time and again, the cry from the political system is, in effect: 'We Must Do Something!'[1] 'We' must save Kuwaiti new-borns flung from their incubators by Iraqi stormtroopers.[2] 'We' must save Iraqi civilians from Saddam's shredding machines.[3] 'We' must save civilians in Kosovo from Milosevic's 'final solution'.[4]

As for the suffering civilians of Aleppo in Syria, Tory MP Andrew Mitchell demanded, not merely that 'we' save them, not merely that 'we' engage in war to save them, but that 'we' must confront Russia, shoot down their planes if necessary, and risk *actual thermonuclear war* – complete self-destruction – to save them:

> If that means confronting Russian air power defensively, on behalf of the innocent people on the ground who we are trying to protect, then we should do that.[5]

State-corporate propaganda is full of 'shoulds', all rooted in 'our' alleged 'responsibility to protect'. Why 'us'? Because 'we' care. 'We' *really* care. A key task of the corporate media is to pretend this is something more than a charade. The truth is only ever hinted at in BBC political programmes that open with jovial, bombastic, comical music, as if introducing some kind of music-hall farce. The cast is currently led by Foreign Secretary Boris Johnson. After joshing about how: 'There is no other country that comes close to [Britain's] record of belligerence' in invading or conquering 178 out of 200 countries existing today, Johnson opined:

As our American friends instinctively understand, it is the existence of strong and well-resourced British Armed Forces that gives this country the ability to express and affirm our values overseas: of freedom, democracy, tolerance, pluralism.[6]

This was a near-exact reversal of the truth. As Johnson himself noted in 2014 of the 2003 Iraq invasion:

It looks to me as though the Americans were motivated by a general strategic desire to control one of the biggest oil exporters in the world.[7]

If politicians are clearly bluffers, corporate journalists are selected because they powerfully echo and enhance the alleged need for compassionate 'intervention'. Armchair warriors like David Aaronovitch, Nick Cohen, John Rentoul, Jonathan Freedland and Oliver Kamm earn their salaries by appearing to tear their hair out in borderline self-harming outrage at the crimes of official enemies and at the 'useful idiocy' of the perennial, naysaying 'leftists'.

By some strange quirk of independent judgement, Aaronovitch of *The Times* has supported just about every opportunity to wage war for decades, whether under Labour or the Tories (see 'Intermission' below).

The armchair warriors' message is always the same: we understand you're sincere, but sometimes you simply have to drop your reflexive 'anti-Americanism', drop your blinkered adherence to 'principled opposition' and live in the real world. You can't just sit on your hands, you can't just righteously preach – *you have to act!*

This is the shtick of the corporate warmonger, and it is repeated over and over again. It appears to be the key function that determines whether a commentator is granted job-for-life privileges at newspapers like the *Guardian*, *The Times* and the *Telegraph*.

In reality, compassion – the kind rooted in an understanding that all suffering is equal, the kind that feels even more responsibility for suffering caused by our own government – is not partial;

it does not defer to power. It does not fall silent when 'we' are committing crimes; quite the reverse.

Britain's Complicity in War Crimes in Yemen

Consider the case of Yemen. Since March 2015, a 'coalition' of Sunni Arab states led by Saudi Arabia, and supported by the US, Britain and France, has been dropping bombs on neighbouring Yemen.

The scale of the bombing was indicated in a September 2016 article by the independent journalist Felicity Arbuthnot: in one year, 330,000 homes, 648 mosques, 630 schools and institutes and 250 health facilities were destroyed or damaged.[8] In December 2016, it was reported that more than 10,000 people had died and three million had been displaced in the conflict.[9]

The stated aim of Saudi Arabia's devastating assault is to reinstate the Yemeni president, Abd-Rabbu Mansour Hadi, and to hold back Houthi rebels allied with the former president, Ali Abdullah Saleh.[10] The Saudis assert that the Houthis, who control Yemen's capital, Sanaa, are 'proxies' for Iran: a convenient propaganda claim to elicit Western backing and 'justify' intervention. Gareth Porter, an independent investigative journalist and winner of the 2012 Gellhorn Prize for journalism, disputes this claim:

Although Iran has certainly had ties with the Houthis, the Saudi propaganda line that the Houthis have long been Iranian proxies is not supported by the evidence.[11]

Philip Hammond, who was UK Defence Secretary when the Saudi bombing began in 2015, promised:

We'll support the Saudis in every practical way short of engaging in combat.[12]

The British government has been true to its word. In August 2016, Campaign Against Arms Trade reported that UK sales to Saudi Arabia since the start of the attacks on Yemen included £2.2 billion of aircraft, helicopters and drones, £1.1 billion of missiles, bombs and grenades, and nearly half a million pounds' worth of armoured vehicles and tanks.[13] In 2015 alone, the United States approved more than $20 billion in military sales to Saudi Arabia. Around the same time, it was revealed that Britain was now the second biggest dealer of arms in the world, beaten only by the US. Is there any clearer sign of the corrupt nature of UK foreign policy?[14]

Perhaps there is. In August 2016, Oxfam reported that in excess of 21 million people in Yemen, out of a total population of around 27 million, were in need of humanitarian aid, more than in any other country.[15] In December 2016, a new study by UNICEF, the UN children's agency, reported that at least one child was dying every 10 minutes in Yemen. The agency also found that there had been a 200 per cent increase since 2014 in children suffering from severe acute malnutrition, with almost half a million affected. Nearly 2.2 million children were in need of urgent care.

But Yemen's health system teetered on the verge of collapse. Journalist Iona Craig, formerly a Yemen-based correspondent for *The Times*, noted that 'more than 58 hospitals now have been bombed by the coalition airstrikes, and people just do not have access to medical care in a way that they did before the war'.[16] Meanwhile, a brutal blockade on Yemen by Saudi Arabia was preventing vital commodities from getting into the country. Children were dying because Saudi Arabia was delaying shipments of aid for months, denying hundreds of thousands of people urgently-needed medical aid.[17]

Grant Pritchard, interim country director for Save the Children in Yemen, said:

These delays are killing children. Our teams are dealing with outbreaks of cholera, and children suffering from diarrhoea, measles, malaria and malnutrition.

With the right medicines these are all completely treatable – but the Saudi-led coalition is stopping them getting in. They are turning aid and commercial supplies into weapons of war.[18]

He added:

> To see the Saudi-led coalition blocking shipments of humanitarian supplies is simply unforgivable.

As one doctor at the Republic teaching hospital in Sanaa commented:

> We are unable to get medical supplies. Anaesthetics. Medicines for kidneys. There are babies dying in incubators because we can't get supplies to treat them.

The doctor estimated that 25 people were dying every day at the Republic hospital because of the blockade. He continued:

> They call it natural death. But it's not. If we had the medicines they wouldn't be dead. I consider them killed as if they were killed by an air strike, because if we had the medicines they would still be alive.

Amnesty International reported that British-made cluster bombs were being used in deadly attacks on civilians.[19] Children were among those killed and maimed. The human rights organisation said that the UK should stop all arms sales to Saudi Arabia.[20] Amnesty also called for Saudi Arabia to be dropped from the United Nations Human Rights Council because of 'gross and systematic violations of human rights', both at home and abroad.[21]

In October 2016, a Saudi bombing raid killed 140 people and wounded 525 at a funeral.[22] British-manufactured cluster bombs were found in Yemeni villages, all but confirming that banned weapons were being used.[23] The United Nations reported that the Saudi-led coalition is responsible for nearly two-thirds of civilian deaths.

Yemeni Prime Minister Abdulaziz bin Habtour was adamant that the UK was guilty of war crimes:

> They have sold cluster bombs to Saudi Arabia. They know the Saudis are going to drop them on Yemen [...] in Saadah and in Sana'a and other provinces.

I don't think they are guilty of war crimes, I believe so. They are participating in the bombing of Yemen people.[24]

But *why* would Britain continue to be complicit in Saudi war crimes? The clue was provided by Adel al-Jubeir, the Saudi Foreign Minister, when he declared that it was 'in Britain's interest' to continue supporting Saudi Arabia in its murderous assault on Yemen. A report in the *Telegraph* spelt out why:

Apart from maintaining traditional links on military and intelligence cooperation, Mr Jubeir also said post-Brexit Britain could look forward to forging new trade links with the kingdom as Saudi Arabia embarks on its ambitious plan to restructure its economy under a plan called Saudi Vision 2030. 'We are looking at more than $2 trillion worth of investment opportunities over the next decade, and this will take the relationship between Saudi Arabia and Britain to an entirely new level post-Brexit.'[25]

Saudi pressure was presumably considerable, and the UK government was unable to resist; or, more accurately, happy to go along with the decades-old policy of appeasement for the sake of power and money. A post-Brexit, $2 trillion Saudi carrot trumps any concerns over war crimes.

In June 2016, it was reported that even the UN had succumbed to Saudi pressure when it removed Saudi Arabia from a blacklist of countries responsible for child casualties in conflicts around the globe.[26] Saudi Arabia had been placed on the list for killing and maiming children in Yemen bombing attacks.[27] The Saudis, along with other Arab and Muslim countries, had reportedly threatened to withdraw funding from vital UN humanitarian programmes.[28] One anonymous diplomat spoke of 'bullying, threats, pressure', and summed it up as 'real blackmail'.[29]

Intermission: David Aaronovitch, Perpetual Warmonger

In March 1999, in an article graciously titled, 'It's because we're rich that we must impose peace for others', David Aaronovitch supported war on Sierra Leone:

Given a choice, do we really think that the suffering civilians of Sierra Leone would object to a military presence by the British?[30]

Two months later, in support of NATO's war in Serbia, Aaronovitch wrote:

Is this cause, the cause of the Kosovar Albanians, a cause that is worth suffering for? ... Would I fight, or (more realistically) would I countenance the possibility that members of my family might die?

His answer: 'I think so.'[31]

In the aftermath of the 11 September attacks on the United States, Aaronovitch supported war on Afghanistan:

For a fair-minded progressive the call should not be Stop the War. That slogan is now irrelevant and harmful. The requirement is surely to win the peace ...

So on Sunday, instead of listening to the same old tired stuff about cowboys with rockets and selective horror stories from Mazar; instead of marching along with mouth open and ears closed (however comforting that can be); instead of indulging yourself in a cosmic whinge, why not do something that might help the people of Afghanistan?[32]

In supporting war on Iraq in January 2003, Aaronovitch wrote of Saddam Hussein:

I want him out, for the sake of the region (and therefore, eventually, for our sakes), but most particularly for the sake of the Iraqi people who cannot lift this yoke on their own.[33]

In 2011, Aaronovitch supported the war on Libya in an article titled: 'Go for a no-fly zone over Libya or regret it.' He commented:

We have a side here, let's be on it.[34]

In 2012, Aaronovitch supported war on Syria:

I say we could arm the rebels so that they can defend themselves from the weapons supplied by the Russians. And I argue for safe havens inside Syrian territory for civilians and have to agree that this may well require military action to deal with Syrian air defences.[35]

In June 2014, Aaronovitch once again supported the bombing of Iraq:

We must do everything short of putting boots on the ground to help the Kurds to defend themselves against Isis and similar groups.[36]

On Twitter in 2016, he was asked about Yemen:

How do you feel then about Britain's role in what the Saudis are doing (providing arms, advisers etc.)?[37]

Aaronovitch responded:

I haven't looked at it, and you're right, I must.[38]

Since then, Aaronovitch has written not one word about the Yemen War, or Britain's role in it.

Callously Waving Away Evidence of War Crimes

The *Guardian*'s 'liberal' soft-pedalling of UK complicity in war crimes and humanitarian nightmares was summed up by one editorial which lamented that Britain was 'sitting by as disaster unfolds'. There was but a token mention that the war in Yemen was 'fuelled in part by British and US bombs'.[39] However, as pointed out by US-based media analyst Adam Johnson, there was vital context that was absent from the *Guardian* editorial: the British government's £3.3 billion in arms sales, as well as logistical support, surveillance assistance and political cover.[40]

In contrast to the *Guardian*'s hand-wringing, Peter Oborne is a rare example of a Western journalist pointing unequivocally to British complicity in Yemen's nightmare. Together with Nawal Al-Maghafi, Oborne reported in 2016 that:

> We discovered indisputable evidence that the coalition, backed by the UK as a permanent member of the UN Security Council, is targeting Yemeni civilians in blatant breach of the rules of war.[41]

This was shocking enough. But Oborne added that there was:

> powerful evidence that the Saudi-led coalition has deliberately targeted hospitals across the country. Four MSF [Médecins Sans Frontières] hospitals had been hit by Saudi air strikes prior to the organisation's withdrawal from the country, even though MSF were careful to give the Saudi authorities their GPS positions.

Oborne, who resigned as political commentator from the *Telegraph* in 2015,[42] placed Western complicity in Yemen's war and humanitarian crisis at the front and centre of his reporting. He pointed out that Britain was continuing to sell arms to Saudi Arabia and its partners, despite copious evidence of breaches of international humanitarian law presented by human rights organisations.

This was an echo of Britain's shameful role in arming Indonesia while it crushed tiny, independence-seeking East Timor, killing around 200,000 people in the years following the 1975 invasion. Noam Chomsky described that as a 'slaughter' of 'near-genocidal' levels.[43] He noted:

> By 1998, Britain had become the leading supplier of arms to Indonesia ... over the strong protests of Amnesty International, Indonesian dissidents, and Timorese victims. Arms sales are reported to make up at least a fifth of Britain's exports to Indonesia (estimated at one billion pounds), led by British Aerospace.[44]

In the case of Yemen, the British Foreign Office repeatedly denied that Saudi Arabia had broken humanitarian law, asserting for months that the Foreign Office's own 'assessment' had cleared the Saudis of any wrong-doing. As Oborne noted, however, on 21 July 2016, the last day of Parliament before the long summer recess:

the British government was forced to admit that it had repeatedly misled parliament over the war in Yemen.[45]

It turned out that no such 'assessment' had taken place; a grudging and damaging admission that ministers had clearly hoped to slip out quietly just before summer without proper scrutiny. Oborne described it as 'a dark moment of official embarrassment'. You had to dig deep in the BBC News website to find even scant mention of this disgraceful episode.[46] Moreover, Britain supported a UN Security Council resolution backing a Saudi blockade, and the UK also provided the Saudis with intelligence and logistical support.

Oborne continued:

Perhaps most crucially of all, Britain and the United States have provided Saudi Arabia with diplomatic cover. Last year [2015], Britain and the United States helped to block *a Dutch initiative at the UN Human Rights Council for an independent* investigation into violations of international humanitarian law.[47]

In a powerful accompanying filmed report on the destruction of Yemen's capital Sanaa, Oborne concluded:

This city of old Sanaa is as extraordinary, as priceless, as unique as any of the masterpieces of western civilisation like Florence or Venice. Just imagine the outcry if bombs were falling on Florence or Venice. But because this is old Sanaa, in forgotten Yemen, nobody cares a damn.[48]

Least of all Boris Johnson, who callously waved away copious evidence of Saudi breaches of international humanitarian law. The *Guardian*'s Diplomatic Editor, Patrick Wintour, noted of Johnson's assertion that the Saudis are not 'in clear breach' of humanitarian law:

His judgment is based largely on a Saudi-led inquiry into eight controversial incidents, including the bombing of hospitals.[49]

To his credit, Wintour observed that Johnson was 'defending the credibility of a Saudi-led inquiry exonerating Saudi targeting'.

Comment seemed superfluous. He then added Johnson's own unwittingly self-damning statement:

> They [the Saudis] have the best insight into their own procedures and will be able to conduct the most thorough and conclusive investigations. It will also allow the coalition forces to work out what went wrong and apply the lessons learned in the best possible way. This is the standard we set ourselves and our allies.

Indeed, this is the same standard that the world observed with horror in 2015,[50] when the US investigated, and largely exonerated, itself[51] over its bombing of an MSF hospital in Kunduz, Afghanistan.[52]

Meanwhile, on 5 September 2016, the Foreign Office minister, Tobias Ellwood, addressed the Commons after being requested to do so by the Speaker, John Bercow, because of previously misleading statements on Yemen given by ministers to Parliament. Wintour claimed in his *Guardian* report that Ellwood 'apologised' for these 'inaccurate answers'.[53] But the quoted wording is far from a proper apology. Indeed, the minister obfuscated further in support of Saudi Arabia. Ellwood:

> said it was not for the UK government to conclude whether individual bombing incidents by the Saudis represented breaches of international humanitarian law (IHL), but instead to 'take an overall view of the approach and attitude by Saudi Arabia to international humanitarian law'.

In effect, the UK had ignored numerous evidence-based objections to its policy, and the government would continue to rely on Saudi Arabia's own assertions that it was not breaching international humanitarian law. Worse, while Yemenis continued to die under US/UK-supported bombing, Ellwood continued to back the Saudis, as Wintour noted:

> Defending the Saudi response to criticisms of its campaign, Ellwood said: 'It was new territory for Saudi Arabia and a conservative nation was not used to such exposure.'

This was sophistry of the worst order. 'New territory' was newspeak for a murderous bombing campaign and a crippling blockade. And describing Saudi Arabia, a brutal and repressive regime that ranks amongst the world's worst violators of human rights, as merely 'a conservative nation', speaks volumes about the mental and ethical contortions required to defend British foreign policy.

In December 2016, Defence Secretary Sir Michael Fallon finally admitted to the House of Commons that British-made cluster bombs had been dropped by Saudi Arabia in Yemen.[54] Shamefully, Fallon continued to defend Britain's staunch support for Saudi Arabia and insisted there was no breach of international law because cluster bombs were being used against 'legitimate military targets'. Prime Minister Theresa May also affirmed that Britain would carry on arming Saudi Arabia, even as the Yemeni death toll continued to mount.[55]

The Yemen Motion Gives the Lie to 'Responsibility to Protect'

British state prioritising of *realpolitik* over human rights concerns was dramatically brought to the fore in Parliament in October 2016. That month, Emily Thornberry, Labour Shadow Foreign Secretary, placed the following motion before the House of Commons:

> That this House supports efforts to bring about a cessation of hostilities and provide humanitarian relief in Yemen, and notes that the country is now on the brink of famine; condemns the reported bombings of civilian areas that have exacerbated this crisis; believes that a full independent UN-led investigation must be established into alleged violations of international humanitarian law in the conflict in Yemen; and calls on the Government to suspend its support for the Saudi Arabia-led coalition forces in Yemen until it has been determined whether they have been responsible for any such violations.[56]

At this time, Yemen was truly facing disaster. As the *Guardian* reported:

There are 370,000 children enduring severe malnutrition that weakens their immune system, according to Unicef, and 1.5 million are going hungry. Food shortages are a long-term problem, but they have got worse in recent months. Half of children under five are stunted because of chronic malnutrition.[57]

Oxfam's humanitarian policy adviser, Richard Stanforth, said:

Everything is stacked against the people on the brink of starvation in Yemen.

Martha Mundy, Professor Emeritus at the London School of Economics, commented:

The [Saudi-led] coalition was and is targeting intentionally food production, not simply agriculture in the fields.[58]

She added:

According to the Food and Agriculture Organisation, 2.8 per cent of Yemen's land is cultivated. To hit that small amount of agricultural land, you have to target it.

Saudi Arabia's blockade has worsened the crisis. A World Food Program official warned: 'An entire generation could be crippled by hunger.' At least 14 million Yemenis, more than half of the country's population, were going hungry.[59] More than one-third of all Saudi-led air raids on Yemen have hit civilian sites, such as schools, hospitals, markets, mosques and economic infrastructure, including factories and power stations.[60]

As for Thornberry's motion, more than 100 Labour MPs – almost half the parliamentary Labour Party – failed to support it. As a result, the motion was defeated by 283 votes to just 193, a majority of 90.[61]

Labour MP John Woodcock had dismissed the motion in advance as mere 'gesture politics'. In justifying his stance, he even welcomed the involvement of UK personnel in the Saudi bombing campaign:

the support we are giving is largely to help train pilots in targeting practices that reduce civilian casualties.[62]

As revealed by Campaign Against Arms Trade, Woodcock attended a dinner in February 2015 in support of the arms trade as a guest of BAE Systems, the huge 'defence' company.[63] As the chairman of Labour's backbench Defence Committee, he is an ardent supporter of Trident,[64] describing the announcement in 2016 that Labour would support it as a 'very thoughtful birthday present'.[65]

As Peter Oborne wrote:

To sum up ... the British parliament sent the green light to Saudi Arabia and its allies to carry on bombing, maiming and killing. I have reported politics from Westminster for almost 25 years and can recall few more shocking parliamentary events.

Shocking – but not surprising. The Yemen vote demonstrates something that has been apparent ever since the vote on 18 March 2003 to support the invasion of Iraq: the party of war holds a majority in the Commons.

It comprises virtually all of the Conservative Party and the Blairite wing of Labour.[66]

Since the rejection of the motion, 'Do something!' crusaders Aaronovitch and Cohen have, as far as we can see, printed not a word about 'our' 'responsibility to protect' civilian life in Yemen.

In the entire UK 'mainstream' press, we found a single opinion piece, in the *Guardian*, condemning the vote, headlined, 'The Labour rebels who didn't back the Yemen vote have blood on their hands.'[67] A curiously vague *Guardian* leader commented merely of the Yemen motion:

Though admirable, it could change government policy only indirectly, by contributing to moral pressure.[68]

Apart from that, the only other mention was in passing in a comment piece on the Yemen disaster in the *Telegraph*.[69]

No corporate journalist raised the question that cried out to be asked: if Britain cares enough about civilian suffering in Kosovo,

Iraq, Libya and Syria *to go to war*, then how can it not even suspend support for Saudi Arabia while potential war crimes are investigated?

Literally no journalist made the point that the vote makes a complete nonsense of the UK's famed enthusiasm for 'responsibility to protect'. The warmongers' silence tells us their 'compassion' is a tool of *realpolitik*, nothing more.

'The BBC Has Betrayed its Own Rules of Impartiality'

In May 2017, 'mainstream' media coverage of a trip by US President Trump to Saudi Arabia, where he signed trade deals worth around $350 billion, virtually ignored Yemen.[70] The trade agreement included an arms deal of $110 billion, which the White House described as 'the single biggest in US history'. Around the same time, the World Health Organization warned of the rising numbers of deaths in Yemen due to cholera, saying that it was 'unprecedented'.[71] Save the Children said that the cholera outbreak could well become 'a full-blown epidemic'. Moreover:

> The upsurge comes as the health system, sanitation facilities and civil infrastructure have reached breaking point because of the ongoing war.[72]

As Gareth Porter observed via Twitter:

> World leaders are silent as #Yemen faces horrible cholera epidemic linked to #Saudi War & famine. Politics as usual.[73]

Yemen's nightmare was deemed irrelevant by the corporate media in comparison to Trump's signing of the arms deal with Saudi Arabia. BBC News focused instead on inanities such as Trump 'to soften his rhetoric', 'joins Saudi sword dance' and 'no scarf for Melania'.[74] But then, it is standard practice for the BBC to absolve the West of any blame for the Yemen war and humanitarian disaster.

British historian Mark Curtis posed a vital question that journalists fear to raise, not least those at the BBC: is there, in effect, collusion between the BBC and UK arms manufacturer BAE Systems not to report on UK support for the Saudi bombing of Yemen, and not to make it an election issue?[75] Curtis pointed out that the BAE Systems Chairman, Sir Roger Carr, was also Vice-Chair of the BBC Trust until April 2017 (when the Trust was wound up at the end of its 10-year tenure). The BBC Trust's role was to ensure the BBC lived up to its statutory obligations to the public, including news 'balance' and 'impartiality'. How could Sir Roger's dual role *not* suggest a major potential conflict of interest?

Curtis gave a damning assessment of BBC reporting on foreign affairs, particularly during the 2017 general election campaign. First, he made the point that:

> One aspect of a free and fair election is 'nonpartisan' coverage by state media.[76]

He continued:

> Yet BBC reporting on Britain's foreign policy is simply amplifying state priorities and burying its complicity in human rights abuses. The BBC is unable to report even that Britain is at war – in Yemen, where the UK is arming the Saudis to conduct mass bombing, having supplied them with aircraft and £1 billion worth of bombs, while training their pilots.

Curtis then provided some telling statistics:

> From 4 April to 15 May, the BBC website carried only 10 articles on Yemen but 97 on Syria: focusing on the crimes of an official enemy rather than our own. Almost no BBC articles on Yemen mention British arms exports. Theresa May's government is complicit in mass civilian deaths in Yemen and pushing millions of people to the brink of starvation; that this is not an election issue is a stupendous propaganda achievement.

Our own newspaper database searches reveal that, during the 2017 general election campaign, there was no significant journalistic scrutiny of May's support of Saudi Arabia's bombing of Yemen.

The subject was even deemed radioactive during a public meeting in Rye, Sussex, when Home Secretary Amber Rudd, standing for re-election, appeared to shut down discussion of arms sales to Saudi Arabia. Electoral candidate Nicholas Wilson explained what happened:

> At a hustings in Rye on 3 June, where I am standing as an independent anti-corruption parliamentary candidate, a question was asked about law & order. Home Secretary Amber Rudd, in answering it referred to the Manchester terrorist attack. I took up the theme and referred to UK arms sales to Saudi Arabia & HSBC business there. She spoke to and handed a note to the chairman who removed the mic from me.[77]

The footage of this shameful censorship deserves to be widely seen. If a similar event had happened in Russia or North Korea, it would have received intensive media scrutiny here. Once again, we note the arms connection with the BBC through BAE Systems Chairman, Sir Roger Carr. Wilson has also pointed out a potential conflict of interest between HSBC and the BBC through Rona Fairhead, who was a non-executive director of HSBC while serving as Chair of the BBC Trust.[78]

These links, and Theresa May's support for the Saudi regime, went essentially unexamined by the BBC. And yet, when BBC Political Editor Laura Kuenssberg responded to Corbyn's manifesto launch, her subtle use of language betrayed an inherent bias against Corbyn and his policies on foreign affairs.[79] She wrote: 'rather than scramble to cover up his past views for fear they would be unpopular', he would 'double down ... proudly'. Kuenssberg's pejorative vocabulary – 'scramble', 'cover up', 'unpopular' – delivered a powerful negative spin against Corbyn policies that, in fact, were hugely to his credit.

When has Kuenssberg *ever* pressed May over her appalling voting record on Afghanistan, Iraq, Libya, Syria and Yemen? In fact, there was no need for May to 'scramble' to 'cover up' her past views. Why not? Because the 'mainstream' media rarely, if ever, seriously challenged her about being consistently and disastrously wrong in her foreign policy choices; not least, on decisions to go to war.

8

The BBC as a Propaganda Machine

When we started Media Lens in 2001, our aim was to test the limits of free speech in all corporate media, but particularly in media famed for their fairness and honesty. As should be obvious, the limits of rational thought are *not* set by right-wing press like *The Times* and the *Sun*; they are set by the *Guardian*, the *Independent*, Channel 4 News and the BBC.

We began Media Lens with the expectation that professional journalists would be willing to engage in rational debate. We assumed that journalists would be keen to defend themselves against evidence-based charges of bias and distortion. In support of this aim, we were determined to do our best to maintain a polite and non-aggressive tone. As quickly became clear, high-profile journalists – feted as 'stars' and even 'celebrities' – respond to even gentle criticism like scalded cats. Aggression gives them a welcome excuse to dismiss a challenge as mere 'rudeness'. We used a non-aggressive approach based only on highly credible, referenced sources and solid arguments. Often, we were simply asking questions: 'Why did you say or write this, given that X and Y said that?' We didn't expect an easy ride: we initially worked on Media Lens in our spare time with zero resources challenging full-time journalists supported by teams of researchers, high-level sources, insider access and so on. Surely, they knew far more than we did? Surely, we would be severely tested?

In the early years of Media Lens, and indeed just prior to setting it up, we had extensive email exchanges with journalists. Edwards conducted telephone interviews with senior journalists Jon Snow of Channel 4 News, Roger Alton, then Editor of the *Observer*, and Alan Rusbridger, then Editor of the *Guardian*. Snow set the tone for many of the interactions we have experienced in the subsequent 17 years with shocking aggression and rudeness. He dismissed our media analysis out of hand as 'bollocks. Total bollocks!' 'I think you're *bananas* … You're completely off the clock!', despite professing to be 'Chomsky fan *numero uno*'. Did the corporate nature and funding of mass media mean there was a problem with structural bias? No, the problem was 'lazy journalism'. 'But isn't there a pattern to the lazy journalism?' 'No, unfortunately there is *not!*'[1]

Alton was amiable but bewildered. Rusbridger set the other major tone – canny obfuscation and bland diversion. He surely understood exactly what we were talking about – his long pauses and careful replies made clear that he was trying hard not to say too much.[2] In subsequent years, Rusbridger responded to our emails on several occasions. But this stopped after we highlighted the deceitful way the *Guardian* had treated Noam Chomsky in a 2005 interview, which had generated hundreds of emails in complaint.[3] Rusbridger's respect for free speech stopped at the point where he felt we were actually damaging the business, Guardian Media Group plc. (We sometimes wonder how Media Lens would have been received, if we had limited our criticisms to the *Guardian*'s enemies in the right-wing press. All we had to do was to insist that the Tory press was *incomparably worse* than the left-liberal press like the *Guardian* and the *Independent*, and that it was absurd to attack the only sources of honest news. We suspect we would have been feted as heroes by the *Guardian* and other corporate leftists. Certainly, it would have been a much easier life. And far less fun!)

As for the BBC, in the early days of Media Lens we had respectful, serious exchanges with Richard Sambrook, then Head of BBC News. His successor, Helen Boaden, was initially open to email exchanges when she took over in 2004. However, this again changed when we started having an impact, ramping up our questions about evidence of US war crimes in Iraq – for example, in the devastating assaults on Fallujah – that BBC News was underreporting, or reporting in a way that appeared to justify US force.[4] By now, many Media Lens readers were also challenging the BBC about the corporation's biased coverage of the Iraq War. Coincidentally or not, around this time the BBC launched a new website and television programme called 'Newswatch', supposedly intended to respond to public scrutiny.[5] Moreover, the BBC 'complaints system' was also 'streamlined' with challenges to individual editors and journalists deflected with instructions to use the 'official' route (with farcical consequences, as we will see later).

The impossibility of ever extracting any admission from BBC News that it could possibly be biased about *anything* was demonstrated when Boaden proclaimed, using standard BBC-speak:

I always think that impartiality is in our DNA – it's part of the BBC's genetic make-up.[6]

In fact, Boaden supplied one of the most ludicrous responses we have ever received from a journalist when she sent us the equivalent of six A4 pages of quotes from George W. Bush and Tony Blair as 'proof' of their good intentions: that they had indeed invaded Iraq for the stated propaganda reason of disarming Saddam of WMD.

During Boaden's tenure, email exchanges with the BBC dropped off, perhaps as journalists grew more wary of engaging with us. Who knows; perhaps there were even internal memos warning BBC employees to steer clear of us. As we wrote one media alert after another, gathering evidence of the BBC's lack of scrutiny of government policy, we saw ever more clearly how the broadcaster was actually *complicit* in state crimes: Afghanistan, Iraq, Israel's oppression of Palestinians, Libya, Syria, climate chaos. No wonder they respond to rational challenges with Kafkaesque confusion or, best of all, silence.

BBC News: 'A Twin of Rupert Murdoch's Sky News'

And yet, through constant repetition of BBC advertising messages, the public is *trained* to believe that the BBC is the world's 'best' news broadcaster; a relentlessly fair, honest and impartial provider of facts about national and international events. In reality, as critical theory academic Gavin Lewis notes, BBC News is:

> a twin of Rupert Murdoch's Sky News. Its editorial values are so identical that viewers get exactly the same hierarchy of news stories, at the same time of day, and predominantly from the same ideological viewpoint.[7]

Coverage of Western policy is, says Lewis, 'driven by a crude, skewed "good guy versus bad guy" narrative formula'. This BBC agenda is shaped by the compelling need of the state broadcaster to serve power. As a result, 'it has aligned itself with deeply undemocratic, unrepresentative forces and values.'

As the writer and activist Steve Rushton observes, the BBC habitually protects power, the monarchy, and an unjust and inequitable class system:

> The BBC should be seen as no less of an old boys' network than any other of the UK's institutions. From the top flights of big business, to the judiciary, to the civil service, to Westminster, the same pattern persists. This problem takes a particularly insidious form in the BBC because of its enormous influence, allowing it both to gloss and to normalise these dynamics not only for its audience in Britain, but around the world.[8]

Sarah O'Connell, who has worked for BBC News for many years, gives an insider view of the organisation:

> not many national BBC news journalists see enough of life at the 'bottom' of society to report on it properly or accurately. If most of my colleagues at the BBC didn't start life with a silver spoon in their mouths, by the time they've served ten years at the BBC (and the longevity and security of a BBC news staff job is recognised industry wide), they've pretty much gained honorary status of the establishment class.[9]

She continues:

> when you walk into a BBC newsroom you can see and hear the privilege. There are only a few genuinely working-class voices. There are hardly any black faces at all.

As an example, O'Connell describes how the widespread abuse of the parliamentary expenses system by MPs, a major scandal that emerged in 2009, was essentially ignored by the BBC. When she tried to report the scandal, she was told by BBC News editors that 'this isn't a story, MPs have to eat.' She adds:

> But it was a story. It was one of the biggest political stories of the decade. And the BBC missed it, because, to most of their journalists at that time, the idea of having lunch for £150 on expenses, well, it just wasn't a story, was it? Not when it was exactly the kind of thing BBC news executives might be doing as well.

And yet, high-profile BBC News professionals are sufficiently schooled in doublethink that they can routinely proclaim their adherence to the highest standards of journalism without batting an eye. For instance, Jon Sopel, BBC North America Editor, asserted with metaphorical hand on heart:

> It is our job to test our elected officials, to subject them to scrutiny, to ask the questions the public want answering and hopefully to be fearless in our pursuit of those questions.[10]

It takes great chutzpah, or overweening pride in institutional BBC myths, to try to get away with such remarks. But it's no surprise to hear boilerplate guff like this from BBC journalists. After all, the man who was leading Sopel from atop BBC News was James Harding, a former *Times* editor under Rupert Murdoch, who churned out corporate PR-speak, piously declaring that BBC journalism has an:

> uncompromising commitment to accuracy, to impartiality, to diversity of opinion, and to the fair treatment of people in the news.[11]

Harding added:

> If you make a mistake, you should correct it as soon as you become aware of it – particularly in live and continuous news or on a website.

But what happens when the BBC's 'mistake' is to channel and amplify pro-government and pro-business ideology, day after day, as we have seen throughout this book? When has this ever been 'corrected' by the BBC?

When Harding migrated from Murdoch's empire to UK public broadcasting, he famously urged BBC journalists:

> not to shy away from investigative reporting and difficult issues in the wake of the Jimmy Savile and Lord McAlpine affairs.[12]

He described the corporation as 'the best news organisation in the world', and he promised a renewed commitment to 'curious, inquisitive journalism in the public interest'. He claimed that he wanted BBC News to devote more resources to 'original journalism' and to focus on 'story-getting'.

But the claim was farcical. When asked whether the BBC would have run with whistle-blower Edward Snowden's revelations, if the news organisation had been approached first, he said no.[13] Why not? Because that would have been 'campaigning' journalism. Just consider that for a moment. Presenting the truth of US government deceptions is 'campaigning'!

As Glenn Greenwald wrote:

> his reasoning shows how neutered state-funded media inevitably becomes. Here's one of the biggest stories in journalism of the last decade, one that sparked a worldwide debate about a huge range of issues, spawned movements for legislative reform, ruptured diplomatic relationships, changed global Internet behavior, and won almost every major journalism award in the West. And the director of news and current affairs of BBC says they likely would not have reported the story, one that — in addition to all those other achievements – happened to have enraged the British government to which the BBC must maintain fealty.[14]

But there is no end to the ideological shibboleths that establishment figures churn out. Tony Hall, the BBC's Director-General, once told an interviewer:

One of the things that has always amazed me about the BBC is that it is the most self-questioning organisation I've ever worked in. It asks itself questions all the time about whether it's doing the right thing, could we have done that better.[15]

Jenni Russell, a former BBC editor, takes a very different view:

Nothing makes the BBC as nervous as the prospect of its own journalists inquiring into its behaviour. [...] No one in the organisation is ever unaware of the possible damage to the BBC's brand when news starts asking critical questions of the BBC itself. The corporate centre's instinctive response is to block and discourage criticism, and any ambitious editors and executives in news are constantly aware of that. [...] Trying to get a reaction out of senior executives either in news or the corporate centre always sent it into hedgehog mode, making it bristling, fearful and unresponsive.[16]

'The World Wants America as its Policeman'

Spare a thought for those brave people who enter the labyrinthine den of the BBC 'complaints system', mentioned earlier. This is a soul-crushing experience that even the former BBC Chairman Lord Grade once described as 'grisly', due to a system that is 'absolutely hopeless'.[17] So what hope for us mere mortals? Anyone who makes the attempt is surely forever disabused of the notion that BBC News engages with, or indeed serves, the public in any meaningful way. Helen Boaden, then Head of BBC News, once joked about how she evaded public complaints that were sent to her on email:

Oh, I just changed my email address.[18]

This was not long after Media Lens and many of our readers had repeatedly challenged the BBC over its biased reporting, notably on Iraq (see above).

One of our favourite cases was a challenge made about an article by that avuncular epitome of BBC gravitas, World Affairs Editor

John Simpson. As noted in Chapter 6, in a 2014 BBC website article entitled, 'Barack Obama's best years could still be ahead of him', Simpson claimed that:

The world (well, most of it) wants an active, effective America to act as its policeman, sorting out the problems smaller countries can't face alone.[19]

One of our readers studied the article, then submitted a complaint to the BBC in November 2014, noting that:

In an international opinion poll by Gallup this year the US was found to be the greatest threat to peace in the world, voted three times more dangerous to world peace than the next country. The BBC article is therefore, at worst, incorrect and biased or at best highly inaccurate. Will you be retracting the statement?[20]

Needless to say, the BBC did no such thing. In fact, Sean Moss, whose job title reads 'BBC Complaints Adviser for BBC News Website', delivered a comical reply:

In fact the poll referenced in your complaint was from the end of last year rather than this year. It is an annual end of year survey which in this edition 'explores the outlook, expectations, hopes and fears of people from 65 countries around the world' from 2013.

Given that we're now nearly at the end of 2014 and they will be conducting a new poll next month we're unclear on what basis you feel these views are still applicable.

'Unclear' if 'still applicable'? Far from being a rogue result, the US *regularly* tops polls of global public opinion as the country posing the greatest threat to peace. As Noam Chomsky noted in a 2016 interview when discussing nuclear weapons:

Iran is not a threat, period. The world doesn't regard Iran as a threat. That's a U.S. obsession. You look at polls of global opinion taken by Gallup's international affiliate, the leading U.S. polling agency, one of the questions that they ask is, 'Which country is the greatest threat to world peace?' Answer: United States, by a huge margin. Iran is barely mentioned. Second place is Pakistan, inflated by the Indian vote, that's way behind the United States. That's world opinion. And there are reasons for it. Americans are protected from this information.[21]

Not only Americans. British – indeed, global – audiences, too; thanks in no small measure to the BBC.

The requirement to keep awkward facts hidden or marginalised is especially pressing on those BBC journalists who report from the United States. Thus, in an online report titled 'The decline of US power?', the BBC New York correspondent Nick Bryant had to tread carefully in mentioning America's 'approval rating', as measured by Gallup:

> In Asia, America's median approval rating in 2014, as measured by Gallup, was 39%, a 6% drop since 2011.
> In Africa, the median approval went down to 59%, the lowest since polling began, despite Obama hosting the US-Africa Leaders' Summit in Washington in August, last year.[22]

There was no mention of the finding that, as noted above, global public opinion regularly regards the US as the country that is the greatest threat to world peace, and by a considerable margin.[23]

However, there was plenty of space for Bryant to churn out the usual BBC boilerplate about America's 'national interest' and Obama's 'pragmatism' and 'diplomatic dexterity'; all this about a leader who boasted he had bombed seven countries,[24] rapidly escalated a killer drone programme[25] and broken his pledge to shut down the US Guantanamo torture camp in Cuba.

'A Load of Tosh'

On 22 January 2018, BBC 'News at Ten' broadcast a piece by Defence Correspondent Jonathan Beale reporting a speech by General Sir Nick Carter, the British Army's Chief of General Staff. Carter gave his speech, pleading for more resources in the face of the Russian 'threat', at the Royal United Services Institute (RUSI), an establishment thinktank with close links to the military and corporate media.

Beale began his BBC News piece with a prologue of raw propaganda, delivered in an urgent and impassioned tone:

> Russia's building an increasingly modern and aggressive military. Already tested in battle in Syria, using weapons Britain would struggle to match – like long-range missiles. In Ukraine, they've been using unconventional warfare, electronic cyber and misinformation. And they're even on manoeuvres on Europe's doorstep, with large-scale exercises near NATO's borders. Enough to worry the head of the British army who tonight gave this rare public warning.

The essence of Carter's 'rare public warning' was that:

> Russia was building an increasingly aggressive expeditionary force and the potential military threats to the UK 'are now on Europe's doorstep'... the Kremlin already boasted an 'eye-watering quantity of capability' – a level the UK would struggle to match ... Britain 'must take notice of what is going on around us' or ... the ability by the UK to take action will be 'massively constrained'.[26]

Carter continued:

> Rather like a chronic contagious disease, it will creep up on us, and our ability to act will be markedly constrained – and we'll be the losers of this competition.

The BBC reported that the army chief's warning had been approved by the Defence Secretary, Gavin Williamson. On 'News at Ten', Beale's reporting of the speech amplified the army chief's message – in other words, the Defence Secretary's stance – by deploying such key phrases as:

> increasingly aggressive', 'tested in battle', 'Britain would struggle to match', 'manoeuvres on Europe's doorstep', 'near NATO's borders'.

There was, of course, no mention of US/NATO encroachment towards Russia since the fall of the Soviet Union (contravening assurances given to Gorbachev[27]), or the US bases[28] and military exercises[29] close to Russia's borders as well as globally, or the long history[30] of US threats and major crimes[31] around the world. Nor was there any reference to Ukraine, which has routinely been reported as an example of Russian 'aggression'. John Pilger observes that the BBC, along with others, including CNN, the *New York Times* and the *Guardian*:

> played a critical role in conditioning their viewers to accept a new and dangerous cold war.
>
> All have misrepresented events in Ukraine as a malign act by Russia when, in fact, the coup in Ukraine in 2014 was the work of the United States, aided by Germany and NATO.[32]

Beale's credulous reporting of the army chief's speech was an exemplar of 'public broadcast' media whipping up fear to promote state interests.

Later, standing outside the Ministry of Defence, Beale said:

> This intervention by the head of the army is as much an appeal for more money for defence as it is a warning about the threat posed by Russia.

And yet Beale had earlier dramatically highlighted the 'worrying' facts, asserting they were 'enough to worry the head of the British army'; in other words, that the army chief really *was* worried. Beale's subsequent comment was a token, blink-and-you'll-miss-it acknowledgement of the reality: that Carter's speech was aimed at propping up UK military power.

Note that Beale's 'neutral' reporting was not about an 'alleged threat posed by Russia'; simply the 'threat posed by Russia'. This subtly insidious use of language occurs daily on 'impartial' BBC News.

And, as ever, such a report would be incomplete without an establishment talking head from a 'defence and security' thinktank. Professor Michael Clarke, a senior RUSI fellow, was on hand to perform the required role. This was BBC News in standard establishment/state/military/corporate mode.

Later, Beale was duly confronted by several people on Twitter about his promotion of UK state and military propaganda on the Russian 'threat'. One Twitter user asked the BBC journalist:

> The only thing the MSM [mainstream media] is good for is fake news, falsification and manipulation of truth & propaganda. Ask yourself for whose benefit?[33]

This is a reasonable starting point for a debate about the major news media. But Beale did not distinguish himself with the quality of his response:

> What a load of tosh.[34]

In contrast, Beale's 'opinion-free' response to the army chief's propaganda speech was:

> Coherent, detailed and impressive speech by @ArmyCGS @RUSI_org tonight making the case for investment in #defence. CDS [Chief of Defence Staff] in waiting?[35]

Imagine if the BBC man's observations had been reversed. It is, of course, completely unthinkable that a BBC reporter would respond to a major military or political speech with:

> What a load of tosh.

It would be equally unthinkable for a BBC journalist to respond to a speech by, for example, Noam Chomsky, with:

> Coherent, detailed and impressive speech tonight exposing Western war propaganda.

And likewise, a dissident expert would never be invited to respond scornfully, or even sceptically, to a speech by the likes of Sir Nick Carter on the BBC's 'News At Ten'.

Dying in a Ditch for BBC News 'Impartiality'

The irony in the ongoing corporate media allegations about 'fake news' (see Chapter 12) is that, as Glenn Greenwald noted, 'those who most loudly denounce Fake News are typically those most aggressively disseminating it.'[36] That is because the corporate media fears losing control of the media agenda.

As for BBC News, its privileged, publicly-funded position as supposedly the world's most trusted broadcaster is under threat. So, while reasonable questions can be asked[37] of the growing behemoths of the media landscape – Google, YouTube and Facebook – 'mainstream' journalists know full well not to scrutinise publicly their own industry's output of state-corporate 'fake news'.

Thus, following the US presidential election in November 2016, BBC Technology Correspondent Rory Cellan-Jones could safely hold Facebook up to the light and ask:

> If Facebook or something similar had not existed, would Donald Trump still be heading for the White House?
>
> That is hard to say but what does seem likely is that social media served to polarise views in what was already a bitter election and may have encouraged a few hesitant voters to come out for Mr Trump.
>
> This makes Facebook's claims that it is just a technology platform, rather than a hugely powerful media company with Mark Zuckerberg as editor-in-chief, look very thin indeed. But *there are few signs that the company is ready to face up to this heavy responsibility or engage in some serious soul-searching* [our emphasis].[38]

It would be remarkable if a BBC journalist were to write of his or her employer:

> there are few signs that the broadcaster is ready to face up to this heavy responsibility or engage in some serious soul-searching.

But then, as John Pilger noted:

> Propaganda is most effective when our consent is engineered by those with a fine education – Oxford, Cambridge, Harvard, Columbia — and with careers on the BBC, the *Guardian*, the *New York Times*, the *Washington Post*.[39]

As a prime example, consider Laura Kuenssberg, the BBC's Political Editor. In 2016, *Press Gazette* awarded her the accolade of 'Journalist of the Year'.[40] She told the trade paper proudly that:

> I would die in a ditch for the impartiality of the BBC.[41]

Two former senior BBC figures would dispute that self-serving depiction of die-hard BBC impartiality. Greg Dyke, a former BBC Director-General, made no bones about it when he declared:

> The BBC is part of a 'conspiracy' preventing the 'radical changes' needed to UK democracy.[42]

Dyke argued that a parliamentary commission should look into the 'whole political system', adding that:

> I fear it will never happen because I fear the political class will stop it.

And Sir Michael Lyons, former Chairman of the BBC Trust, admitted in 2016 that there had been 'some quite extraordinary attacks' on Labour leader Jeremy Corbyn by the BBC.[43]

Up to and including dying in a ditch, Kuenssberg would do anything to defend the impartiality of the BBC. Well, perhaps not *anything*. Asked for her 'impartial' view on why 35,000 members of the public had signed a petition[44] calling for her to be sacked for her bias, Kuenssberg replied rather less heroically: 'I'm not going to get into that.'[45]

Des Freedman, Professor of Media and Communications at Goldsmiths, University of London, says of the kind of anti-Corbyn bias displayed by Kuenssberg (see Chapter 2) that it:

> isn't an accident or a one-off example of 'bad journalism' but is built into a media system that is intertwined with the interests that run the country.[46]

He adds:

> This doesn't mean that there's a smoke-filled room somewhere where anti-Corbyn people get together. I think you just call it a routine editorial meeting. The point is many senior journalists ...

reflect the dominant strain that runs through their newsrooms – one based on the assumed benefits of neoliberalism and foreign intervention and the undesirability (or the sheer madness of the idea) of redistribution, nationalisation and people like Jeremy Corbyn who don't share the same social circles or ideological commitments.

As Freedman rightly concludes:

We need a wholly different media system: one that's not afraid to challenge power because it's not steeped in power in the first place.

9

Dismantling the National Health Service

Noam Chomsky once described the standard state-corporate strategy for handing over public services to private interests:

> If you want to privatize something and destroy it, a standard method is first to defund it, so it doesn't work anymore, people get upset and accept privatization.[1]

Few political acts have illustrated this better, and simultaneously exposed the sham of British 'democracy', than the decision to dismantle the National Health Service. The Health and Social Care Act 2012 has an innocuous title, but the consequences have been enormous:

1. The long-standing obligation of the UK government to provide universal healthcare was ditched.
2. The NHS was carved open for exploitation by private interests.

Most fundamentally, the new act removed the formal commitment of the Secretary of State for Health to provide healthcare for every man, woman and child in England. In effect, this removed the founding principle of the NHS, set up in 1948. It means that one of the finest health services anywhere, created by the British people in the wake of the Second World War, had just been primed for demolition.

Private companies would now be able to move in and take over NHS infrastructure such as hospitals. The new law also allowed hospitals to earn up to 49 per cent of their revenue from private patients; previously the limit was 2 per cent. Doctors and nurses warned this would create a two-tier system, with one queue for the rich and one for the poor, with the rich having priority regardless of the seriousness of their condition. People could wave farewell to one of the founding principles of the NHS: to supply care based on need, not on the ability to pay.

In 2006, then Conservative leader David Cameron had spoken out passionately in support of the NHS:

> When your family relies on the NHS all the time – day after day, night after night – you know how precious it is. So for me, it's not just a question of saying the NHS is safe in my hands. My family is so often in the hands of the NHS. So I want them to be safe there.

Cameron had pledged that a Tory government would not bring in any more 'pointless and disruptive reorganisations'. He added:

> Yes, change is necessary in the NHS. But that change must come from the bottom up; driven by the wishes and needs of NHS professionals and patients.[2]

The coalition agreement between the Tories and the Lib Dems of May 2010, following the general election that spring, had promised: 'We will stop the top-down reorganisation of the NHS.'[3] That promise was well and truly smashed.

The government tried to justify the bill by arguing that the NHS was 'not working' and that it must be 'reformed'. In fact, a study published in the *Journal of the Royal Society of Medicine* found that the NHS is one of the fairest, most cost-effective and efficient healthcare systems in the world.[4]

The NHS bill was hideously complicated and virtually unreadable. Critics claimed this was intentional, serving to hide the bill's true purpose: selling off more and more of the NHS to private companies. For example, the British Medical Association (BMA) denounced the bill as 'complex, incoherent and not fit for purpose, and almost impossible to implement successfully, given widespread opposition across the NHS workforce'.[5]

Richard Horton, Editor of *The Lancet*, the prestigious medical journal, warned that instigating a new era of private sector colonisation of health services was 'simply reckless. Not one expert inside or outside government believes this is a sensible strategy.'[6] As a result, he said, there would be 'unprecedented chaos' in the NHS. He continued:

People will die, thanks to the Government's decision to focus on competition rather than quality in healthcare. The coming disaster puts even greater responsibility on us to overturn this destructive legislation.

No wonder that the NHS bill was opposed by 27 professional medical bodies, including the Royal College of GPs, the BMA and the Royal College of Nurses: that's *all but one of the relevant medical bodies*. Only the Royal College of Surgeons did not actually call for the bill's withdrawal, but they did argue that it 'would damage the NHS'.[7]

The BMA warned before the bill became law:

... if passed the Bill will be irreversibly damaging to the NHS as a public service, converting it into a competitive marketplace that will widen health inequalities and be detrimental to patient care.[8]

The Royal College of General Practitioners said they were:

concerned that the Bill will cause irreparable damage to patient care and jeopardise the NHS. Three quarters of respondents to a poll carried out by the RCGP said they thought it appropriate to seek the withdrawal of the Health and Social Care Bill.[9]

The Royal College of Midwives also called for the bill to be scrapped:

This bill is a massively expensive distraction from the challenges that the NHS faces in trying to improve healthcare at a time of severe spending restraint ... We join the growing chorus of voices calling for the bill to be withdrawn, and the proposed reforms stopped in their entirety.[10]

It was all to no avail. The government bulldozed the bill through Parliament into law.

SERCO, described by one *Guardian* columnist as 'probably the biggest company you've never heard of',[11] and Virgin were two of the corporate giants who were quick to move in. Virgin Care won a £500 million contract to provide community services across Surrey and began running these services, as well as the county's prison healthcare, on 1 April 2012. Max Pemberton, a junior doctor 'writing about life on the NHS frontline', noted that Virgin Care's takeover in Surrey exposed two fundamental lies propagated by the government, with media collusion:

> The first is the flat denial that the Bill represented any sort of privatisation of the NHS, despite it being obvious to anyone who read it that this is precisely what it was.[12]

The NHS will become 'a nominal logo', warned Pemberton, and 'a bureaucratic governing body dishing out public money to private companies.'

The second lie exposed was the lunatic government claim that the reforms were underpinned by 'the concept of choice within a nationalised healthcare system'. Pemberton asked pointedly:

> What real choice did the people of Surrey have in who provided their community health services?

The answer?

> None. The choice was made by unelected, unaccountable bureaucrats who use 'public consultation' as a fig leaf for fundamentally changing the nature of how healthcare is delivered. Increasingly, the details of these decisions and the contracts that are drawn up are deemed commercially sensitive, so we are not privy to what is happening to our NHS and our money.

What about choice of healthcare providers? There was none; it's Virgin Care or nothing. So much for the much-touted 'market'. The outcome is 'perverse, warped and corrupt'.

Dr John Lister, of the campaign group London Health Emergency, said:

Now we can see [then Health Secretary Andrew] Lansley's nightmare vision of the NHS taking shape, as the full chaos of cuts coupled with privatisation hits services around the country.[13]

Lister warned:

Report after report highlights the chronic, systemic failure of home care services and nursing homes for frail older people – services entirely dominated by for-profit private providers, offering clients the spurious 'choice' of uniformly awful services at extortionate rates while paying most of their exploited staff just the minimum wage. The chaos in this sector gives a real flavour of what many other sectors of health care will look like once they have been carved up between 'any qualified provider'.

He cited just one disturbing example from Camden in London, following a long-running fiasco in which a local GP surgery was handed over to US multinational, United Health, on a cut-price contract. The multinational then pulled out and the practice was taken over by the blandly-titled The Practice plc. But this company then failed to secure premises or invest in services, leaving 3,000 or more patients without a GP, at least temporarily.

'Much Profit to be Made!' Vested Interests of MPs and Lords

On 20 March 2012, MPs passed the Health and Social Care Bill (commonly called 'the NHS bill') more than 14 months after it was first put before Parliament. There had been numerous public protests[14] and, as we saw above, virtually every major professional medical body had fought against it.

Many of the MPs and Lords who voted the bill through stood to gain financially from the Health and Social Care Act. 225 parliamentarians had recent or current financial private healthcare connections, and 145 Lords had recent or ongoing financial connections to companies involved in healthcare.[15] In a responsible democracy, this would be deemed a serious conflict of interest, and yet it would presumably not come as a shock to a British electorate used to unpleasant surprises: if they ever got to hear of it.

Research by Labour activist Éoin Clarke revealed that 333 donations from private healthcare sources totalling £8.3 million were gifted to the Tories.[16] Moreover, the website Social Investigations, run by blogger Andrew Robertson, compiled an extensive list of the financial and vested interests of MPs and Lords in private healthcare. This list, said Robertson, 'represents the dire state of our democracy'.[17] Here is a sample from the list:

Lord Bell: Conservative – Chairman of Chime Communications group, whose companies include Bell Pottinger, and whose lobbying clients include Southern Cross, BT Health and Astra-Zeneca.

Lord Blyth of Rowington: Conservative – senior adviser to investment bankers Greenhill. Former Boots Chemists Deputy Chairman. Tory donor.

Nick de Bois, [then] Conservative MP for Enfield North: the majority shareholder in Rapier Design Group, an events management company heavily involved with the private medical and pharmaceutical industries, and whose clients include leading names such as AstraZeneca. A number of the company's clients are 'partners' of the National Association of Primary Care (NAPC), a lobby group that supported the NHS bill. Rapier Design Group's biggest clients stand to profit now that the NHS has been opened up to wider private-sector involvement. The GP commissioning consortium for south-west Kent, covering 49 GP practices and known as Salveo, has already signed a contract with the pharmaceuticals giant AstraZeneca.

And then there is Andrew Lansley himself, who was the Tory Secretary of State for Health at the time. John Nash, the Chairman of Care UK, gave £21,000 to fund Lansley's personal office in November 2009. According to a senior director of the firm, 96 per cent of Care UK's business, which amounted to more than £400 million in 2011, comes from the NHS. Hedge-fund boss Nash is one of the major Conservative donors with close ties to the healthcare industry. Nash is also a founder of City firm Sovereign Capital, which runs a string of private healthcare firms. And so on.

Robertson rightly pointed to 'the network of vested interests that runs between Parliament and the private healthcare industry. This cosy, toxic relationship,' he warns, 'threatens not only the future of the NHS but that of democracy in the UK.' This insidious network linking healthcare companies, politicians, thinktanks, lobbyists and big money is yet another example of how public interests and accountability are seemingly forever bypassed by powerful elite forces.[18]

If this had been happening in an officially-declared enemy state, the British news media would have been shouting themselves hoarse about corruption, greed and the pathetic state of 'democracy' over 'there'. If this had been happening in Libya under Gaddafi, or Syria under Assad, or Iran under any leader, the airwaves and newspapers in this country would have been filled with condemnations and scorn about the oppression of the people by an unaccountable, tyrannical government.

That it was happening under their noses here at home, largely with the corporate media's connivance, said it all.

Dear BBC: Where Were You When the Tories Dismantled the NHS?

Given such a momentous attack on one of the UK's most cherished institutions – if not, *the* most cherished – it should have been incumbent upon the media to report honestly and accurately what was happening. And, as several of the references in this chapter show, there *was* some good reporting in the *Guardian*, the *Independent*, the *Telegraph* and other papers. But surely this requirement for honest and challenging coverage applies above all to the BBC? After all, as it so incessantly reminds us, it is a globally respected news organisation. Moreover, BBC News has a statutory commitment to 'impartiality', 'providing a breadth of view' and properly informing the public of 'matters of public policy'.[19]

The NHS affects every man, woman and child in the country. And yet we suspect very few members of the public realised then, or even now, just what had been happening to our healthcare system. The BBC mostly failed to cover the story, and otherwise offered coverage heavily biased in favour of the government's perspective. On the very day the bill passed into law, the tagline across the bottom of BBC News broadcasts said 'Bill which gives power to GPs passes'. This assessment could have come from a government press release. It was a propaganda line that had been rejected by an overwhelming majority of GPs.[20] The BBC also repeatedly failed to cover public protests, including one outside the Department of Health which stopped traffic in Whitehall for an hour (see below).

A media activist who followed the NHS story closely over an extended period sent us this in 2012:

> For the past two years there has been so little coverage of this bill that even as some were desperately fighting to stop it – through e-petitions, lobbying campaigns and even demonstrations – many people did not appear to be even aware of it. I have been on a demonstration in which people sat down in the road in Whitehall, outside the Department of Health and blocked the traffic, yet this was not mentioned at all on the news.
>
> When the BBC have reported on the bill they have been sparse with their explanations of its implications or the reasons why so many – including most medical professionals – have objected to it. They have tended to limit their comments to those of the type 'Some people say it's privatisation' without explaining why or exploring the issue.
>
> There have not been – as we might have expected for so momentous a change – debates on the Today Programme, on BBC Newsnight, or background analysis programmes, with politicians being challenged and questioned on the policy. Radio 4 ran a programme at 8pm ['The Report', on 22 March 2012] which appeared to be very biased in favour of the bill, with opposing views not adequately represented.

The activist summed up:

Whatever one's views on the Health and Social Care bill, surely such large scale changes which may affect the health of so many, should have been widely reported and debated, especially when you consider that the [Tory-Liberal Democrat] coalition government was not elected and did not put this issue in their manifestos.[21]

Why did we never see a BBC television news report like this one from RT: 'UK govt bill opens up NHS to private profiteering'?[22]

On the day the NHS bill was passed, insightful and outraged public comments on the BBC's paltry coverage were tracked by activist Isobel Weinberg on Twitter:[23]

As the sun sets on the #NHS isn't it great to know what a nice dress Kate Middleton was wearing. Thanks #tvnews #BBC #ITV #media

Did anything happen to the #NHS today, OECD leading health system? Who IS making these editorial decisions? #BBCnews @BBCNews @BBCNewsnight

Dear #BBC where were you when the #Tories dismantled the #NHS? Just checked to see and tis indeed true not a word on the NHS bill on the BBC – unbelievable.

It is our arrogance that makes us mistrust every other state-run media but believe ours to be independent and free. #NHS #BBC

And Clive Peedell, Deputy Chair of the NHS Consultants' Association, observed:

England's biggest ever robbery took place today – The #NHS was stolen from under the noses of the public by the Health & Social Care Act.[24]

Author and journalist Marcus Chown, a consultant for *New Scientist*, distributed examples via Twitter of protests against the bill that made no inroads into corporate news coverage (Chown's wife is an NHS nurse). These included:

- Unreported 'Drop the NHS bill' protest on Mothers' Day in Parliament Square, London.
- Unreported doctors' 'Drop the NHS bill' protest.
- Unreported 'Drop the NHS bill' sit-down protest that blocked traffic for an hour in Whitehall, London.
- Unreported 'Drop the NHS bill' candle-lit vigil, St Thomas' Hospital, London.

Dorothy Bishop, Professor of Developmental Neuropsychology at Oxford University challenged the BBC about its supposed 'extensive coverage' of the NHS bill. She described 'a remarkable disconnect between what was being reported on BBC News outlets and what was concerning many members of the public'.[25]

Liz Panton, a speech and language therapist who has worked for the NHS for over 30 years, said:

> The BBC seems completely out of touch with the general mood of public opinion and widespread fear and anxiety about the changes to our way of life as a result of the NHS Bill.[26]

In a rare instance of the BBC actually putting a senior politician on the spot about something that matters, Dr Phil Hammond challenged Andrew Lansley, then Secretary of State for Health, on 'Question Time' about the disaster the bill would create for genuine healthcare, for cooperation between medical professionals and for basic human compassion.[27] Imagine if news editors and journalists had been consistently making this kind of challenge in the 14 months before the bill became law.

So why *was* the BBC coverage so appalling?

The BBC's Private Healthcare Perks and the Lord Living it Large

As discussed in the previous chapter, the BBC habitually protects power, not least the state, to which it is closely tied. Tom Mills, author of *The BBC: The Myth of a Public Service*, explains:

> First it is important to state from the outset what is rarely acknowledged in discussions about the BBC: that it isn't

independent from governments, let alone from the broader Establishment. The BBC has always been formally accountable to ministers for its operations. Governments set the terms under which it operates, they appoint its most senior figures, who in future will be directly involved in day-to-day managerial decision making, and they set the level of the licence fee, which is the BBC's major source of income. So that's the context within which the BBC operates, and it hardly amounts to independence in any substantive sense.[28]

Consider, then, the ties that link BBC bosses with private health companies. The BBC is managed by an Executive Committee while, at the time, the now defunct BBC Trust was there to ensure that standards such as impartiality and fairness were maintained in the public interest. At least, that is the official line.

For example, take Dr Mike Lynch OBE, who was then on the BBC's Executive Board.[29] Lynch was a non-executive director of Isabel Healthcare Ltd, a private company specialising in medical software. He was a director of Autonomy PLC, a computing company whose customers include Isabel Healthcare, Blue Cross Blue Shield (a health insurance firm), AstraZeneca, GlaxoSmithKline, and several other pharmaceutical companies. He was also on the advisory board of Apax Partners, which describes itself as 'one of the leading global investors in the Healthcare sector' and has invested over €2.5 billion in the area. These medical interests all stand to gain from the new legislation. Is this the resumé of a man who would really insist on impartial reporting of controversial 'reforms' of the NHS?[30]

Lord Patten of Barnes, then Chairman of the BBC, was similarly tied up in private medical and financial interests.[31] Patten was a member of the European Advisory Board for a private equity investment company called Bridgepoint. Alan Milburn, the former Secretary of State for Health under Tony Blair, was chair of Bridgepoint's board. The company had been involved in 17 healthcare deals in previous years. Its current investments in the UK total more than £1.1 billion.

One company acquired by Bridgepoint for £414 million in July 2010 was the residential care company Care UK, whose chairman donated £21,000 in November 2009 to run then Tory Health Secretary Andrew Lansley's personal office. Further transactions for Bridgepoint and a private healthcare company involved Alliance Medical who sold the MRI scan company for £600 million to Dubai International LLC in 2007.

Lord Patten was appointed to the Lords in 2005 and, before being accepted as the head of the BBC, was urged to cut back on his business activities. However, this didn't happen, and in addition to his advisory role in Bridgepoint, he remained a stakeholder of energy giant EDF, adviser to telecom business Hutchison Europe and a member of the advisory board of BP.

None of this is intended to suggest that BBC managers were crudely leaning on BBC editors to suppress news coverage of opposition to the dismantling of the NHS. We are aware of no evidence to that effect. But the interests and priorities of senior managers certainly have a more subtle impact on the culture of the organisation beneath them. As even former *Guardian* Editor Alan Rusbridger, no radical, once told us:

> If you ask anybody who works in newspapers, they will quite rightly say, 'Rupert Murdoch', or whoever, 'never tells me what to write', which is beside the point: they don't have to be told what to write.[32]

The observation, of course, generalises to the broadcast media. And anyway, surely the interlocking links between politics, the media and private financial and industrial interests should have been exposed and widely debated?[33]

As a strong additional factor, it is likely that the Hutton Inquiry, leading to the resignation of the BBC's Chairman Gavyn Davies and Director-General Greg Dyke, generated a climate of fear at the BBC that deters journalists from challenging the government too strongly. We will return to this point below.

A further possible factor behind BBC indifference to the dismantling of the NHS is that many senior BBC staff do not themselves depend on the NHS.

The BBC actually spends millions of pounds on private healthcare for its staff. Under a Freedom of Information request, it was revealed that the BBC shelled out almost £2.2 million of public money on private healthcare for several hundred senior BBC staff between 2008–10.[34]

In 2012, when the NHS bill became law, the *Daily Telegraph* reported that in the previous year, 506 BBC managers benefited from the £1,500-a-year perk. When challenged, the BBC responded that this is 'common industry practice' for senior managers, 'although the BBC has recently announced this benefit will no longer be made available to new senior managers'.[35] There was no word, though, on existing senior BBC managers having to forgo their private health insurance.

Dear Nick Robinson: About That Email ...

Marcus Chown, the science writer, highlighted an extraordinary email that he received from an anonymous BBC employee just after the NHS bill was voted through.[36] The email read:

> The BBC under/non-reporting of the opposition to the bill is even more of a mystery after I've read over the BBC news briefs myself (I don't work in news, but anyone can see the news briefs). There are pages and pages of text on the opposition to the bill. Someone, or some people have clearly gone to a great deal of effort enumerating the objections, documents that have existed for over a month, and there is a long and comprehensive (and regularly updated list) outlining the latest views of all the professional bodies. All the fact checking and detail anyone needs to run a detailed story on the opposition to the bill is there, and there are no official restrictions on reporting it, but somehow it still isn't happening. I can't make sense of it.[37]

This prompted us to email Nick Robinson, the BBC's Political Editor, on 17 April 2012. He had previously written to *us* to say he was investigating 'BBC impartiality' on related issues:

I am looking solely at my own patch ie issues of domestic politics.[38]

We reminded him of this and asked:

Presumably, then, you will examine the evidence that the BBC failed to report impartially on the Health and Social Care Bill?

There are many serious and reputable sources that you could ask, not least the 27 professional medical bodies in this country who opposed the Bill, such as the Royal College of GPs, the British Medical Association and the Royal College of Nurses ...

And what about apparent conflicts of interest at the BBC? Will you investigate the evidence?

For example: 'BBC chief Lord [Chris] Patten of Barnes, Bridgepoint and the Conflicts of Interest' (Andrew Robertson, 'BBC chief Lord Patten of Barnes, Bridgepoint and the Conflicts of Interest', Social Investigations blog, March 22, 2012; http://socialinvestigations.blogspot.co.uk/2012/03/lord-patten-of-barnes-bridgepoint-and.html).

'Why did the BBC ignore the NHS Bill?' (Rusty Light blog, March 31, 2012; http://rustylight.blogspot.co.uk/2012/03/why-did-bbc-ignore-nhs-bill.html)

When you have a moment, could you possibly give us your response, please? Many thanks.

Alas, as so often, we received the familiar BBC response of no-response.

So why the BBC behaved in the way it did over the NHS bill remains an intriguing puzzle. It is not a complete mystery, of course, given that the BBC is dependent on government money (i.e. public money), and given that the UK government sets the BBC Charter and determines who runs the organisation. As we saw with the government's deceptions on Iraq's non-existent WMD, and the subsequent fallout (as noted above, both the BBC Chairman and

Director-General resigned), there is always the threat of reper-
cussions if the state broadcaster becomes too critical of the state.
Whether any actual high-level decision was taken at the BBC to
adopt a government-friendly line on the NHS will never be known,
unless whistle-blowers speak out. It is much more likely that no
executive 'decision' was required and that this has simply become
the default mode of BBC reporting.

We asked Tim Llewellyn, a former BBC Middle East correspondent for over ten years, if his insider perspective could shed some
light on the BBC's performance. He began by candidly admitting
that UK healthcare 'is outside my area of normal close perusal'[39]
But he then continued with refreshing honesty:

> My first observations are, though, to say that I don't think it has
> much to do with Chris Patten [Former Tory minister who was
> Chairman of the BBC Trust from 2011–14], unless the BBC has
> become an even more sinister place than I thought. He would
> not interfere in coverage decisions as such, and I don't think
> even BBC news execs and editors would be so puerile or pusil-
> lanimous as to tailor their coverage of the NHS outrage to suit
> his perceived sensitivities.
>
> Second, what has happened at the BBC is that (as with Israel,
> another area where powerful interests and government forces
> operate), especially since the kicking it got over Iraq from Alistair
> Campbell/Tony Blair in 2004, it has become an institution that
> does not like any longer to take anyone on or to challenge
> received ideas or vested interests or risk being seen to take sides.
> There is no backbone left in current affairs programmes; news
> operates on the principle that X says Y and Y says X and this
> adversarial knockabout is a substitute for real analysis and ques-
> tioning. (Even before Hutton, there was no proper, analytical
> reporting of Northern Ireland until long after the Good Friday
> Agreement had made it to some extent history.)
>
> In this climate of fear, which is what basically it is, reporters
> and producers know what they have to do to get on air. Leave
> well alone, report the surface, filter any controversies through

studio debates and Question Time, arenas in which, of course, 'balance' can be seen to be being practised.

I don't suppose the medical health bandits sit on the BBC's shoulders in the same way the Zionist lobby does, it's a different kind of thing.

But it's part of the argument why the BBC fails over Israel/Palestine and reports the US so blandly. The organisation is big and rich and potentially powerful, but it is scared of everybody and does not wish to rattle any important cages in case something nasty leaps out.

Jeremy Hunt, Andrew Lansley's successor as Health Secretary, has continued the Tory policy of weakening the NHS for corporate takeover. Professor Raymond Tallis, who has worked as an adviser to the Chief Medical Officer and served with the National Institute for Clinical Excellence, does not mince his words. Hunt, Tallis says, 'has contempt for the NHS' and is 'destroying the NHS' through creeping privatisation and spending cuts. He has 'blood on his hands'.[40]

In February 2017, Rachel Clarke, a doctor in Oxford, pointed out the Tory strategy of blaming others for the fragile state of the NHS:

As the NHS quietly implodes around us, Downing Street's media tactics exhibit a disturbing trend. Just like her special friend across the pond [i.e. President Trump], Theresa May has fully embraced the power of migrant-bashing to divert attention away from inconvenient news. Those NHS disasters you've been hearing so much about – the patients dying in corridors or waiting years for surgeries – that's right, it's those filthy foreigners to blame. You know, the migrants clogging up the system, pinching all the GP slots and essentially stealing all of our precious NHS cash. Anyone would think it was time to seal ourselves within a great big British wall.[41]

Clarke continued:

As Theresa May is, of course, fully aware, it is her Government's cost-cutting agenda, not migrants, that imperils our NHS. To inject some facts into Downing Street's grubby post-truth narrative, so-called health tourism is responsible for a mere 0.3 per cent of NHS spending. The NHS loses more money on missed GP appointments and spends more on stationery. Yet the political choice to impose £22bn of 'efficiency savings' is decimating our ability to provide safe, reliable care to our patients. Whipping up anti-immigrant feeling to divert attention from the crisis state of our NHS is like accusing 'bad hombres' and Muslims of ruining America – this is cynical, sinister stuff.

Clarke's observations are exactly the kind of vital context that is routinely buried by the BBC. Rarely, if ever, does BBC News put the government's cost-cutting agenda upfront in its NHS reporting. The extreme right-wing ideological agenda driving the 'deliberate destruction' of the NHS, ready for acquisition by private companies, is simply ignored.[42]

A segment on BBC 'Newsnight' in February 2017 encapsulated this. Cancer specialist Karol Sikora was given a slot to attack the NHS as 'the last bastion of communism'. But there was no mention of Sikora's links to private interests working hard to benefit from the destruction of the NHS.[43]

But then, as many readers will be only too aware, BBC News reporting fits snugly within the skewed constraints set by elite interests. Over the years, Media Lens has tended to focus on exposing the biased, marginal or missing news coverage of 'our' crimes abroad; for example, in Iraq, Afghanistan, Libya and Syria. But powerful state and corporate forces are obviously dominant here at home as well. There is no reason to believe that BBC News coverage of domestic issues would be any different. Its shameful lack of coverage of opposition to the corporate takeover of the NHS highlights the BBC's structural failure to report in the public interest – yet again.

10

Scottish Independence: An 'Amazing Litany' of Bias

The Corporate Media's 'Jocky Horror Show'

The ludicrous claim that corporate media are objective, balanced and impartial can become so unsustainable that laughter is the only sane response. Just one week before the Scottish independence referendum on 18 September 2014, a YouGov opinion poll showed that the 'Yes' vote (51 per cent) for independence had edged ahead of 'No' (49 per cent). Westminster, business elites and their media cheerleaders went into full panic mode. Newspaper headlines exposed the truth of the supposed media 'spectrum' of opinion on key issues of this kind:

'Ten days to save the Union' (*Daily Telegraph*)
'Parties unite in last-ditch effort to save the Union' (*The Times*)
'Ten days to save the United Kingdom' (*Independent*)
'Scotland heads for the exit' (*i*, a tabloid version of the
   Independent)
'Last stand to keep the union' (*Guardian*)
'Queen's fear of the break up of Britain' (*Daily Mail*)
'Don't let me be last Queen of Scotland' (*Daily Mirror*)

And, of course, the laughably biased *Sun*:

'Scots vote chaos. Jocky horror show'

By contrast, Craig Murray, the former UK Ambassador to Uzbekistan, was scathing about a last-ditch trip to Scotland to 'save the Union' made by the leaders of the main Westminster political parties:

> Cameron, Miliband and Clegg. Just typing the names is depressing. As part of their long matured and carefully prepared campaign plan (founded 9 September 2014) they are coming together to Scotland tomorrow to campaign. In a brilliant twist, they will all come on the same day but not appear together. This will prevent the public from noticing that they all represent precisely the same interests.[1]

Murray nailed what was at stake when he said that the 'three amigos' 'offer no actual policy choice to voters', and he gave a list showing how tightly they marched together:

> They all support austerity budgets
> They all support benefit cuts
> They all support tuition fees
> They all support Trident missiles
> They all support continued NHS privatisation
> They all support bank bail-outs
> They all support detention without trial for 'terrorist suspects'
> They all support more bombings in Iraq
> They all oppose rail nationalisation

In short:

> The areas on which the three amigos differ are infinitesimal and contrived. They actually represent the same paymasters and vested interests.

Centralised power hates uncertainty, especially any threat to its grip on the political, economic and financial levers that control society. And so elites reacted with horror when the United Kingdom, formed by the 1706–7 Acts of Union, appeared to be on the verge of unravelling. Scottish independence would represent a tectonic and historic shift in power. There would be significant consequences for the Trident nuclear missile system, the future of the NHS and the welfare state, education, climate policy, energy generation and other industry sectors, the media and many additional issues; not just in Scotland, but beyond, including NATO and the European Union. There was clearly a lot at stake and established power was *seriously* concerned.

Ramping Up the Patronising and Deceitful Rhetoric

Corporate media scaremongering over Scottish independence was thus relentless. In the *Telegraph*, Business News Editor Andrew Critchlow intoned ominously:

Scottish homeowners face mortgage meltdown if Yes campaign wins.[2]

The same newspaper published a piece by Boris Johnson arguing:

Decapitate Britain, and we kill off the greatest political union ever. The Scots are on the verge of an act of self-mutilation that will trash our global identity.[3]

A *Times* editorial twitched nervously:

The British political class is in a fight for which it seemed unprepared. It needs to find its voice.[4]

Larry Elliott, the *Guardian*'s Economics Editor, warned that an independent Scotland 'would not be a land flowing with milk and honey'.[5] Jonathan Freedland, then the *Guardian*'s Executive Editor, who oversaw the paper's opinion section and editorials, bemoaned that:

If Britain loses Scotland it will feel like an amputation ... the prospect fills me with sadness for the country that would be left behind.[6]

Freedland sighed:

When I contemplate the prospect of waking up on 19 September to discover the union has been defeated, I can't help but feel a deep sadness.

Given Freedland's role as a *Guardian* mover and shaker, with a big input to its editorial stance, it was no surprise when a *Guardian* leader followed soon after, firmly positioning the flagship of liberal journalism in the 'No' camp under the pleading title, 'Britain deserves another chance'.[7] But the appeal for the Union was propped up by a sly conflation of independence with 'ugly nationalism', notwithstanding a token nod towards 'socialists, greens and other groups'. The paper continued with the unsubstantiated assertion that 'a coded anti-English prejudice can lurk near the surface of Alex Salmond's pitch'.

Ironically, one of the *Guardian*'s own columnists, Suzanne Moore, had a piece two days earlier that inadvertently pre-empted the stance now being adopted by her paper's own editors:

> The language of the no camp – Westminster, bankers, Farage, Prescott, the Orangemen and Henry Kissinger – is innately patronising.[8]

To which we could now add the *Guardian*.

She continued:

> Do not give in to petty nationalism, they say. Just stick with the bigger unionist nationalism; it's better for you.

In the *Observer*, sister paper of the *Guardian*, Will Hutton was virtually inconsolable:

> Without imaginative and creative statecraft, the polls now suggest Scotland could secede from a 300-year union, sundering genuine bonds of love, splitting families and wrenching all the interconnectedness forged from our shared history.[9]

He ramped up the rhetoric still further:

> Absurdly, there will be two countries on the same small island that have so much in common. If Britain can't find a way of sticking together, it is the death of the liberal enlightenment before the atavistic forces of nationalism and ethnicity – a dark omen for the 21st century. Britain will cease as an idea. We will all be diminished.

Writing for the pro-independence *Bella Caledonia* website, Mike Small responded to Hutton's apocalyptic warnings:

> Unfortunately he has misunderstood the basic tenor of the British State, that is to cling to power, to centralise it, and to shroud it in obscurity.[10]

Small added that Hutton's caricature of the 'Yes' camp as 'the atavistic forces of nationalism and ethnicity' is 'such an absurd metropolitan misreading of what's going on as to be laughable'. Small's crucial point is one we should remember when listening to senior politicians; that their first priority is always to cling to power. These 'paymasters and vested interests' surely trembled with fear at the power residing in the hands of voters in Scotland. As George Monbiot observed:

> A yes vote in Scotland would unleash the most dangerous thing of all – hope.[11]

He expanded:

> If Scotland becomes independent, it will be despite the efforts of almost the entire UK establishment. It will be because social media has defeated the corporate media. It will be a victory for citizens over the Westminster machine, for shoes over helicopters. It will show that a sufficiently inspiring idea can cut through bribes and blackmail, through threats and fear-mongering. That hope, marginalised at first, can spread across a nation, defying all attempts to suppress it.

The frantic and intense campaign for 'the Union' and 'stability' paid off. The referendum result was 55.3 per cent in favour of the status quo and 44.7 per cent for independence. Disaster for the UK's elites had been averted, and they breathed a huge collective sigh of relief.

Auntie Beeb Does Big Brother

The pro-Union bias of 'mainstream' coverage was made clear by a careful academic study of media output over the period of one year, which was then subjected to a concerted BBC attempt to rubbish both the work and its author. The research was conducted by a small team led by Professor John Robertson of the University of the West of Scotland.[12]

Between 17 September 2012 and 18 September 2013, the team recorded and transcribed approximately 730 hours of evening TV news output broadcast by BBC Scotland and Scottish Television (STV). The study concluded that 317 news items broadcast by the BBC favoured the 'No' campaign compared to just 211 favourable to the 'Yes' campaign. A similar bias in favour of the 'No' campaign was displayed by STV. Overall, there was a broadcaster bias favouring the 'No' campaign by a ratio of 3:2. In other words, 50 per cent of coverage was more favourable to the 'No' campaign.

'More importantly', Robertson told Media Lens, there was also:

undue deference and the pretence of apolitical wisdom in [official] reports coming from London – the Office for Budget Responsibility and Institute for Fiscal Studies, for example; but, also, Treasury officials [were] presented as detached academic figures to be trusted.[13]

The broadcasters also personalised Scottish independence by constantly linking the aims and objectives of the 'Yes' campaign with the 'wishes' of Alex Salmond, then Scotland's First Minister and leader of the Scottish National Party. It was as if the 'Yes' campaign was all about what Salmond wanted. This was not the case with media coverage of the 'No' campaign. The objectives of the 'No' campaign were not routinely portrayed as the 'wishes' of senior Labour politician Alastair Darling, leader of the 'Better Together' group campaigning to keep Scotland within the United Kingdom.

Robertson told us that:

the conflation of the First Minister's wishes with the YES campaign seems a classic case of undermining ideas by association with clownish portrayal of leading actors [in the campaign].

This media performance was, he said, reminiscent of corporate media demonisation in the 1980s of miners' leader Arthur Scargill and Labour leaders Neil Kinnock and Michael Foot. One might now add the media campaign that relentlessly demonised and undermined Labour leader Jeremy Corbyn (see Chapter 2).

Finally, Robertson noted that there was a strong 'tendency to begin [news] reports with bad economic news for the Yes campaign [...]. Reports leading off with bad news or warnings against voting Yes were more common than the opposite by a ratio of 22:4 on Reporting Scotland (BBC) and a ratio of 20:7 on STV.'

Craig Murray gave a dramatic illustration of this biased tendency to report bad news for the 'Yes' campaign with the following list of BBC headlines:[14]

'Scottish independence: Pension shortfall warning'[15]
'Scottish independence: Warning over "weakened military"'[16]
'Scottish independence: "Havoc" warning from pensions firm'[17]
'Scottish independence: Luxembourg warns against "going separate ways"'[18]
'Scottish independence: Barroso warning on EU membership'[19]
'Scottish independence: Michael Moore issues warning over vote question'[20]
'Scottish independence: "Border checks" warning from home secretary'[21]

Murray commented:

Please note this amazing litany – and I use the word litany carefully, a verbal repetition to inculcate belief – includes only those where the deliberate practice of repetitive coupling of 'independence' and 'warning' has been captured by being written on the [BBC] website; there are hundreds of other examples of broadcast, spoken use of the words 'Warning' and 'Scottish independence' in the same sentence by the BBC.

The presentation of every one of the above stories was in the most tendentious and anti-independence manner conceivable. They have all been countered and comprehensively rebutted.

Surely BBC 'impartiality' would suggest that there should be a roughly equal number of headlines extolling the possible benefits of Scottish independence? This did not happen.

So how did BBC Scotland respond to Robertson's documented evidence of clear bias in its coverage of the Scottish independence referendum? Derek Bateman, a retired BBC journalist with decades of experience at the Corporation, summed up the broadcaster's reaction thus:

> Instead of doing what any self-confident public service broadcaster should do and produce a news item out of a critical report from one of our own universities, they seem to have hidden it from the licence-fee paying public who bankroll them and then mounted a sabotage operation against the author.[22]

Amazingly, BBC Scotland sent a 6,000-word letter to Robertson attacking both his study and his credibility, copying it to the professor's Principal at the University of the West of Scotland. This unprecedented move seemed deliberately calculated to intimidate the researcher. This was described by Bateman and other commentators, as well as Robertson himself, as 'bullying'.

Bateman noted BBC Scotland's 'fury at being found out misleading viewers', and he concluded:

> It strikes me as the height of hypocrisy for the BBC to try to badger an independent organization because it can't stand it revealing the truth – that it is failing in its primary duty to the Scots ... and they didn't even report it.

In a careful and detailed response, Robertson rebutted the BBC criticism of his one-year study, commenting:

> I think I've answered all the questions needed to contest these conclusions. [...] The BBC response is a remarkably heavy-handed reaction. Why did they not report the research, let their experts critique it on air and then ask me to defend it? Instead we see a bullying email to my employer and a blanket suppression across the mainstream media in the UK. I'm shocked.[23]

The BBC Corporate 'Gang of Four' Emerge from the Shadows

On 11 March 2014, Robertson appeared in front of the Scottish Parliament's Education and Culture Committee in Edinburgh.[24] He had been invited to present the main findings of his study and to answer questions from those sitting on the Committee, all members of the Scottish Parliament (MSPs). Four senior staff from BBC Scotland also appeared before the Committee later that same day.

Robertson told the Committee:

> much has happened in the month or so since I released the research paper. Much of it has been quite upsetting for me. So, I want to begin by saying some fairly strong things about my experience in the last month or so.
>
> I'd like to condemn the behaviour of BBC Scotland's Department of Policy and Corporate Affairs in suppressing the dissemination of my research, and in circulating an insulting and ill-informed critique of my research directly to my Principal, bypassing my Head of School, my Dean, straight to the Principal. [...]
>
> I'd like to condemn the silence and collusion of almost all of Scotland's mainstream media in disappearing my research, despite this massive online presence [of Robertson's study]. Its online presence is a news item which has been ignored. [...]
>
> And thirdly I'd like to, unfortunately, condemn the silence of almost all Scottish academics with an interest in this field who might have been expected to challenge censorship of intellectual material.
>
> I've been personally hurt by the above combination of threat from a powerful institution. [...] I interpret [what has happened] as an attempt at thought control in a democracy, and, of all democracies, the one I like the best. And I'm very upset by that.[25]

Robertson was asked by one MSP what kind of research he'd conducted in the past. He responded:

My interest is in, dare I say it, thought control in democracies. Everyone knows in a totalitarian state you can't trust the media. Everyone knows they're being lied to. Thought control in totalitarian states is totally ineffective because the entire population pretty much know: don't trust that stuff from the party.

In democracies, there is thought control. There's undeniably thought control. Media and political elites often work in each other's interests. They don't go round in a big cauldron saying, 'Let's do down the working classes and send our boys off to die, because we want them to do that.' They just mix. They go to the same schools. Their children go to the same schools. They share the same interests, the same cultural interests.

So, we *do* end up with a degree of thought control without conspiracy ...

Robertson added that he'd conducted research for many years into media coverage of war and the economy. That research was '*more controversial*' than the work he'd just published. But:

This is the first piece of research I've ever done that's attracted any interest.

Following Robertson's solo appearance before the Parliamentary Committee, BBC Scotland put up a four-man panel to counter him. This heavyweight squad comprised Ken MacQuarrie (Director of BBC Scotland), John Boothman (Head of News and Current Affairs), Bruce Malcolm (Head of Commonwealth Games coverage) and John Mullin (Editor, Referendum Unit). It is worth noting that Mullin is a former editor of the *Independent on Sunday*: his role there has previously been scrutinised by Media Lens.[26]

This was a rare outing for senior BBC management being compelled to answer questions in public on BBC coverage, and it was fascinating to watch.[27] Many Media Lens readers will be all too painfully aware of the boilerplate text that is routinely generated whenever complaints are submitted to the broadcaster: copious and vacuous prose about how 'BBC News adheres to impartiality', 'we are confident that our standards have been upheld', and so on, *ad nauseam*.

Here, then, was an opportunity for the public to see what it looks like when the standard text is read out loud in all seriousness by a senior BBC manager. Much of the BBC's stonewalling of the Parliamentary Committee's questions was characterised by stock evasive phrases and corporate-speak padding, trying to buy time to think and to shrug off challenges. It consisted largely of a verbal shuffling of the feet, a feeble attempt to project an illusion of responding with something, *anything*, of substance.

The very first question from the Committee Chairman, Stewart Maxwell, and the shifty response from the Head of BBC Scotland was emblematic of the proceedings:

> Could you tell us, Mr MacQuarrie, why you took the view that it was necessary to respond in the way you did to Professor Robertson's research?

MacQuarrie responded woodenly with a prepared script about the supposed 'fundamental errors' in the study, but singularly failed to answer Maxwell's question.

Maxwell persisted:

> We know what you did with this research [i.e. did not report it, but instead issued a 6,000-word response to Professor Robertson, copied to his Principal]. What I'm asking about is, in all of the many hundreds of other bits of academic research that you report every year, can you name the number of occasions where you did a similar thing?

MacQuarrie:

> No, in general terms, I can't name a specific instance where we would have copied the Principal in a piece in academic research.

Maxwell continued:

> Don't you find it rather peculiar – wouldn't an ordinary person looking at this event find it rather peculiar – that the BBC accept academic research, day in day out, respond to that by publishing stories on it, having debates on that research? But on this one

occasion, when the research is about your own output, that's not how you respond; you respond in an entirely different way.

MacQuarrie:

I don't think it's peculiar in the slightest. We wanted to correct the errors of fact that, you know, were in the report. And I think it's perfectly reasonable when it is about our own output, and it was on a question, if you like, of our impartiality that we would get the facts on the table. And that we wrote only to Professor Robertson and copied to the Principal.

There followed a comical interlude in which Maxwell tried to determine the number of complaints that the BBC had received about its coverage of the Scottish independence referendum. MacQuarrie stonewalled and refused to say.

Derek Bateman summed it up in his blog:

From what I saw, the BBC are in full assault mode and totally unapologetic and as a result look unreasonable, defensive and flustered. It has become the default position of an organisation caught out by events and floundering.[28]

'Dark Omens' and 'Horror Shows'

As mentioned above, just over a week before the referendum, to the consternation of Westminster elites and their cheerleaders in media circles, a YouGov opinion poll showed that the 'Yes' vote (51 per cent) had edged ahead of 'No' (49 per cent) for the first time in the campaign, having at one point trailed by 22 per cent.

The *Observer* noted 'signs of panic and recrimination among unionist ranks', adding that 'the no campaign is desperately searching for ways to seize back the initiative'.[29] The panic was marked by 'intensive cross-party talks' and underpinned George Osborne's announcement on the BBC's Andrew Marr show eleven days before the referendum, that 'a plan of action to give more powers to Scotland' in the event of a No vote would be detailed in the coming days.[30]

Confusion reigned in the unionist camp as well as in corporate media reporting of their befuddlement. According to the rules governing the referendum, the UK and Scottish governments were forbidden from publishing anything which might affect the outcome during the so-called 'purdah period' of 28 days leading up to the referendum on 18 September. So, how would corporate media deal with the opportunistic 'promise' during purdah to grant Scotland new powers following a 'No' vote? BBC News dutifully reported the government sleight-of-hand that:

> the offer would come from the pro-Union parties, not the government itself.[31]

Voters, then, were supposed to swallow the fiction that the announcement came, not from the UK government represented by Chancellor George Osborne, but from the pro-union parties represented by senior Tory minister George Osborne!

However, Labour's Alastair Darling, leading the 'Better Together' campaign, told Sky News that all new powers for Scotland had already been placed on the table before the purdah period. What had been announced was 'merely ... a timetable for when the Scottish Parliament could expect to be given the limited powers already forthcoming'.[32]

Thus, an announcement setting out a timetable for enhanced powers was completely above board and not at all designed to influence the very close vote on independence. This was establishment sophistry and a deeply cynical attempt at manipulation of the voting public.

Media manipulation was exposed in stark form when Nick Robinson, then the BBC's Political Editor, was rumbled by viewers able to compare his highly selective editing of an Alex Salmond press conference with what had actually transpired.[33] Robinson had challenged Salmond about claims made by company bosses and bankers that independence would damage the Scottish economy:

> Why should a Scottish voter believe you, a politician, against men who are responsible for billions of pounds of profits?

Salmond responded comprehensively to these assertions, which he called 'scaremongering'. He then turned the tables on Robinson by rightly calling into question the BBC's role as an 'impartial' public broadcaster.[34]

When Robinson presented his report on the exchange with Salmond that evening on BBC 'News at Ten', he claimed that Salmond had *not responded* to the charge that independence would harm Scotland's economy:

> He didn't answer, but he did attack the reporting.[35]

But by viewing the full exchange on YouTube, people could see for themselves that it was simply not true that Salmond hadn't answered the question. He had, in fact, very carefully addressed the claims made by business leaders and bankers.

Robinson's misleading reporting of Salmond's remarks sparked huge discussion across social media. It even led to public protests outside the BBC headquarters in Glasgow.[36] Some called for Robinson to resign.[37] The protests involved thousands of pro-independence campaigners,[38] although Nicola Sturgeon, Salmond's then deputy and now leader of the SNP, distanced her party from the demonstration outside the BBC when she 'emphasised it was not organised by the official Yes Scotland campaign'.[39] The Glasgow protest was but one episode in a bigger picture of considerable public dissent against BBC News; indeed, against corporate news bias generally.

The BBC's dismissive response to the public complaints about Robinson's skewed report concluded with the usual worn-out boilerplate text:

> the overall report [was] balanced and impartial, in line with our editorial guidelines.[40]

'Bullying': BBC Political Editor's Bizarre Term for Public Dissent

Nick Robinson has made a career out of telling the public what leading politicians say and do; sometimes even what they 'think'. This stenography plays a key role in the 'mainstream' media, given that a vital part of statecraft is to keep the public suitably cowed and fearful of 'threats' from which governments must 'protect' us. But when a senior journalist complains of 'intimidation and bullying' *by the public*, making comparison's to 'Vladimir Putin's Russia', such a distortion of reality is mind-boggling. These were claims made by Robinson, as the BBC's outgoing Political Editor, using an appearance at the 2015 Edinburgh international book festival, almost a year after the referendum, to settle a few scores.

As noted above, Robinson was guilty of media manipulation in reporting that Alex Salmond had not answered the claims of big business and bankers that independence would harm the Scottish economy. Robinson was in Edinburgh to promote his latest book *Election Diary*. He spoke defiantly about what had happened when his reporting was exposed for what it was:

> Alex Salmond was using me to change the subject. Alex Salmond was using me as a symbol. A symbol of the wicked, metropolitan, Westminster classes sent from England, sent from London, in order to tell the Scots what they ought to do.
>
> As it happens I fell for it. I shouldn't have had the row with him which I did, and I chose a particular phrase ['He didn't answer, but he did attack the reporting.'] we might explore badly in terms of my reporting and that is genuinely a sense of regret.[41]

So, Robinson's distorted reporting, caught and exposed in public, had led merely to 'a sense of regret' which 'we might explore badly'. He then launched a bizarre attack on the public:

> But as a serious thought I don't think my offence was sufficient to justify 4,000 people marching on the BBC's headquarters, so that young men and women who are new to journalism have, like they do in Putin's Russia, to fight their way through crowds of protesters, frightened as to how they do their jobs.

The hyperbole continued:

> We should not live with journalists who are intimidated, or bullied, or fearful in any way.

And yet, a couple of months earlier, Robinson had *played down* the alleged bullying as ineffectual:

> In reality I never felt under threat at all.[42]

Given that the protest was triggered by *Robinson*'s propaganda, one might wonder to what extent the 'young men and women who are new to journalism' at the BBC were 'intimidated, or bullied, or fearful', or whether this was more tragicomic bias from Robinson. Needless to say, Robinson was silent about how the corporate media routinely acts as an echo chamber for government propaganda,[43] scaremongering the public about foreign 'enemies' and security 'threats'.[44]

A couple of days later, Salmond responded to Robinson. He told the Dundee-based *Courier* newspaper:

> The BBC's coverage of the Scottish referendum was a disgrace.
>
> It can be shown to be so, as was Nick's own reporting of which he should be both embarrassed and ashamed.[45]

Salmond continued:

> To compare, as Nick did last week, 4000 Scots peacefully protesting outside BBC Scotland as something akin to Putin's Russia is as ludicrous as it is insulting.
>
> It is also heavily ironic given that the most commonly used comparison with the BBC London treatment of the Scottish referendum story was with Pravda, the propaganda news agency in the old Soviet Union.

The *Guardian* then gave ample space to Robinson to respond to Salmond with an ill-posed defence of the BBC's slanted coverage of the independence debate.[46] This was followed by a news piece by Jane Martinson, then Head of Media at the *Guardian*, about the 'row' between the two.[47]

'The BBC', declaimed Robinson, 'must resist Alex Salmond's attempt to control its coverage.' In fact, Salmond had rightly pointed out that the BBC's broadcasting had been biased and 'a disgrace'; a view held by many people in Scotland and beyond.

Robinson's response was that, all too often, politicians 'simply do not understand why the nation's broadcaster doesn't see the world exactly as they do'. Case dismissed.

The BBC Political Editor then fell back on the old canard that complaints from both sides implied that reporting had been balanced:

> There were many complaints about our coverage of the Scottish referendum – although interestingly just as many came from the No side as the Yes.

How convenient. Deploying this fatuous argument means that serious evidence of bias against 'Yes' of the kind supplied by Professor John Robertson of the University of the West of Scotland need not be examined.

In its place, Robinson painted a heroic picture of himself and the BBC rejecting demands from 'politicians' to 'control' news reporting. Robinson declared his unshakeable confidence in:

> the BBC's high journalistic standards, which are recognised around the world.

No evidence to the contrary can ever persuade well-rewarded BBC journalists otherwise.

On Twitter, George Monbiot succinctly made the point that matters about the Robinson-Salmond 'row':

> Establishment unites to crush popular movements. If movements protest, they're accused of bullying.[48]

For many years now, Media Lens has cast a sceptical eye over Robinson's reporting. Notoriously, he was guilty of repeating false government claims about weapons of mass destruction in Iraq, like so many other journalists. When challenged about this, Robinson wrote in a column for *The Times*:

> It was my job to report what those in power were doing or thinking ... That is all someone in my sort of job can do.[49]

As the US journalist Glenn Greenwald remarked:

That'd make an excellent epitaph on the tombstone of modern establishment journalism.[50]

But Robinson had also made a solemn promise back then:

Now, more than ever before, I will pause before relaying what those in power say. Now, more than ever, I will try to examine the contradictory case.[51]

To little or no avail, as we have seen in the intervening years. Robinson hates to be reminded of this. He once replied on Twitter to one of our challenges with a seemingly exasperated 'zzzzzzzzzzzz'.[52]

11

Climate Chaos: An Inconvenient Emergency

Temperatures are 'Off the Charts'

In previous chapters, we have seen how Western governments insistently claim that they are willing to spend billions of taxpayers' money on 'interventions' to protect the lives, not just of Britons and Americans, but of Iraqis, Libyans and Syrians.

As we have also seen, a key task of the corporate media is to defy all known evidence, including recent history, by taking these claims of 'humanitarian' intent seriously. This is amazing enough. But we truly have to stand aghast at the spectacle of the same corporate journalists failing to notice that the same political leaders are working hard to ignore a climate crisis that is neither faked nor hyped, but that genuinely threatens the near-term survival of the human race.

In 2012, leading NASA climate scientist James Hansen bluntly declared: 'We are in a planetary emergency.'[1] In mid-March 2016, other climate scientists similarly warned of a 'climate emergency'. The *Guardian* reported:

> February [2016] smashed a century of global temperature records by a 'stunning' margin, according to data released by Nasa. The unprecedented leap led scientists, usually wary of highlighting a single month's temperature, to label the new record a 'shocker' and warn of a 'climate emergency'.[2]

When dispassionate climate scientists use this kind of language, it's time to start paying attention; assuming you care about the life-expectancy of your children and grandchildren, and indeed of yourself.

In January 2017, the world's major climate agencies confirmed 2016 as the hottest since modern records began.[3] The global temperature is now 1C higher than preindustrial times, and the three years from 2014 to 2016 saw the record broken successively; the first time this has happened. The record-breaking heat had pushed the world into 'truly uncharted territory', according to the World Meteorological Organisation.[4] Professor David Reay, an emissions expert at the University of Edinburgh, said that the WMO report was 'startling'. He added:

> The need for concerted action on climate change has never been so stark nor the stakes so high.[5]

Towards the end of 2016, scientists reported 'extraordinarily hot' Arctic conditions.[6] Danish and US researchers were 'surprised and alarmed by air temperatures peaking at what they say is an unheard-of 20C higher than normal for the time of year'. One of the scientists said:

> These temperatures are literally off the charts for where they should be at this time of year. It is pretty shocking.

Another researcher emphasised:

> This is faster than the models. It is alarming because it has consequences.

These 'consequences' will be terrible. Scientists have warned that increasingly rapid Arctic ice melt 'could trigger uncontrollable climate change at global level'.[7]

It gets worse. A study in 2017 suggested that global warming is on course to raise global sea levels by between six and nine metres, wiping out coastal cities and settlements around the world.[8] Professor Michael Mann, the well-known climate scientist from Pennsylvania State University who devised the classic 'hockey stick' diagram of rising global temperatures, described the finding with classic scientific understatement as 'sobering' and added that:

we may very well already be committed to several more metres of sea level rise when the climate system catches up with the carbon dioxide we've already pumped into the atmosphere.[9]

It gets worse still. The Paris Climate Accord of 2015 repeated the international commitment to keep global warming below 2C. Even this limited rise would threaten life as we know it. When around a dozen climate scientists were asked for their honest opinion as to whether this target could be met, not one of them thought it likely.[10] Bill McGuire, Professor Emeritus of Geophysical and Climate Hazards at University College London, was adamant:

there is not a cat in hell's chance [of keeping below 2C].

And it gets even worse. Global warming could well be happening so fast that it is 'game over'.[11] In other words, the Earth's climate could be so sensitive to greenhouse gases that we may be headed for a temperature rise of *more than 7C within a lifetime*. Mark Lynas, author of the award-winning book, *Six Degrees: Our Future on a Hotter Planet*, was 'shocked' by the researchers' study, describing it as 'the apocalyptic side of bad'.[12]

To put this in stark perspective, Professor John Schellnhuber, one of the world's leading climate scientists, observes that 'the difference between two degrees and four degrees' of warming 'is human civilisation'.[13] We are literally talking about the end of human life as we know it. And the corporate media, politicians, business and modern societies carry on regardless. If this doesn't equate to madness, we don't know what does.

Human stress on the Earth's environment has become so severe that the planet has entered the 'danger zone', making it much less hospitable to our continued existence. Researchers warn that life support systems around the globe are being eaten away 'at a rate unseen in the past 10,000 years'. It is 'a death by a thousand cuts', shifting the world to 'a warmer state, 5–6C warmer, with no ice caps'.[14]

Professor Will Steffen, of the Australian National University and the Stockholm Resilience Centre, is the lead author of two studies published in 2015 on the 'planetary boundaries' that are being breached by human activity around the globe. He warned that although there would still be life on Earth, it would be disastrous for large mammals such as humans:

> Some people say we can adapt due to technology, but that's a belief system, it's not based on fact. There is no convincing evidence that a large mammal, with a core body temperature of 37C, will be able to evolve that quickly. Insects can, but humans can't and that's a problem.

He added ominously:

> It's clear the economic system is driving us towards an unsustainable future and people of my daughter's generation will find it increasingly hard to survive. History has shown that civilisations have risen, stuck to their core values and then collapsed because they didn't change. That's where we are today.[15]

Commenting on Steffen's analysis of the planet's life support systems now collapsing, Jon Queally, senior editor of the progressive *Common Dreams* website, observed:

> the world's dominant economic model – a globalized form of neoliberal capitalism, largely based on international trade and fueled by extracting and consuming natural resources – is the driving force behind planetary destruction ...[16]

Climate expert Jørgen Randers, who co-authored *The Limits to Growth* in 1972, was similarly scathing about the current system of economics:

> It is cost-effective to postpone global climate action. It is profitable to let the world go to hell.[17]

Unsurprisingly, then, at the start of 2018, the *Bulletin of the Atomic Scientists* moved their symbolic Doomsday Clock forward another thirty seconds, towards apocalypse. At the time of writing, it is now two minutes to midnight, the closest since 1953.[18] Historically, the Doomsday Clock represented the threat of nuclear annihilation. But global climate change is now also recognised as a 'looming threat'.[19]

Hurricanes Harvey and Irma – and the Elephant in the BBC Living Room

In 2017, Hurricane Harvey hit the United States and provided a genuinely terrifying glimpse of our destiny. And yet, even then, corporate media continued to suppress the truth.

On 25 August, Hurricane Harvey made landfall near Corpus Christi on the southern coast of Texas. Harvey's progress then stalled over Houston, the fourth largest city in the United States, dumping 'unprecedented' quantities of water, creating 'a 1-in-1,000-year flood event'.[20] Over 60 people were killed, around one million residents displaced and 200,000 homes damaged in a 'path of destruction' stretching for over 300 miles.[21] The *Washington Post* reported that:

> the intensity and scope of the disaster were so enormous that weather forecasters, first responders, the victims, everyone really, couldn't believe their eyes.[22]

Meteorologist Eric Holthaus surveyed the deaths and devastation caused by Harvey and said bluntly: 'this is what climate change looks like'.[23] He added:

> The symbolism of the worst flooding disaster in U.S. history hitting the sprawled-out capital city of America's oil industry is likely not lost on many. Institutionalized climate denial in our political system and climate denial by inaction by the rest of us have real consequences. They look like Houston.

Meanwhile, halfway around the planet in South Asia, an even greater climate-related catastrophe was taking place. Reuters observed that 'the worst monsoon floods in a decade' killed over 1,400 people across India, Nepal and Bangladesh.[24] Around 41 million people were displaced. That number is simply staggering. And in areas with little infrastructure and financial resources, the consequences are almost unthinkable. The *Times of India* reported that rains had brought Mumbai, a city of 18 million people, 'to its knees'.[25]

Although coverage of the flooding in South Asia was not entirely absent in British media by any means, it was swamped by the coverage devoted to Harvey in Texas and Louisiana. We conducted a newspaper database search on 4 September 2017 for the period since 25 August (the day Hurricane Harvey hit Texas). Our search yielded just 26 stories in the UK national press on the South Asian flooding, while there were 695 articles on Harvey. Thus, coverage from the US dominated South Asia by a factor of *almost 30 to 1*, even though the scale of deaths and flooding was far greater in the latter. Somehow, people in South Asia just don't matter as much as Americans; or Westerners in general.

Climate writer David Roberts noted that 'it's grossly irresponsible to leave climate out of the picture'.[26] That, however, is overwhelmingly what the BBC did in its coverage. It is significant that when the flagship BBC 'News at Ten' programme had extensive coverage of Harvey on three successive nights (28–30 August 2017), there was not a single mention of global warming. Likewise, when BBC2's 'Newsnight' devoted fully 14 minutes to the hurricane on 29 August 2017, references to climate change were conspicuously absent.

To its credit, the BBC did publish an article on its website, 'Hurricane Harvey: The link to climate change'; and it is possible they made reference to it somewhere in their television or radio coverage.[27] But this hardly compensated for the seeming reluctance to utter the words 'climate change' in its extensive coverage over several days in its most high-profile news programmes. This black hole in BBC coverage continued when, just days after Hurricane Harvey, Hurricane Irma swept through the Caribbean, then towards Florida. As Holthaus observed: 'Harvey and Irma aren't natural disasters. They're climate change disasters.'[28] But not in the eyes of BBC News.

It is not merely that this climate silence is a dereliction of the BBC's responsibility to the public that pays for it. In not giving climate change the prominent coverage it deserves, the BBC is obstructing the public debate that is vital to prevent climate catastrophe. In effect, the BBC is firmly on the side of the state and corporate forces that have been fighting a decades-long, heavily-funded campaign (see below) to prevent the radical measures needed to avoid climate chaos.

Could it be that BBC News editors took a decision not to 'politicise' Hurricane Harvey by discussing climate change? Naomi Klein hit the 'don't politicise hurricanes' argument on the head with a cogent article in which she argued that:

> Now is exactly the time to talk about climate change, and all the other systemic injustices – from racial profiling to economic austerity – that turn disasters like Harvey into human catastrophes.[29]

To provide perspective, extensive biodiversity evidence shows that Earth is entering its sixth mass extinction event in geological history, posing a 'frightening assault on the foundations of human civilization', according to a new study co-authored by Professor Gerardo Ceballos at the University of Mexico. All five previous mass extinction events were natural. This is the first one caused by human activity, especially a dangerous increase of atmospheric greenhouse gases that may well cause runaway heating. The authors warn that:

> the window for effective action is very short, probably two or three decades at most. [...] All signs point to ever more powerful assaults on biodiversity in the next two decades, painting a dismal picture of the future of life including human life.[30]

The Great Derangement

How has the world reacted to this extraordinary evidence of rapidly approaching calamity? The barely believable truth is described in an article by climate reporter Barry Saxifrage in the *National Observer*.[31] Using data compiled from the latest 'BP Statistical Review of World Energy', one of the most respected and widely referenced analyses of energy use, Saxifrage was able to track 'most of the important trends in global energy'. There was this striking omission:

> Conspicuously absent was the basic statistic on fossil fuels that I, as a climate reporter, was looking for: how much fuel is the world burning each year?

Given the evidence of a crisis, one might think this would be a major focus. Oil giant BP chose not to mention it. That already tells its own story.

Saxifrage heroically decided to crunch the numbers and made his own charts, the first of which found:

> Last year humanity set another fossil fuel energy record of 11.4 billion tonnes of oil equivalent (Gtoe). A decade ago we were at 10 Gtoe of energy. In 2000, we were at 8 Gtoe.

Quite simply, we are at an 'all-time record' for burning fossil fuels. But there is more. In 25 of the last 26 years, we burned more fossil fuels than the year before. Since 1990, the fossil fuel share of global energy has barely declined from 88 per cent to 86 per cent.

Saxifrage concluded with what reads like a death sentence for our species:

> Together, these three 'missing' charts of BP's fossil fuel data – ever rising amounts; increasing every year; and maintaining uncontested dominance – paint a sobering picture of humanity's lackluster response to the growing threat ...
>
> Those three missing charts illustrate our inadequate response quite clearly. Perhaps that is why BP (an oil & gas company after all) left them out of their report.

In a landmark book published in 2016, the Indian writer Amitav Ghosh describes the present era of corporate-driven climate crisis as *The Great Derangement*.[32] Future generations, warns Ghosh, may well look back on this time and wonder whether humanity was deranged to continue on a course of business-as-usual. Indeed, it has become abundantly clear that governments, at best, pay lip service to the urgent need to address global warming, or dismiss it altogether, while pursuing policies that deepen climate chaos. As climate writer and activist Bill McKibben pointed out, when US President Donald Trump took office in 2017, he granted senior energy and environment positions in his administration to men who:

> know nothing about science, but they love coal and oil and gas – they come from big carbon states like Oklahoma and Texas, and their careers have been lubed and greased with oil money.[33]

Rex Tillerson, then Trump's US Secretary of State, was the former Chairman and CEO of oil giant, ExxonMobil. He once told his shareholders that cutting oil production is 'not acceptable for humanity', adding: 'What good is it to save the planet if humanity suffers?'[34]

As for former US President Barack Obama's 'legacy' on climate, renowned climate scientist James Hansen only gave him a 'D' grade.[35] Obama had had a 'golden opportunity', stated Hansen. But while he had said 'the right words' as US president, for eight years he had avoided 'the fundamental approach that's needed'.

Contrast this with the *Guardian*'s starry-eyed view on Obama's legacy.[36] Writing in the *Morning Star*, Ian Sinclair noted the stark discrepancy between Obama's actual record on climate and fawning media comment, notably by the BBC and the *Guardian*:

> Despite the liberal media's veneration of the former US president, Obama did very little indeed to protect the environment.[37]

In 2017, the British government even worked hard to bury its own alarming report on the likely impacts of climate change on the UK. These impacts include:

> the doubling of the deaths during heatwaves, a 'significant risk' to supplies of food and the prospect of infrastructure damage from flooding.[38]

An exclusive article in the *Independent* noted that the climate report made virtually no impact when it was published on the government website of the Department for Environment, Food and Rural Affairs (Defra) on 18 January 2017:

despite its undoubted importance, Environment Secretary Andrea Leadsom made no speech and did not issue her own statement, and even the Defra Twitter account was silent. No mainstream media organisation covered the report.[39]

The government said in the ignored report that climate change meant that 'urgent priorities' needed to be addressed, including a dramatic rise in heat-related deaths, coastal flooding and 'significant risks to the availability and supply of food in the UK'. So, lip service at least. But Bob Ward, Policy and Communications Director at the Grantham Research Institute on Climate Change and the Environment in London, said he was 'astonished' that the government had done so little to publicise the report:

It's almost as if they were trying to sneak it out without people realising.[40]

At a time of manufactured fear[41] by 'mainstream' media about 'fake news'[42] and 'post-truth' politics, the government's rejection of reality is clear. It would rather ignore such an important report, far less address seriously the urgent truth of climate chaos.

As Hurricanes Harvey and Irma devastated the US Gulf Coast, Green Party MP Caroline Lucas insisted in Parliament that now was time to talk about climate change and for the government to deliver 'leadership' rather than fine words. Foreign Office minister Sir Alan Duncan replied:

May I just say that I think the honourable lady has deeply misjudged the tone of this house today. We are seeing people in deep and urgent, immediate need ... And she ought to show a bit more urgent and immediate humanity than make the point she's made today.[43]

This was a shameful response. As mentioned earlier, leading politicians, intelligence chiefs and their media allies are forever warning the British public of 'security threats' which are so often blowback from Western foreign policy;[44] or the warnings are overhyped claims to justify their own fear-mongering agendas.[45] But when it comes to the greatest threat of all – climate change – they are either silent or mendacious.

This exposes as a lie the rhetoric from government and security services that they are motivated by genuine concern for the well-being of the population. The truth is that such powerful forces are driven primarily by the desire to preserve and boost their own interests, their own profits, their own dominance. Tackling climate change requires tackling global inequity. This means a deep-rooted commitment not just to 'a redistribution of wealth, but also to a recalibration of global power'. Ghosh makes the crucial point that:

> from the point of view of a security establishment that is oriented towards the maintenance of global dominance, this is precisely the scenario that is most greatly to be feared; from this perspective *the continuance of the status quo is the most desirable of outcomes.*[46]

And so while political 'leaders' refuse to change course to avoid disaster, bankers and financial speculators continue to risk humanity's future for the sake of money; fossil fuel industries go on burning the planet; Big Business consumes and pollutes ecosystems; wars, 'interventions' and arms deals push the strategic aims of Western geopolitical power, all wrapped in newspeak about 'peace', 'security' and 'democracy'; and corporate media promote and enable it all, deeply embedded and complicit as they are. This is indeed 'The Great Derangement'.

Breaking the Back of 'The Beast'

Action to avert this looming, terminal threat to our existence is being obstructed by literally hundreds of millions of dollars of organised propaganda.

In February 2014, US senator Sheldon Whitehouse made a courageous and crucial speech to the US Senate.[47] He commented:

I have described Congress as surrounded by a barricade of lies. Today, I'll be more specific. There isn't just lying going on about climate change; there is a whole, carefully built apparatus of lies. This apparatus is big and artfully constructed: phoney-baloney organisations designed to look and sound like they're real, messages honed by public relations experts to sound like they're truthful, payrolled scientists whom polluters can trot out when they need them. And the whole thing big and complicated enough that when you see its parts you could be fooled into thinking that it's not all the same beast. *But it is.* Just like the mythological Hydra – many heads, same beast.

Whitehouse's speech made repeated reference to a ground-breaking 2013 study by Robert J. Brulle, Professor of Sociology and Environmental Science at Drexel University, which describes the organisational underpinnings and funding behind climate denial.[48] This is the first peer-reviewed, comprehensive analysis ever conducted on the topic.

Brulle found that from 2003 to 2010, 140 foundations made 5,299 grants totalling $558 million to 91 major climate denial organisations. These 91 organisations have an annual income of just over $900 million, with an annual average of $64 million in identifiable foundation support. Disturbingly, Brulle observed that 'while the largest and most consistent funders behind the counter-movement are a number of well-known conservative foundations, the majority of donations are "dark money", or concealed funding.' This is part of a trend:

> The data also indicates that Koch Industries and ExxonMobil, two of the largest supporters of climate science denial, have recently pulled back from publicly funding countermovement organizations. Coinciding with the decline in traceable funding, the amount of funding given to countermovement organizations through third party pass-through foundations like Donors Trust and Donors Capital, whose funders cannot be traced, has risen dramatically.[49]

In other words, as scientific evidence of looming climate disaster has become simply overwhelming, the funders blocking action to prevent disaster have knowingly hidden their support for fear of negative publicity.

The UK also has its own denial network 'where wealthy rightwing donors secretly finance a highly professional campaign against policies to reduce greenhouse gases', as climate expert Bob Ward pointed out in 2013.[50] The main UK lobby group is the notorious Global Warming Policy Foundation, established by Lord Lawson, a Conservative peer. The climate activist group DeSmog UK has mapped a US-UK climate denier network, with links to Trump and Brexit, and underpinned in large part by the extreme right-wing Heritage Foundation.[51]

As for the high-profile 'deniers' embraced by the media, Brulle commented:

> Like a play on Broadway, the countermovement has stars in the spotlight – often prominent contrarian scientists or conservative politicians – but behind the stars is an organizational structure of directors, script writers and producers, in the form of conservative foundations. If you want to understand what's driving this movement, you have to look at what's going on behind the scenes.[52]

An oft-quoted figure is that 97 per cent of published scientific papers on climate change agree that global warming is real, dangerous and caused by humans.[53] But what about the other 3 per cent? A team of researchers investigated the 38 peer-reviewed papers published in scientific journals in the past decade that deny human-induced global warming. Katharine Hayhoe, an atmospheric scientist at Texas Tech University who worked with the team, concluded:

> Every single one of those analyses had an error – in their assumptions, methodology, or analysis – that, when corrected, brought their results into line with the scientific consensus.[54]

The truth, then, is this: that climate denial is *a wholly artificial, manufactured creation*; a gigantic corporate fraud. Without the 'apparatus of lies' it simply would not exist as a 'serious' argument and would certainly not be able to challenge the overwhelming consensus of climate scientists on the reality of the threat posed by climate change.[55] It is this outright fraud subordinating human welfare to profit that the corporate media continues to indulge in the name of 'balance'.

Senator Whitehouse summed up the significance of corporate attempts to block climate action:

> This apparatus is a disgrace. When the inevitable happens and the impact of climate change really starts to hit home, people will want to know: why? Why we didn't take proper steps in time. It's not as if there's not enough scientific evidence out there for us to act. Why not?
>
> This denial operation – The Beast – will then go down as one of our great American scandals, like Watergate or Teapot Dome – a deliberate, complex scheme of lies and propaganda that caused real harm to the American people, and to our country. All so that a small group of people could make more money a little longer.

Intermission: Turned Out Nice Again?

'Little darling, it's been a long, cold, lonely winter.' So sang George Harrison of the Beatles. 'Upon us all a little rain must fall', crooned Robert Plant of Led Zeppelin.

The weather has always seemed the closest metaphor for human emotions and experience. These metaphors are often optimistic because, of course, after the cold, after the rain: 'Here comes the sun.' We find solace and hope in the idea that good times follow bad, summer follows winter, calm follows the storm. Nature seems to be full of 'moments of reprieve' in this way.

But a destabilising climate is not like the weather. It does not get worse, then better. It gets worse and worse for thousands, perhaps hundreds of thousands, of years. Could it be that our faith in the rhythm of nature, in the seasons as we have known them, has helped lure us into a fatal complacency? Perhaps we can't quite believe that Mother Nature could turn on her children, not just to teach us a lesson – supplying us with stern tests to help us grow – but to annihilate us from the face of the Earth?

Frank Fenner, Emeritus Professor in Microbiology at the Australian National University and an authority on extinction, told the *Australian* newspaper in 2010:

We're going to become extinct. Whatever we do now is too late.[56]

Professor Fenner added:

Climate change is just at the very beginning. But we're seeing remarkable changes in the weather already ... Homo sapiens will become extinct, perhaps within 100 years. A lot of other animals will, too. It's an irreversible situation. I think it's too late. I try not to express that because people are trying to do something, but they keep putting it off.

Mitigation would slow things down a bit, but there are too many people here already.

And since 2010, we have seen no mitigation – we have seen only an acceleration in fossil-fuel consumption and emissions.

Fatal complacency also seems to inhere in the idea of 'progress', viewed as the 'manifest destiny' of our species. The rapid empowerment of science and technology naturally gave the impression that they were leading somewhere better, not worse. As environmental writer Paul Kingsnorth commented:

A society that takes progress as its religion does not look kindly on despair. If you are expected to believe everything will keep getting better, it can be difficult to admit to believing otherwise.[57]

This is especially so when billions of advertising dollars – all promising a better, more comfortable life – have a vested interested in this religion. It surely seems inconceivable to many people in awe of the high-tech digital revolution that an iPad could appear shortly before *we* disappear. Even committed atheists may have a subtle faith in the idea that the human story cannot be merely absurd – that we could not develop, flourish and suddenly just vanish. Surely science and technology will save the day; surely the great adventure of 'progress' will not collapse from glittering 'peak' to nothingness. Science has long given us a sense that we have 'conquered' and 'escaped' nature. It is humbling and humiliating to imagine that we might yet be destroyed by nature.

And, of course, science fiction writers and film-makers have saturated society with the idea that our manifestly unsustainable way of life is part of an almost preordained journey to an ever more high-tech, high-consuming lifestyle. A glamorous, pristine future among the stars seems to have been mapped out for us. What if the reality of our situation on this planet has made a complete nonsense of this science fictional vision of 'progress'?

Similarly, is it really possible for the many believers in a theistic God to accept the possibility of near-term human extinction? Can they conceive that we were created by a divine being only to be wiped out by a giant fart of industrial gas? Theists precisely reject the idea of a random, meaningless universe. But what could be more nihilistic than industrial 'progress' culminating in self-extinction? What does it mean for the promise of 'the second coming', for the teaching of the prophets down the ages?

The Myth of 'Fearless and Free Journalism'

So why has the climate denial 'Beast' not been exposed? The reason is that, for the last three decades, corporate politics and corporate media, closely allied 'limbs' of 'the Beast', have censored the truth about its workings.

By way of a bitter irony, we need only consider the media response to Brulle's study. When we searched the Lexis database of the UK press in February 2014, we found that Brulle's ground-breaking, peer-reviewed research, published three months earlier, had been mentioned in just one article in the *Guardian*,[58] with a further mention in passing in the *Daily Mail*. It was not mentioned by any other UK newspaper. A Factiva database search of US newspapers by media analyst David Peterson[59] found that the study had been mentioned in a single, 500-word piece in the *Washington Post*.

This is consistent with a growing trend of corporate media suppression. In 2012, Douglas Fischer reported that corporate media coverage of climate change 'continued to tumble in 2011, declining roughly 20 percent from 2010's levels and nearly 42 percent from 2009's peak'.[60]

Here in the UK, Justin Lewis, Professor of Communication at Cardiff University, says that studies suggest that 'media coverage of climate change – and environmental issues more generally – has declined precipitously since 2009/10.'[61] In particular, British press coverage of climate change in 2012 was just 20 per cent what it was in 2007, even as the warning signs of climate chaos have become clearer. This is truly a scandal, even if entirely predictable.[62]

A quarter of a century ago, Frank Mankiewicz, a senior executive at PR firm Hill and Knowlton, provided a clue to corporate strategy in referring to the fall of the Romanian dictator Ceausescu:

> I think the companies will have to give in only at insignificant levels. Because the companies are too strong, they're the establishment. The environmentalists are going to have to be like the mob in the square in Romania before they prevail.[63]

This may well be the case. Senator Whitehouse told Congress:

> We must break the back of the beast ... For the sake of our democracy, for the sake of our future, for the sake of our *honour* – it is time to wake up.

As NASA climate scientist James Hansen has suggested, senior executives should be held legally accountable for crimes against humanity and the planet that almost defy belief.[64]

The 'mainstream' media are not somehow separate from this state-corporate status quo, selflessly and valiantly providing a neutral window into what powerful sectors in society are doing. Instead, the major news media are an intrinsic component of this system run for the benefit of elites. The media are, in effect, the public relations wing of a planetary-wide network of exploitation, abuse and destruction. The climate crisis is the gravest symptom of this dysfunctional global apparatus.

Typically, the climate crisis was ignored as an election issue during the UK general election campaign in 2017. A leading group of media academics at Loughborough University produced weekly reports during the election campaign and regularly found that climate change was blanked.[65]

Some readers will say: 'But surely the best media – the likes of the BBC, the *Guardian* and Channel 4 News – report climate science honestly and accurately?' Yes, to a large extent, they do a good job in reporting the science (though the BBC has often been guilty of 'false balance' on climate[66]). But they rarely touch the serious, radical measures needed to address the climate crisis, or the nature and extent of the climate denial 'Beast'. This is taboo; not least because it would raise awkward questions about rampant neoliberalism addressed, for example, by Naomi Klein in her books *The Shock Doctrine* and *This Changes Everything*.

The failure of BBC environment, economics and business journalists to explore these issues is scandalous; all the more so for their avowed responsibility to the public who funds them. This is no surprise. As we have seen, the BBC still reflects its origins in empire and the establishment while proclaiming falsely its 'independence' and 'impartiality'.[67]

In January 2017, Sir David Clementi, former Deputy Governor of the Bank of England, was confirmed as the new BBC Chair.[68] He replaced former *Financial Times* Chief Executive, Rona Fairhead. This, in a nutshell, is how the state-corporate media system operates – no controversy is perceived in a former banker becoming the new Chair of the 'independent' BBC, appointed by the government. So much for the fiction of 'media plurality', 'impartiality' and 'freedom' from 'political interference'.

Even when the *Guardian* ran a live page on climate change on the day that President Trump took office,[69] with a follow-up entitled, 'So you want to be a climate campaigner? Here's how', the paper's compromised worldview was all too apparent.[70] The top of the *Guardian*'s website proudly proclaimed:

With climate sceptics moving into the White House, the *Guardian* will spend the next 24 hours focusing on the climate change happening right now, and what we can do to help protect the planet.[71]

But you would have searched in vain for any in-depth analysis of how big business, together with co-opted governments, have mobilised massive resources in order to stifle any real progress towards tackling climate change, and 'what we can do' about that.

Significantly, the *Guardian's* 'focused' climate coverage once again steered clear of its own questionable behaviour,[72] including its structural ties to elite money and power.[73] In particular, there was no *Guardian* commitment to drop any, never mind all, fossil-fuel advertising revenue. A proposal to reject ads from 'environmental villains' had been put to the paper by its own columnist George Monbiot[74] in 2009, following a challenge from Media Lens.[75] It got nowhere. Meanwhile, the paper continues to be riddled with ads promoting carbon emissions – notably short-haul flights[76] and cars[77] – ironically appearing right beside articles about dangerous global warming.

In an online debate on the *Guardian* website in 2015, just after then Editor Alan Rusbridger had made a commitment to give serious attention to the climate threat, one reader asked him:

Will [the] *Guardian* refuse advertising from fossil fuel companies?

This would send a powerful signal that as an organisation you would not accept money from those engaged in continued climate destruction.

Rusbridger's reply was a classic of the 'buying time' genre:

Fair question. As I wrote at the start, we're looking at our own investments. We publish an annual sustainability report about the progress we're making on the cost and impact of our own operations. As for the advertising question, I'll discuss it with our commercial director. When I last saw him, he didn't think we took vast sums from fossil fuel companies![78]

Two months later, we asked on Twitter about the outcome of this discussion. There was no response: a sign of the *Guardian*'s lack of commitment to genuine environmental sustainability.

Even as such glaring contradictions, omissions and silences became ever more apparent to *Guardian* readers, the paper was ramping up its appeals for readers to dip into their pockets. When Trump triumphed in the US election in November 2016, Lee Glendinning, editor of *Guardian* US, pleaded:

> Never has the world needed independent journalism more. [...] Now is the time to support journalism that is both fearless and free.[79]

She deployed standard, self-serving *Guardian* rhetoric:

> Because the *Guardian* is not beholden to profit-seeking share-holders or a billionaire owner, we can pursue stories without fear of where they might take us, free from commercial and political influence.

In repeatedly churning out the myth that the *Guardian* is 'free from commercial and political influence', any public doubts about its pure nature are supposed to be dispelled. But there comes a point where readers know their intelligence is being insulted. And we are now well past that point.

'We're Destroying the Rest of Life in One Century'

For years, the corporate media, notably the *Guardian*, has selected and promoted high-profile green spokespeople; like the Green Party's Jonathan Porritt and Sara Parkin, Greenpeace's Lord Peter Melchett and Stephen Tindale, Friends of the Earth's Charles Secrett and Tony Juniper, authors Mark Lynas and George Monbiot – who have then come to limit and dominate the environment debate within 'respectable' bounds.

Porritt, once the darling of the green movement in Britain, suggested in 2015 that he may finally have woken up. A *Guardian* confessional by Porritt had the subheading:

Leading UK environmentalist Jonathon Porritt calls his years working on green energy projects with Shell and BP a 'painful journey' that have led him to believe no major fossil fuel company will commit to renewables in the near future.[80]

Many radicals will feel they could have told him this 25 years earlier; as indeed several did, Media Lens included.

For Porritt himself:

This has been quite a painful journey for me personally. I so badly wanted to believe that the combination of reason, rigorous science and good people would enable elegant transition strategies to emerge in those companies.

Porritt's 'pragmatic' approach of working with 'good, far-sighted people' inside companies 'capable of conducting their business "on a truly sustainable basis"' has failed abysmally. Worse than that, as *Guardian* reader 'kalahari' asked Porritt in the comments section online:

Has your involvement not to some extent legitimated these companies' activities and actually forestalled the emergence of more radical political responses?[81]

This is a good question that the *Guardian's* more progressive writers might also wish to address when mulling over their continued employment by a media organisation that is so often complicit in shielding elite power from public challenges, not least on climate change.

In 2012, the acclaimed biologist and conservationist Edward O. Wilson put the scale of the climate crisis bluntly:

We're destroying the rest of life in one century. We'll be down to half the species of plants and animals by the end of the century if we keep at this rate.[82]

And yet 'very few people are paying attention' to this disaster. Wilson, then 82, directed his warning to the young in particular:

Why aren't you young people out protesting the mess that's being made of the planet? Why are you not repeating what was done in the '60s? Why aren't you in the streets? And what in the world has happened to the green movement that used to be on our minds and accompanied by outrage and high hopes? What went wrong?

The trouble is that most of what the public hears about politics, including environmental issues, comes from the corporate media. This is a disaster for genuine democracy. As we have frequently noted, the media industry is made up of large profit-seeking corporations whose main task is to sell audiences to wealthy advertisers – also corporations, of course – on whom the media depend for a huge slice of their revenues. It's blindingly obvious that the corporate media is literally not in the business of alerting humanity to the real risk of climate catastrophe and what needs to be done to avert it.

And yet even liberal media outlets repeatedly present as fact that there has been government 'failure' to respond to climate change. They do very little to report that, as discussed earlier in this chapter, big business, acting through and outside government, and the corporate media itself, has been fighting tooth and nail to prevent the required radical action.

Indeed, media debate on how best to respond to environmental crisis has barely moved in a generation. For years, the public has been assailed by the same anodyne editorials urging 'the need for all of us to act now'. Meanwhile, for obvious reasons, corporate media organisations are silent about the inherently biocidal logic of corporate capitalism. They are silent about the reality that politics in the US and UK is largely in thrall to giant corporations, as Ralph Nader has observed.[83] They are silent about the role of the mass media, especially advertising, in normalising the unthinkable of unrestrained consumption.

The typical, ubiquitous corporate advert depicts modern men and women using high-tech vehicles and gadgets to solve even tiny problems on the way to a brighter, ever more comfortable future. We can argue about imbalance in news reporting and commentary, but not in advertising, because there is *no balance whatever* – no counter-force opposing this utterly fraudulent view of 'progress'. The truth is that the animals and plants that share this planet with us, together with the formerly stable climate on which we all depend, *are not surviving* our disastrous, high-tech rush to 'a better world'. Virtually every advert depicts our pathological state of denial as 'normal', suggesting that nothing is terribly wrong, and much right, with the way we are living. This deluge of advertising is arguably even more influential than news and commentary in shaping our view of the world. Where is the counter-advertising to 'balance' this incessant and insidious propaganda?

The corporate media, including the liberal media wing, are a vital cog of the rampant global capitalism that threatens our very existence. With humanity heading for the climate abyss, it's time for the green movement and those on the left to wake up to the reality that the *Guardian*, the BBC and the rest of the corporate media, are not in favour of the kind of radical change that is desperately needed. In short, the current era of 'great derangement' will last as long as the public allows news and debate to be manipulated by a state-corporate media system that is complicit in killing the planet.

12

'Fake News', Objective Journalism and the No-Business Model

In 2016, in the wake of Corbyn, Brexit and Trump, 'mainstream' media did the formerly unthinkable by focusing on mass media bias spreading 'fake news' to a 'post-truth' society. The intensity of focus was such that Oxford Dictionaries announced that 'post-truth' was their 'Word of the Year 2016', referring to 'circumstances in which objective facts are less influential in shaping public opinion than appeals to emotion and personal belief'.[1]

Students of 'brainwashing under freedom' will notice that this bears a striking resemblance to twentieth-century US public intellectual Reinhold Niebuhr's insistence on the use of 'emotionally potent over-simplifications' to control the public mind.[2] But, of course, this ongoing elite attempt to manipulate society with fake news – the kind of thing seen in the 'free press' on a daily basis – was not part of the discussion.

We learn from an article on Wikipedia that 'post-truth politics' is driven by 'fake news':

Fake news websites ... are Internet websites that deliberately publish fake news – hoaxes, propaganda, and disinformation purporting to be real news – often using social media to drive web traffic and amplify their effect.[3]

This 'fake news' is being harvested by social media that seal unwitting users in airtight 'filter bubbles':

A filter bubble is a state of intellectual isolation that can result from personalized searches when a website algorithm selectively guesses what information a user would like to see based on information about the user, such as location, past click-behavior and search history. As a result, users become separated from information that disagrees with their viewpoints, effectively isolating them in their own cultural or ideological bubbles.[4]

In one news report, seven different *Guardian* journalists – all apparently trapped within their own corporate 'filter bubbles' – discussed the rise of 'fake news' around the world without once mentioning the role of 'mainstream' media. This led to remarkable conclusions:

Fake news is not a problem of any scale in Australia: the media market, dominated by a handful of key players serving a population of just over 21 million people, does not seem fragmented enough.[5]

No fake news in Australia? Some perspective was supplied by former CIA counterterrorism official Philip Giraldi in 2009:

The Rupert Murdoch chain has been used extensively to publish false intelligence from the Israelis and occasionally from the British government.[6]

Also in the *Guardian*, author Andrew Smith argued that, post-Trump and Brexit, future historians would decide 'whether this will go down as the year democracy revealed itself unworkable in the age of the internet'.[7]

It was hard not to interpret this as a *cri de coeur* from the propaganda establishment. As Trump, Brexit, Bernie Sanders in the US, Podemos in Spain, and, above all, Corbyn in the UK, have shown, elite control of *managed* democracy may have become unworkable. The forecast is grim:

One day, I suspect, we will look back in disbelief that we let the net-induced friction on civil society reach this pitch, because if we didn't know before, we know now that our stark choice is between social networks' bottom line and democracy. I know which I prefer.

These words appeared less than two years after the January 2015 Charlie Hebdo massacre, when a *Guardian* editorial had opined:

Any society that's serious about liberty has to defend the free flow of ugly words, even ugly sentiments.[8]

Now, it seems, anyone 'serious about liberty' has to resist the free flow of ugly words for fear of 'net-induced friction on civil society'. What does 'net-induced friction' mean? Yes, it can mean Trump's racist provocations. But it can also mean Sanders' and Corbyn's successful mobilisation of young people to oppose war and injustice.

Smith was reacting to 'the accidental or deliberate propagation of misinformation via social media'. Many millions of people 'saw and believed fake reports that the pope had endorsed Trump; Democrats had paid and bussed anti-Trump protesters ...'; and so on. Curiously, Smith made no mention of the relentless 'mainstream' and social media efforts to link Trump with Putin. Nor did he mention the upside of social media – the democratisation of outreach and related empowerment of a more compassionate politics.

Smith had nothing to say about the leading role played by traditional corporate media in the 'deliberate propagation of misinformation'. A remarkable omission, given the unprecedented ferocity of the smear campaign against Jeremy Corbyn. As Adam Johnson of Fairness and Accuracy in Reporting noted, 'mainstream' commentators 'have carved out such a narrow definition of "fake news" that it excludes anything emanating from establishment news sources'.[9]

Johnson noted that a YouGov poll showed that a shocking 46 per cent of Trump supporters had believed the 'pizzagate' scandal – a bizarre conspiracy spread on alternative media about Clinton's campaign manager running a child sex ring from a Washington DC pizza restaurant. This led to widespread outrage over fake news by 'MSM' journalists. Johnson added:

But most missed that the same poll found that 50 percent of Clinton supporters believed the Russian government had tampered directly with vote tallies – as in, Putin agents directly manipulated election results. While these fears are based, at least in part, on actual (though still unproven) assertions by US intelligence that Russian hackers leaked unflattering DNC emails in an effort to influence the election, the idea that Russia actually hacked the voting process itself is an ungrounded conspiracy theory, and one the White House has repeatedly insisted didn't happen.

In 2017, there was considerable media hysteria over 'Russiagate' that focused obsessively on outraged claims of supposed pivotal Russian interference in Trump's election as US President. But, as Glenn Greenwald noted:

> Inflammatory claims about Russia get mindlessly hyped by media outlets, almost always based on nothing more than evidence-free claims from government officials, only to collapse under the slightest scrutiny, because they are entirely lacking in evidence.[10]

Greenwald was not arguing that there was definitely no Russian interference. But the 'evidence' for decisive intervention presented at that stage was unconvincing, to say the least. A related point is that Western corporate media have only ever given minimal coverage to longstanding US government efforts to intervene in other countries – from propaganda campaigns, meddling in foreign elections, and all the way up to assassinations, coups and full-blown invasions. A *Time* magazine cover story in 1996 even boasted that US interference helped Boris Yeltsin to be re-elected as president of Russia:

> Exclusive: Yanks to the Rescue. The Secret Story of How American Advisers Helped Yeltsin Win.[11]

Another *Guardian* piece was titled:

> Bursting the Facebook bubble: we asked voters on the left and right to swap feeds – Social media has made it easy to live in filter bubbles, sheltered from opposing viewpoints. So what happens when liberals and conservatives trade realities?[12]

The problem being:

> Facebook users are increasingly sheltered from opposing viewpoints – and reliable news sources [sic] – and the viciously polarized state of our national politics appears to be one of the results.

Facebook readers, then, are sheltered from the giant, global corporate media that dominate our newspapers, magazines, publishing companies, cinema, TVs, radios and computer screens – even though social media are themselves corporate media. And, presumably, we are to believe that readers of 'reliable news sources' – the BBC, the *Guardian*, *The Times*, the *Telegraph* and other traditional outlets – are forever being exposed to 'opposing viewpoints' by these media, for example on Corbyn, Iraq, Libya, Syria and Israel-Palestine.

If we beg to differ, having studied the media intensively for two decades, it may be because we should be added to a list of 200 websites that 'are at the very least acting as bona fide "useful idiots" of the Russian intelligence services, and are worthy of further scrutiny', according to the PropOrNot group. The *Washington Post* reported:

> PropOrNot's monitoring report, which was provided to [the] *Washington Post* in advance of its public release, identifies more than 200 websites as routine peddlers of Russian propaganda during the election season, with combined audiences of at least 15 million Americans. On Facebook, PropOrNot estimates that stories planted or promoted by the disinformation campaign were viewed more than 213 million times.[13]

Matt Taibbi noted in *Rolling Stone* that outlets as diverse as AntiWar.com, LewRockwell.com and the Ron Paul Institute are on the list, although the *Washington Post* offered no information about the PropOrNot group, 'which offered zero concrete evidence of coordination with Russian intelligence agencies'.[14]

Chris Hedges of Truthdig, which is on the list, describes the *Post*'s report as an 'updated form of Red-Baiting.' He added:

> This attack signals an open war on the independent press. Those who do not spew the official line will be increasingly demonized in corporate echo chambers such as the Post or CNN as useful idiots or fifth columnists.[15]

With perfect irony, this focus on 'fake news' was itself a classic example of fake news. The theme of social media manipulating voting and democracy more generally arose only because social media were manifestly threatening elite control of voting and democracy. In other words, the issue of 'fake news' only emerged because the elite monopoly of fake news was under threat.

Fake news is not just limited to stories wholly and consciously fabricated to deceive people – the 'threat' of Iraqi WMD being launched within 45 minutes of an order being given, the 'threat' of Gaddafi massacring civilians in Benghazi. Fake news can simply be news coverage that excludes one side of an argument. It is in this sense that corporate coverage of 'fake news' is itself fake.

Thus, our search of the Lexis newspaper database (25 July 2017) for the terms 'fake news' and 'Noam Chomsky' threw up 10 hits, none of them discussing fake news in the context of Chomsky's media analysis. A search for 'fake news' and Edward Herman and Chomsky's 'propaganda model' found zero hits.

Intermission: Standing Up for the 'Mainstream'

Once again, left commentators have played a key role in marginalising rational dissent on this issue. Aaron Bastani, co-founder of Novara Media – ostensibly a radical left site challenging the 'mainstream' – tweeted a follow-up to his own tweet criticising the *Guardian*:

> Some responding to this tweet saying @guardian is 'fake news' – it isn't. Most of its stuff is crucial and world class[16]

As we have shown, this is a fake assessment of the *Guardian*'s role in producing fake news.

Salaried corporate dissidents are also, of course, to be found leaping to the defence of their employers. In December 2014, former *Guardian* journalist Jonathan Cook challenged George Monbiot of the *Guardian*:

> @GeorgeMonbiot *Guardian*, your employer, is precisely part of media problem. Why this argument [on the need for structural reform] is far from waste of energy. It's vital.[17]

Monbiot replied:

> @Jonathan_K_Cook that's your view. I don't share it. Most of my work exposing corporate power has been through or with the *Guardian*.[18]

In December 2014, Owen Jones lamented the departure of his *Guardian* boss:

> Like so many others, owe so much to Alan Rusbridger. The *Guardian* is a global force, and that's so much down to him. Surreal he's gone[19]

And:

> Surreal he's going, that is. He's still the boss![20]

By March 2015, Jones' mood had brightened:

> Incredible news that @KathViner is new *Guardian* editor! Nearly whooped in the quiet carriage. That's how excited I am.[21]

Much as we might cringe at an ostensible left dissident lauding his corporate boss in this way, a further problem is the background structural bias. In 2017, Jones tweeted:

> I'm barred from criticising colleagues in my column.[22]

Jones was responding to *Guardian* columnist Zoe Williams who had tweeted:

> I've never worked on a paper where you're allowed to openly slate a colleague.[23]

So, Jones is allowed to praise his managers but not *criticise* them, or any other colleagues. This is ugly indeed, and makes the paeans of praise even less palatable.

Naomi Klein is a highly respected social activist much admired by the *Guardian*. Celebrating a long article discussing the future of the media by *Guardian* Editor Katharine Viner, Klein tweeted:

> Brilliant and sweeping essay from *Guardian* editor @KathViner: 'A mission for journalism in a time of crisis.' Don't miss it![24]

In fact, Viner's article was an anodyne annual report-style puff piece for the newspaper. For example, Viner commented:

> After working at the *Guardian* for two decades, I feel I know instinctively why it exists. Most of our journalists and our readers do, too – it's something to do with holding power to account, and upholding liberal values.[25]

This will have come as a surprise to readers who witnessed the *Guardian's* propaganda blitz targeting Corbyn under Viner's editorship. She even wrote:

> In the UK, Jeremy Corbyn appeared to have torn up the rulebook that had governed electoral politics for two decades – finding a surge of support in the June snap election, particularly with young people, by promoting socialist ideas that had long been dismissed.

As we have already seen, the *Guardian* led the way in that dismissal.

Corporate journalists sometimes seem bewildered by our work at Media Lens. We haven't signed any 'gentlemen's agreements', we don't 'play the game' of avoiding the career-damaging 'red lines' that corporate dissidents fear so much. The main prohibition being, as we have seen, against criticising the editors and bosses who pay the salaries, and who can instantly raise or rubbish a writer's public profile.

An amusing example of this befuddlement was provided by Mehdi Hasan, formerly a senior editor at *New Statesman*, now a presenter on Al Jazeera's English news channel. Hasan has sometimes kicked back at our challenges asking journalists like Owen Jones if they are free to challenge their employers:

> @medialens sorry in which world is it acceptable for employees to publicly attack or critique their employers? Do you guys not have bosses??[26]

It was a remarkable question that revealed much about the corporate mind-set. We replied:

> @mehdirhasan No, we don't have bosses, owners, oligarchs, advertisers, or wealthy philanthropist donors. We're independent. How about you?[27]

Asking awkward questions of the handful of corporate leftists with the power to really drive home a propaganda blitz is a risky business. They are key precisely because they have the credibility and also the 'mainstream' outreach to make a difference. And, of course, they will happily use this power against their critics. As discussed in this book, we have been subject to crude smears often imported from the hard-right. By using their very real corporate media power to undermine our credibility, corporate dissidents protect both their own reputations and that of their employers – it is good for their standing and sits extremely well with their editors. The system is well able to protect itself and these dissidents play a crucial and well-entrenched role in support of that.

In an article titled, 'The Fake News Business Exposed', published on the *Event Chronicle* website, Jon Rappoport noted that during his 34 years of working as a reporter, he'd had many illuminating, informal conversations with 'mainstream' journalists. He offered some examples from his notes taken between 1982–2011. One journalist (name withheld) told him:

Most reporters who cover major issues are *de facto* intelligence assets. Some know it, most don't. They're all taking their information from controlled sources. It's like somebody giving you talking points as if they're the honest truth. In these talking points, you're told who the players are in a story and what they're doing. But they aren't the important players, and what they're doing is just a cover for what's really going on. It's all about misdirection.[28]

Another said:

I can write an article that's critical of what a drug company is specifically doing, but I can't criticize the company. If I did, my editor would read me the riot act. He knows if he published that article, his boss would get a visit from the company. They would threaten to pull their advertising. Everybody would be in serious trouble. There is a fine line. Sometimes, the evidence against a drug company is huge, and we can get away with a critical article. But most of the time, it's a no-go area. I could lose my job. If I did, I would have a hell of a time trying to find another position on the same level. I might be subject to an industry-wide demotion.

And another:

We put out provable lies. And they were big ones. It was like being psychologically whipsawed. A few great days, and a lot of bad ones. The worst thing for me was government sources. I was like a horse with a feed bag on, and they were filling it up with rotten food. They knew it, I knew it, and we just kept doing it.

Issues of this kind are simply ignored in 'mainstream' discussion of the 'fake news' phenomenon.

Former *Guardian* journalist Jonathan Cook noted that the claim of 'fake news' usefully offers security agencies, establishment politicians and the corporate media 'a powerful weapon to silence their critics. After all, these critics have no platform other than independent websites and social media. Shut down the sites and you shut up your opponents.'[29]

However ridiculous and biased, the focus on 'fake news' certainly had an effect in preparing the way for attacks on free speech. On 25 April 2017, Google announced that it had made changes to its service to make it harder for users to access what it called 'low-quality' information such as 'conspiracy theories' and 'fake news'. Three months later, in July 2017, the World Socialist Web Site (WSWS) reported:

> In the three months since Internet monopoly Google announced plans to keep users from accessing 'fake news', the global traffic rankings of a broad range of left-wing, progressive, anti-war and democratic rights organizations have fallen significantly.[30]

WSWS added:

> While in April 2017, 422,460 visits to the WSWS originated from Google searches, the figure has dropped to an estimated 120,000 this month, a fall of more than 70 percent.
>
> Even when using search terms such as 'socialist' and 'socialism', readers have informed us that they find it increasingly difficult to locate the World Socialist Web Site in Google searches.

Other sites that have experienced sharp drops in ranking include WikiLeaks, Alternet, Counterpunch, Global Research, Consortium News and Truthout. Even prominent democratic rights groups such as the American Civil Liberties Union and Amnesty International appear to have been hit. This is, in part, the result of the *Guardian* and other media enthusiastically hyping the supposed threat of 'fake news'. In fact, the real threat is that corporate media search engines like Google and corporate social media like Facebook and Twitter will now work to eliminate dissent and restore the 'mainstream' media monopoly that has ensured a steady supply of power-friendly fake news for more than 100 years.

The Media Performance Pyramid

To reiterate, 'fake news' is said to refer to 'websites [that] publish hoaxes, propaganda, and disinformation'. A simple, table-top experiment can help us understand how traditional corporate media do exactly that.

Place a square wooden framework on a flat surface and pour into it a stream of ball bearings, marbles or other round objects. Some of the balls may bounce out, but many will form a base layer within the wooden framework: others will then find a place atop this first layer. In this way, the flow of ball bearings steadily adds new layers that inevitably build a pyramid-style shape.

This experiment is used to demonstrate how near-perfect crystalline structures such as snowflakes are able to arise in nature in the absence of conscious design. We will use it here as a way of understanding Edward Herman and Noam Chomsky's 'propaganda model'[31] of 'mainstream' media performance. It explains how extreme conformity of the kind we have discussed in this book is achieved in the absence of any conscious conspiracy.

Imagine now that the four sides of the wooden framework are labelled to indicate the framing conditions shaping the corporate media:

1. Corporate nature, elite/parent company ownership and profit-maximising orientation
2. Dependence on allied corporate advertisers for 50 per cent or more of revenues
3. Dependence on cheap, subsidised news supplied by state-corporate allies
4. Political, economic and legal carrots and sticks rewarding corporate media conformity and punishing dissent.

When facts, ideas, journalists and managers are poured into this framework, the result is a highly filtered, power-friendly 'pyramid' of media performance. Every aspect of corporate media output is shaped by these framing conditions. Media analyst James Twitchell explained what this means in practice:

> You name it: the appearance of ads throughout the pages, the 'jump' or continuation of a story from page to page, the rise of sectionalisation (as with news, cartoons, sports, financial, living, real estate), common page size, halftone images, process

engraving, the use of black-and-white photography, then colour, sweepstakes, and finally discounted subscriptions were all forced on publishers by advertisers hoping to find target audiences.[32]

This book is packed with examples of fake corporate news. The point is that the performance pyramid ensures that media that flourish do so *because* they serve elite interests. Glenn Greenwald explained:

> They receive most of their benefits – their access, their scoops, their sense of belonging, their money, their esteem – from dutifully serving that role... 'neutrality' means: 'serving the interests of American political and military leaders and amplifying their perspective'.[33]

This is a natural outcome of the performance pyramid, which means that corporate media are in a sense hardwired to boost state propaganda and to stifle honest criticism.

Objective This *Way Not* That *Way*

The standard view of objective journalism was offered in 2001 by the BBC's then Political Editor, Andrew Marr:

> When I joined the BBC, my Organs of Opinion were formally removed.[34]

Nick Robinson offered a similarly hands-off view when describing his role as ITN Political Editor during the Iraq War:

> It was my job to report what those in power were doing or thinking ... That is all someone in my sort of job can do.[35]

Glenn Greenwald remarked:

> That'd make an excellent epitaph on the tombstone of modern establishment journalism.[36]

Amusingly, Robinson subsequently tweeted a picture of a new statue of George Orwell outside the BBC's headquarters bearing the inscription:

If liberty means anything at all, it means the right to tell people what they do not want to hear

Robinson's comment:

I'm proud those words now adorn BBC HQ[37]

Rolling Stone magazine's Matt Taibbi nutshelled the Marr/Robinson take on journalism as 'Just the facts, Ma'am.'[38] The idea being that journalists are able to suppress their personal opinions in simply relaying information that matters.

This is why, if you ask a BBC or ITN journalist to choose between describing the Iraq war as 'a mistake' or 'a crime', they will refuse to answer on the grounds that they are required to be 'objective' and 'impartial'. But actually, there are good reasons for rejecting this idea of objectivity as fundamentally bogus and toxic.

First, it turns out that most journalists are only nervous of expressing personal opinions when criticising *the powerful*. The BBC's Andrew Marr can't call the Iraq War a 'crime', but he *can* say that the fall of Baghdad in April 2003 meant that Tony Blair 'stands as a larger man and a stronger prime minister as a result'.[39] Nick Robinson insists he must limit himself to reporting on the powerful, and yet he *can* report that 'hundreds of [British] servicemen are risking their lives to bring peace and security to the streets of Iraq.'[40] This is closer to a 'Wham, bam, thank you, Ma'am' version of 'impartiality'.

Journalists are allowed to lose their 'objectivity' *this* way, but not *that* way – not in the way that offends the powerful.

The second problem with the no-opinion argument is that it is not possible to hide opinions by merely 'sticking to the facts'. Matt Taibbi gave a striking example:

Try as hard as you want, a point of view will come forward in your story. Open any newspaper from the Thirties or Forties, check the sports page; the guy who wrote up the box score, did he have a political point of view? He probably didn't think so. But viewed with 70 or 80 years of hindsight, covering a baseball game where blacks weren't allowed to play without mentioning the fact, that's apology and advocacy. Any journalist with half a brain knows that the biases of our time are always buried in our coverage ...[41]

A further, closely-related problem is that not taking sides – for example against torture, against big countries exploiting small countries, against selling arms to tyrants, against preventing rather than exacerbating climate change – is monstrous. After all, a doctor treating a patient is certainly *biased* in seeking to identify and solve a health problem. No one would argue that the doctor should stand neutrally between sickness and health. Should we not all be biased *against* suffering, exploitation, torture and environmental suicide?

Finally, why does the journalistic responsibility to suppress personal opinion trump the responsibility to resist crimes of state for which we are accountable as democratic citizens? If the British government was very obviously massacring British citizens, would journalists refuse to speak out? Would the professional media code of conduct – the signed employment contract – outweigh the social contract? Why?

Journalists might respond that supposedly 'opinion-free' journalism is vital for a healthy democracy. But without dissent challenging open criminality, democracy quickly decays into tyranny. This is the case, for example, if we remain 'impartial' as our governments bomb, invade and kill hundreds of thousands of people in foreign countries. A journalist who refuses even to describe the Iraq War as a crime is supporting a process that normalises the unthinkable. In the real world, journalistic 'impartiality' on Iraq helped facilitate subsequent UK and US crimes in Libya, Syria and Yemen.

This is the ugly absurdity of the innocent-looking idea that journalists' 'organs of opinion' can and should be removed before they do their jobs.

Objective Journalism: Equalising Self and Other

The psychologist Erich Fromm rejected the idea that objectivity should be disinterested:

But objectivity is not, as it is often implied in a false idea of 'scientific' objectivity, synonymous with detachment, with absence of interest and care.[42]

Readers may have noticed how professional journalists like to be pictured looking serious, unsmiling, cold. They often wear severe spectacles – harsh, black, oblong – to reinforce this impression of cold detachment. But as Fromm wrote:

> Objectivity does not mean detachment, it means respect; that is, the ability not to distort and to falsify things, persons and oneself. What matters is not whether or not there is an interest, but what kind of interest there is and what its relation to the truth will be.[43]

So: it is okay to take an interest. But what is the ideal kind of interest for objective analysis in this sense?

> Love is the productive form of relatedness to others and to oneself. It implies responsibility, care, respect and knowledge, and the wish for the other person to grow and develop.[44]

Imagine – love should be at the heart of objective, serious journalism! Who would have thought it?

A central claim of Buddhism, Taoism, Sufism and other mystical traditions is that this care and respect for others can become so developed that we can actually come to respect the rights and needs of others as much as we respect our own – no more, no less. In other words, we can equalise our perception of the comparative importance of ourselves and others.

Many Western intellectuals, including leftists, dismiss all such analysis as navel-gazing piffle. But at a time when the Vikings were rampaging through Europe, the eighth-century Buddhist sage Shantideva asked:

> Since I and other beings both,
> In wanting happiness, are equal and alike,
> What difference is there to distinguish us,
> That I should strive to have my bliss alone?[45]

Here is the remarkable prospect of a human being assessing the needs of others rationally, objectively, and asking why his or her happiness should be deemed of greater importance.

But even this question is surpassed by an even more surprising declaration in response:

> The intention, ocean of great good
> That seeks to place all beings in the state of bliss,
> And every action for the benefit of all:
> Such is my delight and all my joy.[46]

After four billion years of evolution ostensibly 'red in tooth and claw', Shantideva was thus asserting that caring for others is *not* a moral responsibility – a dutiful bow to logical fairness – but a source of bliss and delight, of enlightened self-interest, that *far surpasses mere pleasure from personal gain.*

The claim, of course, is greeted with scepticism by a society that promotes unrestrained greed for maximised profit. But if we set aside our groupthink and take another look, it is actually a matter of common (if suppressed) experience. The Indian mystic Osho invited us to look a little closer at what actually makes us happy:

> Have you never had a feeling of contentment after having smiled at a stranger in the street? Didn't a breeze of peace follow it? There is no limit to the wave of tranquil joy you will feel when you lift a fallen man, when you support a fallen person, when you present a sick man with flowers – but not when you do it [out of duty] because he is your father or because she is your mother. No, the person may not be anyone in particular to you, but simply to give a gift is itself a great reward, a great pleasure.[47]

Following one of his solitary reveries, the French philosopher Jean-Jacques Rousseau wrote with great conviction:

> I know and feel that doing good is the truest happiness that the human heart can enjoy.[48]

Objective journalism is thus rooted in two ideas:

1. that human beings are able to view the happiness and suffering of others as being of equal importance to their own.
2. that, perhaps counter-intuitively for a society like ours, individuals and societies dramatically enhance their well-being when they 'equalise self and other' by caring for others in this way.

In other words, this is not a sentimental pipe dream – human beings *can* be fair and just, and they *do* experience delight from being so.

Genuinely objective journalism is thus rooted in the understanding that 'my' happiness does not matter more than 'your' happiness; that it is irrational, cruel, unfair and self-destructive to pretend otherwise. Objective journalism rejects reporting and analysis that prioritises 'my' interests – 'my' bank account, financial security, company, nation, class – over 'your' interests.

Objective journalism does not take 'our' side at 'their' expense. It does not count 'our' dead and ignore 'their' dead. It does not refuse to stand in judgement on 'our' leaders while fiercely condemning 'their' leaders. It does not hold 'them' to higher moral standards than 'us'. It does not accept that 'our' nation is 'exceptional', that 'we' have a 'manifest destiny' to dominate 'them', that 'we' are in some way 'chosen'.

The No-Business Anti-Model Business Model

For as long as we can remember, 'pragmatists' have told us:

> You have to play the game. You have to work with the corporate press and broadcasters to achieve mass outreach, and hope that you can steer them in a more positive direction.

The idea is that some arguments and policies just go 'too far', guaranteeing 'mainstream' rejection and attack, which results in fewer progressive voices being heard, benefiting precisely no-one. Bottom line, again: 'You *have* to play the game!'

We strongly disagree. We know that analysis rooted in compassion that refuses to compromise in exposing the cruelty of state-corporate power has the power to smoke out the corporate media. Alarmed by what they perceive as an 'enemy', even a 'class enemy' – a threatening sign that democratic forces might escape carefully filtered tweedledum-tweedledee choices – elite media will indeed attack. But from our perspective, this is no bad thing. In the process of attacking, supposedly liberal corporate media like the *Guardian*, the *Independent* and the BBC are forced to drop the pretence that they are independent, impartial and progressive. They reflexively leap to the defence of the establishment and thus reveal their true role as powerful supporters of the status quo.

This is important because it is precisely the illusion that 'mainstream' media are fair and impartial that allows them to sell a fake version of democracy as the real thing. In other words, uncompromised analysis *does* come at a cost – it is unpleasant to be subject to attack by 'mainstream' media – but it serves to hold up a mirror to the corporate media system *in a way that erodes its power to deceive*. This is a very different game to careful cooperation, and one that is very much worth the candle. In fact, we believe it has the power to challenge state-corporate power's system of 'managed democracy' favouring elite interests.

This is exactly what we have witnessed in recent years with Jeremy Corbyn's rise to power within British politics. As we have seen, Corbyn's compassionate, people-centred policies were dismissed as a 'loony left' joke, a risible relic of the 1970s. Corbyn would never be able to persuade the public, not least because his views stood no chance of being given a fair hearing by a press that would subject him to relentless attack. He didn't stand a chance.

It was precisely *because* the corporate media subjected Corbyn to such a vicious attack that he prospered. Why? Because it is corporate media credibility *above all else* that keeps a lid on compassionate, people-centred politics – precisely the politics Corbyn espoused.

We have not been focused on corporate media for 20 years because we have some irrational interest in media matters. Our focus is born of the firm, indeed growing conviction that the corporate media system is *the key obstacle to progressive change*. If there is to be change, it will happen only when public perceptions of this toxic system have changed.

The spectacular, relentless ugliness of the attacks on Corbyn made it very easy for the public to see through the illusion of 'mainstream' fairness so that compassionate politics could flourish (see Chapter 2). The New Labour-style argument is a deception – minor gains perhaps *can* be achieved by careful compromise and cooperation; but much more profound changes can be achieved by speaking out honestly, compassionately, selflessly, thus provoking establishment media to reveal themselves in all their soulless, power-friendly cynicism.

Professionally-minded media activists often worry about 'funding models' for media activism: How to escape the advertiser-dependent 'business model' and yet generate revenue? How to emulate best-practice corporate website design and marketing to achieve a comparable mass audience without comparable funding? How to publish dissent that is effective in challenging, without overly alienating, the 'mainstream' in order to retain 'respectability' as part of the 'conversation'?

This is all very much beside the point. If media activists devote themselves sincerely, and wholeheartedly, to working for the benefit of others, the public will be happy to support their efforts. But these efforts do have to be sincere and wholehearted. The focus should be on helping others, not on personal financial gain, status, respectability, profile and applause. We should not even be overly concerned with results, not even on reaching a wide audience: How many hits did this media alert garner? How many shares did that Facebook post get? The German philosopher Arthur Schopenhauer wrote:

> Only he who writes entirely for the sake of what he has to say writes anything worth writing. It is as if there were a curse on money: every writer writes badly as soon as he starts writing for gain. The greatest works of the greatest men [sic: and women] all belong to a time when they had to write them for nothing or for very small payment.[49]

And as Erich Fromm said:

> Our reason functions only to the degree to which it is not flooded by greed. The person who is the prisoner of his irrational passions loses the capacity for objectivity and is necessarily at the mercy of his passions; he rationalises when he believes he is expressing the truth.[50]

As soon as we start worrying about results and 'success' – and above all 'respectability' and financial gain – we enter the realm of the ego; we begin comparing ourselves with others, competing. Jealousy arises and we become reluctant to help even other well-intentioned people striving in the same direction. When we focus on goals – even the goal of making the world a better place – we are placing our attention in the future, which means we are becoming detached from the feelings of compassion and love that exist only in this moment, here and now, our best motivation. The focus should not be on funding, marketing, respectability, status, outreach, success: it should be on maintaining a sincere, honest and uncompromised motivation for what we are doing.

But how can we know if we are staying on the right track or merely fooling ourselves, subtly compromising? The answer lies in how much fun we are having. If our work is genuinely rooted in a desire to share with others, to support others, to increase their happiness and relieve their suffering, this motivation is such a delight, the work such a privilege, that we love doing what we are doing. If the work is a joy in itself – more enjoyable, actually, than a holiday from the work – than we are on the right track.

Rousseau commented:

> I could sometimes gladden another heart, and I owe it to my own honour to declare that whenever I could enjoy this pleasure, I found it sweeter than any other. This was a strong, pure and genuine instinct, and nothing in my heart of hearts has ever belied it.[51]

But Rousseau noted that 'a favour only had to become a duty for me to lose all enjoyment of it. Once that happens, the weight of obligation makes the sweetest pleasures burdensome to me …'[52]

If the work is a grim, grey grind; if we are driven by the hair-shirted idea that we have a 'duty' and 'moral obligation' to help others; if 'fun' is a four-letter word to us, then we are merely spreading misery and boredom. Because then we are operating out of ego-driven thoughts of 'duty', rather than a desire to share with others, and we will be far more likely to feed our egos, to seek to escape this dire situation through 'mainstream' 'respectability' and 'success'.

Again, the key is that the effort should be totally uncompromising, rooted in compassion rather than anger and hatred. The public are very keen to support a challenge to corporate politics and media, the influence of corporate advertising and so on – but the difference needs to be clear. And if they stop supporting us – so what? If we love what we are doing, we can continue in our spare time after doing other paid work. This may even be beneficial. However much we enjoy the work, sitting alone writing all day, full-time, is a somewhat dry, isolated existence. Being more in the world, interacting with other people, can rejuvenate and vivify our work. We at Media Lens produced a huge number of alerts when we were both working full-time on other work.

Our no-business business model draws inspiration from the way the public spontaneously rallied around Bernie Sanders in the US and Jeremy Corbyn in Britain. Heaven knows, it was not slick marketing that persuaded people to give of their time, energy and money to make Bernie dolls or stand in the rain to watch Corbyn splashing around in his sandals. The public was drawn to support a couple of people who were obviously sincere about offering a more compassionate politics.

On 6 September 2017, Craig Murray, former British Ambassador to Uzbekistan, now dissident political activist, revealed that he was being sued for libel in the High Court in England by Jake Wallis Simons, Associate Editor of the *Daily Mail* Online. Wallis Simons was demanding £40,000 in damages and the High Court had approved over £100,000 in costs. One day later, Murray reported:

> The Craig Murray defence fund has just sailed serenely past £50,000 in electronic donations in almost precisely 24 hours

... 2,080 people have donated an average of £24. The largest single donation is £4,000. There are also hundreds of £3 and £5 donations which do really add up. I am absolutely stunned by the outpouring of kindness I have experienced ...[53]

This echoes our experience. We have similarly managed to fund, first one, then – since 2010 – two full-time writers without ever charging for our media alerts or cogitations, without advertising, without big donors or any kind of institutional support (we initially sought out and received small donations from charitable trusts but decided the form-filling was too tedious and time-consuming), and despite very rarely asking for support. Most of our donations come in the form of £2 and £5 donations from 'ordinary' readers. Knowing that Media Lens supporters are people who may themselves have very little inspires us greatly to do the best we can for them – it is incomparably more motivating than a cheque from a media corporation.

The public has immense power to divert resources from corporate media to non-corporate media challenging them. This challenge is no longer a pipe dream; it is very real and already making a big difference. There is no longer any need to pay or otherwise support media corporations selling corporate-owned politics, perpetual war, unsustainable materialism and climate disaster. All we need do is support honest, non-corporate media countering this unaccountable and violent system of disinformation – the public will do the rest.

Visit Media Lens and sign up for Media Alerts and Cogitations: www.medialens.org

You can donate here: http://www.medialens.org/index.php/donate.html

Write to us: editor@medialens.org

Notes

Preface: The Devil's Greatest Trick

1. *The Usual Suspects*, 1995, IMDB.com database, quotes. www.imdb.com/title/tto114814/quotes/?tab=qt&ref_=tt_trv_qu
2. *Guardian* founder, C.P. Scott, Wikipedia, https://en.wikipedia.org/wiki/C._P._Scott
3. Howard Zinn, *The Zinn Reader: Writings on Disobedience and Democracy*, Seven Stories Press, 1997, p. 16.
4. Mark Mardell, BBC Radio 4, 'The World This Weekend', 21 May 2017, 35 mins 19 seconds; www.bbc.co.uk/programmes/bo8qxfcq#play
5. Ralph Nader, interview with Paul Jay, *The Real News Network*, 4 November 2008.

1. Anatomy of a Propaganda Blitz

1. Edward Herman and Noam Chomsky, *Manufacturing Consent: The Political Economy of the Mass Media*, Vintage, 1994, p. 208.
2. Pat Paterson, 'The truth about Tonkin', *Naval History Magazine*, February 2008, Volume 22, Number 1, www.usni.org/magazines/navalhistory/2008-02/truth-about-tonkin
3. James Williamson, 'Getting the Gulf of Tonkin wrong: Are Ken Burns and Lynn Novick "telling stories" about the central events used to legitimize the US attack against Vietnam?', *CounterPunch*, 19 September 2017, https://goo.gl/wVyEqM
4. John Stauber and Sheldon Rampton, 'How PR sold the war in the Persian Gulf', PRWatch, December 2005, www.prwatch.org/books/tsigfy10.html
5. MacArthur, cited, ibid.
6. Ann Clwyd, 'See men shredded, then say you don't back war', *The Times*, 18 March 2003.
7. Brendan O'Neill, 'The media's tall tales over Iraq', *Guardian*, 4 February 2010, www.theguardian.com/commentisfree/2010/feb/04/ann-cwlyd-saddam-shredder-iraq-inquiry

8. Editorial, 'Syria: chemical weapons with impunity', *Guardian*, 22 August 2013, www.theguardian.com/commentisfree/2013/aug/22/syria-chemical-weapons

9. Guido Fawkes blog, 'Labour MP: Israelis should face "transportation" out of Middle East', 26 April 2016, https://order-order.com/2016/04/26/labour-mp-israelis-should-face-transportation-out-of-middle-east/

10. Jonathan Freedland, 'My plea to the left: treat Jews the same way you'd treat any other minority', *Guardian*, 29 April 2016, www.theguardian.com/commentisfree/2016/apr/29/left-jews-labour-antisemitism-jewish-identity

11. Andrew Rawnsley, 'How the parties let the poison of racism seep back into our politics', *Guardian*, 1 May 2016, www.theguardian.com/commentisfree/2016/may/01/parties-let-poison-of-racism-back-into-politics

12. Jonathan Cook, 'The true anti-semites, past and present', blog, 3 May 2016, www.jonathan-cook.net/blog/2016-05-03/the-true-anti-semites-past-and-present/#sthash.r4y3hQg3.00p1JmVB.dpuf

13. Jamie Stern-Weiner and Norman Finkelstein, 'The American Jewish scholar behind Labour's "antisemitism" scandal breaks his silence', Open Democracy UK, 3 May 2016, https://goo.gl/8jM7kr

14. Ibid.

15. Richard Littlejohn, 'The fascists at the poisoned heart of Labour', *Daily Mail*, 19 April 2016, https://goo.gl/d3qoNM

16. Anonymous, 'Labour's shame', *Jewish Chronicle*, 17 March 2016, www.thejc.com/news/uk-news/labour-s-shame-1.61660

17. 'Venezuela protests: Women march against Maduro', BBC website, 6 May 2017, www.bbc.com/news/world-latin-america-39828559

18. Vanessa Buschschlüter, 'Venezuela's irreconcilable visions for the future', BBC website, 22 May 2017, www.bbc.com/news/world-latin-america-39980403

19. Greg Wilpert, 'Time for the "International Left" to take a stand on Venezuela', Venezuelananalysis.com, 15 July 2017, https://venezuelanalysis.com/analysis/13245

20. Vanessa Buschschlüter, 'Inside Venezuela's anti-government protests', BBC website, 11 May 2017, www.bbc.co.uk/news/world-latin-america-3987169

21. Joe Emersberger, 'Comparing Venezuela's media with our own', teleSUR, 16 May 2017, https://goo.gl/gSVb5V

22. Martin Woollacott, 'This drive to war is one of the mysteries of our time', *Guardian*, 24 January 2003, www.theguardian.com/politics/2003/jan/24/foreignpolicy.iraq

23. George Monbiot, 'The Middle East has had a secretive nuclear power in its midst for years', *Guardian*, 20 November 2007, www.theguardian.com/commentisfree/2007/nov/20/foreignpolicy.usa

24. Monbiot, Twitter, 3 October 2011, https://twitter.com/GeorgeMonbiot/status/120955419412791296

25. Owen Jones, Twitter, 20 February 2011, https://twitter.com/owenjones84/status/39416988862382080

26. Jones, 'The case against bombing Libya', *Left Futures*, March 2011, www.leftfutures.org/2011/03/the-case-against-bombing-libya/

27. Jones, Twitter, 18 July 2012, https://twitter.com/OwenJones84/status/225643080747982848

28. Jones, Twitter, 18 July 2012, https://twitter.com/OwenJones84/status/225643764604088320

29. Mark Mazzetti, Adam Goldman and Michael S. Schmidt, 'Behind the sudden death of a $1 billion secret C.I.A. war in Syria', *New York Times*, 2 August 2017, www.nytimes.com/2017/08/02/world/middleeast/cia-syria-rebel-arm-train-trump.html

30. Jones, Twitter, 18 July 2012, https://twitter.com/OwenJones84/status/225646550125252608

31. Jones, Twitter, 27 April 2016, https://twitter.com/OwenJones84/status/725299599708160000

32. Jones, Twitter, 28 April 2016, https://twitter.com/OwenJones84/status/725646692234715138

33. Ali Abunimah, Twitter, 29 April 2016, https://twitter.com/AliAbunimah/status/726007092625154048

34. Abunimah, Twitter, 29 April 2016, https://twitter.com/AliAbunimah/status/726007430358925312

35. Noam Chomsky, ZNet blog, 27 March 2008.

36. Monbiot, Twitter, 3 July 2017, https://twitter.com/GeorgeMonbiot/status/881779007695572993

37. Michael White, Twitter, 25 October 2017, https://twitter.com/michaelwhite/status/923159806394892288

38. Jones, Twitter, 7 February 2013, https://twitter.com/OwenJones84/status/299471529752788992

39. Monbiot, 'Left and libertarian right cohabit in the weird world of the genocide belittlers', *Guardian*, 13 June 2011, www.theguardian.com/commentisfree/2011/jun/13/left-and-libertarian-right

40. Monbiot, 'Media cleanse,' blog, 4 August 2011, www.monbiot. com/2011/08/04/media-cleanse/

41. Monbiot, 'Lord McAlpine – an abject apology', blog, 10 November 2012, www.monbiot.com/2012/11/10/lord-mcalpine-an-abject-apology/

42. Jennifer Cockerell, 'Journalist George Monbiot agrees to £25,000 charity work deal to settle Lord McAlpine Twitter lawsuit', *Independent*, 12 March 2013, https://goo.gl/uR2EoB

43. Monbiot, 'Lord McAlpine – an abject apology', Monbiot website, 10 November 2012, www.monbiot.com/2012/11/10/lord-mcalpine-an-abject-apology/

44. Monbiot, 'My agreement with Lord McAlpine', blog, 12 March 2013, www.monbiot.com/2013/03/12/my-agreement-with-lord-mcalpine/

45. Oliver Kamm, Twitter, 9 May 2016, https://twitter.com/OliverKamm/status/729748760906043392

46. Theodore Sayeed, 'Chomsky and his critics', *Mondoweiss*, 19 February 2016, http://mondoweiss.net/2016/02/chomsky-and-his-critics/

47. Leading article, 'Gloom in Guildhall', *Guardian*, 12 November 2002, www.theguardian.com/politics/2002/nov/12/terrorism.foreignpolicy

48. John Pilger, 'Lies, damned lies and government terror warnings,' *Daily Mirror*, 3 December 2002.

49. George Eaton, 'Labour MPs believe Jeremy Corbyn is incapable of tackling anti-semitism', *New Statesman*, 29 April 2016, www. newstatesman.com/politics/uk/2016/04/labour-mps-believe-jeremy-corbyn-incapable-tackling-anti-semitism

50. International Physicians for the Prevention of Nuclear War, 'Body count. Casualty figures after 10 years of the "War on Terror": Iraq, Afghanistan, Pakistan', first international edition, edited by Jens Wagner, translated from German by Ali Fathollah-Nejad, March 2015, www.psr.org/assets/pdfs/body-count.pdf

51. Machiavelli. Quoted, Howard Zinn, *The Zinn Reader*, Seven Stories Press, 1997, p. 344.

52. Machiavelli, *The Prince*, Dover Publications, 1992, p. 46, our emphasis.

53. Ibid., p. 47.

2. Killing Corbyn

1. Quoted, Noam Chomsky, *Radical Priorities*, Black Rose Books, 1981, pp. 160–4.

2. Peter Oborne, 'Corbyn will confront a bankrupt foreign policy. That's why he must be backed', Middle East Eye, 27 August 2015, www.middleeasteye.net/columns/corbyn-troublemaker-1532484034

3. George Eaton, 'The epic challenges facing Jeremy Corbyn as Labour leader', New Statesman, 12 September 2015, www.newstatesman.com/politics/uk/2015/09/epic-challenges-facing-jeremy-corbyn-labour-leader

4. Peter Oborne, 'Corbyn's election manifesto for the Middle East is radical and morally courageous', Middle East Eye, 19 May 2017, www.middleeasteye.net/columns/corbyns-manifesto-middle-east-well-argued-radical-and-morally-courageous-2036528122

5. 'The Guardian view on the Labour leadership: analogue contest in a digital age', Guardian, 24 July 2015 www.theguardian.com/commentisfree/2015/jul/24/the-Guardian-view-on-the-labour-leadership-analogue-contest-in-a-digital-age

6. Jonathan Freedland, 'The Corbyn tribe cares about identity, not power', Guardian, 24 July 2015, www.theguardian.com/commentisfree/2015/jul/24/corbyn-tribe-identity-politics-labour

7. Polly Toynbee, 'This was the week the Labour leadership contest turned nasty', Guardian, 23 July 2015, www.theguardian.com/commentisfree/2015/jul/23/labour-leadership-contest-jeremy-corbyn

8. Suzanne Moore, 'I could pay £3 to have a say, but why would I intrude on Labour's private grief?', Guardian, 22 July 2015, www.theguardian.com/commentisfree/2015/jul/22/tony-blair-right-labour-past

9. John Pilger, 'Let's face it – the state has lost its mind', New Statesman, 16 May 2005, www.newstatesman.com/node/192496

10. Martin Kettle, 'Labour can come back from the brink. But it seems to lack the will to do so', Guardian, 23 July 2015, www.theguardian.com/commentisfree/2015/jul/23/labour-back-from-brink-unity

11. Comment, 'Labour's leadership crisis just gets worse', Evening Standard, 23 July 2015, www.standard.co.uk/comment/comment/evening-standard-comment-labours-leadership-crisis-just-gets-worse-10410456.html

12. Leader, 'Silence of the lambs: Labour's would-be leaders must stand up to the growing mutiny on the party's left', The Times, 27 July 2015.

13. Leading article, 'Marxed man', Sun, 27 July 2015.

14. Leader, 'Corbyn's Morons have only helped the hard left', Sunday Times, 26 July 2015.

15. David Aaronovitch, Twitter, 15 June 2015, https://twitter.com/DAaronovitch/status/610408642823761920

16. Leading article, 'We need a leader for a new world,' *Mirror*, 27 July 2015.

17. Rachel Sylvester, 'Will a Corbyn victory be the end of Labour?', *The Times*, 1 September 2015, www.thetimes.co.uk/article/will-a-corbyn-victory-be-the-end-of-labour-6lz9tf2krbm

18. Heather Stewart, 'Jeremy Corbyn tells Pride heckler "I did all I could" against Brexit', *Guardian*, 25 June 2016, www.theguardian.com/politics/2016/jun/25/jeremy-corbyn-vows-to-face-down-any-leadership-challenge-brexit

19. Craig Murray, 'How the news agenda is set', blog, 25 June 2016, www.craigmurray.org.uk/archives/2016/06/news-agenda-set/

20. Heather Stewart, Twitter, 25 June 2016, https://twitter.com/Guardian/Heather/status/746743222513319936

21. Craig Murray, Twitter, 25 June 2016, https://twitter.com/CraigMurrayOrg/status/746951250445475840

22. Media Lens Facebook screenshot of BBC live feed, 27 June 2016, https://goo.gl/mT8w4M

23. Paul Mason, 'Corbyn delivered the Labour vote for remain – so let's get behind him', *Guardian*, 26 June 2016, www.theguardian.com/commentisfree/2016/jun/26/corbyn-leader-brexit-labour-rebels-sabotage

24. Dan Hodges, 'Labour MUST dump vampire Jezza: If MPs don't vote for "Jexit" now their party is doomed', *Mail on Sunday*, 26 June 2016, www.dailymail.co.uk/debate/article-3660328/Labour-dump-vampire-Jeremy-Corbyn-DAN-HODGES-says.html

25. Hodges, Twitter, 26 June 2016, https://twitter.com/DPJHodges/status/747113864433639424

26. Damien, Twitter, 26 June 2016, https://twitter.com/Damian0706/status/747138787784986624

27. Dan Hodges, 'March of the Corbinators: Britain's best political columnist DAN HODGES joins the *Mail on Sunday* – and reveals Labour plot to ditch Corbyn', *Mail on Sunday*, 13 March 2016, https://goo.gl/N9DXWD

28. Andrew Marr, *My Trade: A Short History of British Journalism*, Macmillan, 2004, p. 112.

29. Matt Dathan, 'Jeremy Corbyn's weapons pledge makes "nuclear holocaust more likely"', *Independent*, 30 September 2015, www.

independent.co.uk/news/uk/politics/jeremy-corbyns-weapons-pledge-risks-causing-a-nuclear-holocaust-warns-labour-mp-a6674056.html

30. BBC 'News at Ten', 30 September 2015, YouTube capture, www.youtube.com/watch?v=zVNU1Nljs20&feature=youtu.be Discussed at greater length in our media alert, 'Nuclear war and Corbyn – The fury and the farce', 5 October 2015, https://goo.gl/hkaARj

31. See our media alert, '"Our Only Fear Was That He Might Pull His Punches" – BBC caught manipulating the news', 13 January 2016, https://goo.gl/FyjhhJ

32. Peter Curran, The Stephen Doughty resignation sequence on Daily Politics, YouTube, 7 January 2016, www.youtube.com/watch?v=ZcA3hmX5V3g

33. Nicholas Watt and Mark Sweney, 'BBC justifies decision to allow Stephen Doughty to resign live on Daily Politics', *Guardian*, 8 January 2016, www.theguardian.com/media/2016/jan/08/bbc-justifies-decision-to-allow-stephen-doughty-to-resign-live-on-daily-politics

34. Elizabeth Rigby, 'BBC denies arranging live resignation', *The Times*, 9 January 2016, www.thetimes.co.uk/article/bbc-denies-arranging-live-resignation-v7jcq3r8vzh

35. Agency, 'BBC denies orchestrating Stephen Doughty resignation after Labour complaint', *Telegraph*, 9 January 2016, www.telegraph.co.uk/news/bbc/12090599/BBC-denies-orchestrating-Stephen-Doughty-resignation-after-Labour-complaint.html

36. Jane Merrick, 'Stephen Doughty resignation: Why it's fine to resign on air', *Independent*, 9 January 2016, www.independent.co.uk/voices/stephen-doughty-resignation-why-its-fine-to-resign-on-air-a6804521.html

37. Nic Outterside, blog, 8 January 2016, https://seagullnic.wordpress.com/

38. Stephen Doughty, Twitter, 7 January 2016, https://twitter.com/SDoughtyMP/status/685284548922445824

39. Harriet Agerholm, Louis Dore, 'Jeremy Corbyn increased Labour's vote share more than any of the party's leaders since 1945', *Independent*, 9 June 2017, www.independent.co.uk/news/uk/politics/jeremy-corbyn-election-result-vote-share-increased-1945-clement-attlee-a7781706.html

40. Jessica Brown, 'When Rupert Murdoch saw the exit poll "he stormed out of the room", John Prescott tweets', *Independent*, 9 June 2017, www.

indy100.com/article/rupert-murdoch-stormed-out-general-election-exit-poll-hung-parliament-7780951

41. Daisy Wyatt, 'The Jeremy Corbyn critics who admit they were wrong about the Labour leader', iNews, 9 June 2017, https://inews.co.uk/news/politics/jeremy-corbyn-sceptics-admit-wrong-labour-leader/

42. Gaby Hinsliff, 'Jeremy Corbyn is just a symptom of a party that doesn't get why it lost', Guardian, 6 January 2017, www.theguardian.com/commentisfree/2017/jan/06/jeremy-corbyn-symptom-labour-party

43. Hinsliff, Twitter, 8 June 2017, https://twitter.com/gabyhinsliff/status/873047293376647169

44. Hinsliff, Twitter, 12 June 2017, https://twitter.com/gabyhinsliff/status/874212314379104260

45. Media Lens, Twitter, 12 June 2017, https://twitter.com/medialens/status/874218481713106945

46. Media Lens, Twitter, 12 June 2017, https://twitter.com/medialens/status/874218875700883456

47. John Rentoul, 'This election will mark the end of Labour's Corbyn era – but what will come next?', Independent, 13 May 2017, www.independent.co.uk/voices/behind-the-scenes-in-the-election-the-corbyn-era-may-be-coming-to-an-end-a7734026.html

48. Rentoul, 'I was wrong about Jeremy Corbyn', Independent, 9 June 2017, www.independent.co.uk/voices/i-was-wrong-about-jeremy-corbyn-a7781726.html

49. Cathy Newman, Twitter, 8 June 2017, https://twitter.com/cathynewman/status/872927058380423169

50. Piers Morgan, Twitter, 8 June 2017, https://twitter.com/piersmorgan/status/872919228042678272

51. Kyle Griffin, Twitter, 9 June 2017, https://twitter.com/kylegriffin1/status/873325711590916096

52. Rafael Behr, 'Jeremy Corbyn, you broke it – now you must own it', Guardian, 24 February 2017, www.theguardian.com/commentisfree/2017/feb/24/jeremy-corbyn-labour-copeland-stoke-leader

53. Behr, Twitter, 8 June 2017, https://twitter.com/rafaelbehr/status/873007794760409091

54. Nick Cohen, Twitter, 18 March 2017, https://mobile.twitter.com/NickCohen4/status/843177749980368897

55. Nick Cohen, 'Don't tell me you weren't warned about Corbyn', Observer, 19 March 2017, www.theguardian.com/commentisfree/2017/mar/19/jeremy-corbyn-labour-threat-party-election-support

56. Cohen, 'I was wrong about Corbyn's chances, but I still doubt him', *Observer*, 11 June 2017, www.theguardian.com/commentisfree/2017/jun/10/i-was-wrong-about-jeremy-corbyn-still-doubt-him

57. See our media alert: 'Meltdown: The Guardian's Jonathan Freedland writes Jeremy Corbyn's obituary', Media Lens website, 10 May 2017, https://goo.gl/hFsMeP for further discussion.

58. Jonathan Freedland, 'No more excuses: Jeremy Corbyn is to blame for this meltdown', *Guardian*, 5 May 2017, www.theguardian.com/commentisfree/2017/may/05/jeremy-corbyn-blame-meltdown-labour-leader

59. Freedland, Twitter, 8 June 2017, https://twitter.com/Freedland/status/873020631125766144

60. Polly Toynbee, 'Corbyn is rushing to embrace Labour's annihilation', *Guardian*, 19 April 2017, www.theguardian.com/commentisfree/2017/apr/19/general-election-labour-annihilation-jeremy-corbyn

61. Polly Toynbee, 'This is Corbyn's moment: he's rescued Britain from the chains of austerity', *Guardian*, 12 June 2017, www.theguardian.com/commentisfree/2017/jun/12/jeremy-corbyn-austerity-labour-leader

62. Michael White, Twitter, 9 June 2017, https://twitter.com/michaelwhite/status/873153019252285440

63. Jonathan Cook, Twitter, 9 June 2017, https://twitter.com/Jonathan_K_Cook/status/873165132628725760

64. White, Twitter, 10 June 2017, https://twitter.com/michaelwhite/status/873589538681229312

65. Abi Wilkinson, Twitter, June 2017, tweet has been deleted, https://twitter.com/AbiWilks/status/874561022971039744

66. Media Lens, Twitter, 13 June 2017, https://twitter.com/medialens/status/874571324844331009

67. Dr Arshad Isakjee, Twitter, 9 June 2017, https://twitter.com/JasonCowleyNS/status/873053781235163136

68. Jason Cowley, Twitter, 8 June 2017, https://twitter.com/JasonCowleyNS/status/873053781235163136

69. Jason Cowley, 'The Labour reckoning – Corbyn has fought a spirited campaign but is he leading the party to its worst defeat since 1935?', *New Statesman*, 6 June 2017, www.newstatesman.com/politics/uk/2017/06/labour-reckoning

70. Jason Cowley, 'The stench of decay and failure coming from the Labour Party is now overwhelming – Speak to any Conservative MP and they will say that there is no opposition. Period', *New Statesman*,

30 March 2017, www.newstatesman.com/politics/uk/2017/03/stench-decay-and-failure-coming-labour-party-now-overwhelming

71. Owen Jones, Twitter, 8 June 2017, https://twitter.com/OwenJones84/status/872987106750193669

72. Owen Jones, 'Questions all Jeremy Corbyn supporters need to answer', *Medium*, 31 July 2016, https://goo.gl/BEfBtp

73. Owen Jones, *Contexto y Accion*, November 2016. Cited, Guido Fawkes, 'Owen's Paul Mason moment – Corbyn will never win', blog, 17 November 2016, https://order-order.com/2016/11/17/owen-jones-corbyn-will-never-win-election/

74. Owen Jones, 'Owen Jones: "I don't enjoy protesting – I do it because the stakes are so high"', *Evening Standard*, 3 February 2017, https://goo.gl/H4Zm2Q

75. Owen Jones, 'Last words on the Labour leadership', *Medium*, 20 March 2017, https://medium.com/@OwenJones84/last-words-on-the-labour-leadership-bd38667a0a7c

76. Owen Jones, 'Labour is in deep trouble, but it's our only defence against a Tory landslide', *Guardian*, 18 April 2017, www.theguardian.com/commentisfree/2017/apr/18/labour-jeremy-corbyn-time-to-fight-theresa-may

77. Owen Jones, 'Jeremy Corbyn has caused a sensation – he would make a fine prime minister', *Guardian*, 9 June 2017, www.theguardian.com/commentisfree/2017/jun/09/jeremy-corbyn-prime-minister-labour

78. George Monbiot, Twitter, 9 June 2017, https://twitter.com/GeorgeMonbiot/status/873073914989101056

79. Monbiot, Twitter, 9 June 2017, https://twitter.com/GeorgeMonbiot/status/873089986555297792

80. Monbiot, Twitter, 9 June 2017, https://twitter.com/GeorgeMonbiot/status/873425942890393601

81. Monbiot, 'The election's biggest losers? Not the Tories but the media, who missed the story', *Guardian*, 13 June 2017, www.theguardian.com/commentisfree/2017/jun/13/election-tories-media-broadcasters-press-jeremy-corbyn

82. Monbiot, Twitter, 8 December 2014, https://twitter.com/GeorgeMonbiot/status/541909889694851072

83. Monbiot, Twitter, 26 January 2017, https://twitter.com/GeorgeMonbiot/status/824616302010658816

84. Monbiot, Twitter, 26 January 2017, https://twitter.com/GeorgeMonbiot/status/824616646090362881

85. Media Lens, Twitter, 14 June 2017, https://twitter.com/medialens/status/874920967541334016

86. Jonathan Cook, 'Monbiot still can't admit media's core problem', blog, 14 June 2017, www.jonathan-cook.net/blog/2017-06-14/monbiot-still-cant-admit-medias-core-problem/

87. Will Hutton, 'How the right-wing tabloids got it wrong – It was the *Sun* wot hung it', *Guardian*, 10 June 2017, www.theguardian.com/politics/2017/jun/10/sun-election-newspaper-tabloid-corbyn

88. Media Lens, Twitter, 12 June 2017, https://twitter.com/medialens/status/874169583753719808

89. John Simpson, Twitter, 9 June 2017, https://twitter.com/JohnSimpsonNews/status/873204898548109312

90. Media Lens, Twitter, 10 June 2017, https://twitter.com/medialens/status/873486579154780160

91. Michael Lyons, quoted, Rowena Mason, 'BBC may have shown bias against Corbyn, says former trust chair', *Guardian*, 12 May 2016, www.theguardian.com/media/2016/may/12/bbc-bias-labour-sir-michael-lyons

3. Smearing Assange, Brand and Chávez

1. Ray McGovern, 'Assange's asylum', Institute for Public Accuracy, 20 June 2012, www.accuracy.org/release/assanges-asylum

2. Glenn Greenwald, 'Julian Assange's right to asylum', *Guardian*, 20 June 2012, www.theguardian.com/commentisfree/2012/jun/20/julian-assange-right-asylum

3. Dan Ellsberg, interview, 'Assange's asylum', Institute for Public Accuracy, 20 June 2012, www.accuracy.org/release/assanges-asylum

4. Suzanne Moore, Twitter, 19 June 2012, https://twitter.com/suzanne_moore/status/215199979092979712

5. Suzanne Moore, Twitter, 19 June 2012, https://twitter.com/suzanne_moore/status/215209474716209152

6. Media Lens, Twitter, 20 June 2012, https://twitter.com/medialens/status/215393245759410176

7. Moore, Twitter, 20 June 2012, https://twitter.com/suzanne_moore/status/215394860071518208

8. Moore, Twitter, 20 June 2012, https://twitter.com/suzanne_moore/status/215405880877920256

9. Luke Harding, Twitter, 19 June 2012, https://twitter.com/luke harding1968/status/215193536348426240

10. Christina Patterson, Twitter, 20 June 2012, https://twitter.com/queen christina_/status/215380585944842240

11. Charles Arthur, Twitter, 21 June 2012, https://twitter.com/charles arthur/status/215855138039021568

12. David Aaronovitch, Twitter, 21 June 2012, https://twitter.com/DAaronovitch/status/215711554958671873

13. Charlie Beckett, Twitter, 19 June 2012, https://twitter.com/Charlie Beckett/status/215207349051342848

14. Stuart Millar, Twitter, 19 June 2012, https://twitter.com/stuart millar159/status/215158223374782465

15. Joan Smith, 'Why do we buy Julian Assange's one-man psychodrama? The Ecuador government will be a laughing stock if it takes the Assange death penalty sub-plot seriously', *Independent*, 21 June 2012, www.independent.co.uk/voices/commentators/joan-smith/joan-smith-why-do-we-buy-julian-assanges-one-man-psychodrama-7869897.html

16. Tim Dowling, 'Julian Assange: five escape routes from the Ecuadorean embassy', *Guardian*, 21 June 2012, www.theguardian.com/media/2012/jun/21/julian-assange-escape-routes-ecuador-embassy

17. Caroline Hawley, Twitter, 21 June 2012, https://twitter.com/carolinehawley/status/215799199139237889

18. David Aaronovitch, Twitter, 20 June 2012, https://twitter.com/DAaronovitch/status/215499266020487168

19. John Lloyd, 'Julian Assange's fall from the heavens', Reuters, 25 June 2012, http://blogs.reuters.com/john-lloyd/2012/06/25/julian-assanges-fall-from-the-heavens/

20. Deborah Orr, Twitter, 19 June 2012, https://twitter.com/DeborahJaneOrr/status/215193227039473666

21. Deborah Orr, 'Ecuador or Sweden for Assange? Mmm, Sweden, I think', *Guardian*, 23 June 2012 www.theguardian.com/media/2012/jun/23/assange-ecuador-sweden-deborah-orr?newsfeed=true

22. Media Lens, Twitter, 25 June 2012, https://twitter.com/medialens/status/217260373135474690

23. Orr, Twitter, 25 June 2012, https://twitter.com/DeborahJaneOrr/status/217281367266959361

24. Corrections and clarifications, *Guardian*, 26 June 2012, www.theguardian.com/ 2012/jun/26/corrections-and-clarifications

25. Ian Dunt, Twitter, 25 June 2012, https://twitter.com/IanDunt/status/215372504343126016

26. John Pilger, 'Getting Julian Assange: The untold story', blog, 20 May 2017, http://johnpilger.com/articles/getting-julian-assange-the-untold-story

27. Editorial, 'The *Guardian* view on George W Bush: a welcome return', *Guardian*, 27 February 2017, www.theguardian.com/comment isfree/2017/feb/27/the-guardian-view-on-george-w-bush-a-welcome-return

28. Amelia Tait, 'How George W. Bush went from "war criminal" to the internet's favourite grandpa', *New Statesman*, 13 March 2017, www.newstatesman.com/science-tech/2017/03/how-george-w-bush-went-war-criminal-internet-s-favourite-grandpa

29. Matthew d'Ancona, 'Blair has a far bigger vision than saving us from Brexit', *Guardian*, 20 February 2017, www.guardian.com/comment isfree/2017/feb/20/tony-blair-brexit

30. Sonia Sodha, 'Listening to Obama makes me want to be American for a day', *Guardian*, 24 April 2016, www.theguardian.com/commentis free/2016/apr/24/barack-obama-uk-visit-transformed-brexit-referendum-debate

31. Daniel Boffey and Emma Supple, 'Barack Obama: "He has such power … yet such humility"', *Guardian*, 24 April 2016, www.theguardian.com/us-news/2016/apr/24/barack-obama-such-power-such-humility

32. Russell Brand interview, *Newsnight*, YouTube, 23 October 2013, www.youtube.com/watch?v=3YR4CseY9pk

33. Russell Brand, *Revolution*, Century, 2014, ebook, p. 34.

34. Ibid., p. 36.

35. Ibid., p. 36.

36. Ibid., p. 66.

37. Suzanne Moore, 'Russell Brand's revolution or a meaningless two-party system? Politics should be about more than this', *Guardian*, 15 October 2014, https://goo.gl/LNyG2J

38. Oliver Kamm, 'Media Lens tries history, yet again', blog, 21 January 2008, http://oliverkamm.typepad.com/blog/2008/01/media-lens-trie.html

39. Sarah Ditum, 'Stuff your revolution if it doesn't include treating women as people', *New Statesman*, 3 November 2014, www.newstatesman.com/politics/2014/11/stuff-your-revolution-if-it-doesn-t-include-treating-women-people

40. Hadley Freeman, 'Britain, don't put your faith in Russell Brand's revolution', *Guardian*, 24 October 2014, www.theguardian.com/commentisfree/2014/oct/24/britain-russell-brand-revolution-newsnight

41. Yasmin Alibhai-Brown, 'Russell Brand might seem like a sexy revolutionary worth getting behind, but he will only fail his fans', *Independent*, 19 October 2014, www.independent.co.uk/voices/comment/russell-brand-might-seem-like-a-sexy-revolutionary-worth-getting-behind-but-he-will-only-fail-his-9804853.html

42. Howard Jacobson, 'Russell Brand and Miriam Margolyes: Don't fall for the false charms of those two pantomime preachers', *Independent*, 31 October 2014, www.independent.co.uk/voices/comment/russell-brand-and-miriam-margolyes-don-t-fall-for-the-false-charms-of-those-two-pantomime-preachers-9831763.html

43. Boris Johnson, 'The rise of Brandy Wandy signals the end for Silly Mili: Russell Brand has become a prophet of the Left only because of Labour's abject failure', *Telegraph*, 26 October 2014, www.telegraph.co.uk/news/politics/ed-miliband/11189039/The-rise-of-Brandy-Wandy-signals-the-end-for-Silly-Mili.html

44. David Aaronovitch, 'A unique Brand of dozy drivel', *The Times*, 1 November 2014, www.thetimes.co.uk/article/revolution-by-russell-brand-2hvv6t8jr7b

45. Tanya Gold, 'Celebrities trivialise politics – so why must politicians court them?', *Guardian*, 3 July 2014, www.theguardian.com/commentisfree/2014/jul/03/celebrities-trivialise-politics-politicians-david-cameron-cool-britannia

46. Martin Kettle, 'In Scotland the old politics have crumbled, as they once did in Ireland', *Guardian*, 22 October 2014, www.theguardian.com/commentisfree/2014/oct/22/scotland-old-politics-crumbled-young-voters-independence-ireland

47. Nick Cohen, 'Revolution by Russell Brand review – the barmy credo of a Beverly Hills Buddhist', *Observer*, 27 October 2014, www.theguardian.com/books/2014/oct/27/revolution-review-russell-brand-beverly-hills-buddhist

48. Media Lens, Twitter, 27 October 2014, https://twitter.com/medialens/status/526727356745261056

49. Peter Hitchens, 'Why do refugees drown? Because liberals like Dave keep starting wars', *Mail on Sunday*, 2 November 2014, https://goo.gl/omkv5i

50. Stephen Glover, 'Why does anyone take this clown of a poseur seriously ... Russell Brand is a ludicrous charlatan', *Daily Mail*, 25 October 2014, https://goo.gl/MsjZAu

51. Max Hastings, 'The megalomaniac and the narcissist: Two men whose influence you couldn't escape in 2013', *Daily Mail*, 30 December 2013, www.dailymail.co.uk/news/article-2530941/Megalomaniac-narcissist-Two-men-influence-escape-2013.html#ixzz575CJAn30

52. Katie Glass, 'The ultimate Marmite Brand', *Sunday Times*, 22 September 2013.

53. Joan Smith, 'Spare us the vacuous talk and go back to Hollywood', *Independent*, 26 October 2013, www.independent.co.uk/voices/comment/joan-smith-spare-us-the-vacuous-talk-and-go-back-to-hollywood-8906305.html

54. Mark Steel, 'If you think Russell Brand's new book is confused, you should read what his critics have to say about it', *Independent*, 30 October 2014, www.independent.co.uk/voices/comment/if-you-think-russell-brand-s-new-book-is-confused-you-should-read-what-his-critics-have-to-say-about-9829224.html

55. Romesh Ratnesar, 'The unbearable narcissism of Edward Snowden', *Bloomberg BusinessWeek*, 1 November 2013, www.bloomberg.com/news/articles/2013-11-01/the-unbearable-narcissism-of-edward-snowden

56. Jeffrey Toobin, 'Edward Snowden is no hero', *New Yorker*, 10 June 2013, www.newyorker.com/news/daily-comment/edward-snowden-is-no-hero

57. Harold Evans, 'The media has a duty to scrutinise the use of power', *Guardian*, 20 October 2013, www.theguardian.com/commentis free/2013/oct/20/media-duty-scrutinise-use-of-power

58. Chris Evans, cited, 'Corbyn a narcissist, says Labour Islwyn MP Chris Evans', BBC website, 28 June 2016, www.bbc.com/news/uk-wales-politics-36656057

59. Jonathan Freedland, 'The Corbyn tribe cares about identity, not power', *Guardian*, 24 July 2015, www.theguardian.com/commentisfree/2015/jul/24/corbyn-tribe-identity-politics-labour

60. Dominic Sandbrook, 'Putin's useful idiots: Warped, deluded, ignorant. Corbyn's support for Russia shames his party and his country', *Daily Mail*, 13 October 2016, https://goo.gl/MRwL84

61. Janice Turner, 'Seductive Jezza leaves us with a painful choice', *The Times*, 3 June 2017, www.thetimes.co.uk/article/seductive-jezza-leaves-us-with-a-painful-choice-vdsgk9wrc

62. Michael White, 'Media Lens shows it doesn't get the whole picture', *Guardian*, 27 January 2012, www.theguardian.com/global/2012/jan/27/media-lens-picture-michael-white

63. See our media alert, 'I, Fascist Robot', Media Lens website, 26 September 2007, www.medialens.org/index.php/alerts/alert-archive/2007/520-i-fascist-robot-the-bbcs-gavin-esler-lets-rip.html

64. Nick Bryant, 'US election: America the beautiful's ugly election', BBC website, 8 November 2016, www.bbc.com/news/election-us-2016-37903384

65. Craig Murray, 'Chávez', blog, 6 March 2013, www.craigmurray.org.uk/archives/2013/03/chavez/

66. Mark Weisbrot, 'Chávez's legacy', aljazeera.com, 6 March 2013, www.aljazeera.com/indepth/opinion/2013/03/20133663030968692.html

67. Martin Kettle, 'Chávez will continue to inspire – but not in Europe', *Guardian*, 6 March 2013, www.theguardian.com/commentisfree/2013/mar/06/chavez-continue-inspire-but-not-europe

68. Trevor Mostyn, 'Crown Prince Sultan bin Abdul-Aziz obituary', *Guardian*, 23 October 2011, www.theguardian.com/world/2011/oct/23/crown-prince-sultan-bin-abdul-aziz

69. John Sweeney, original URL no longer functional: https://literaryreview.co.uk/sweeney_03_13.php Cited, ' "Berated" and "garlanded as stupid" by Hugo Chávez: John Sweeney's appearance on Aló Presidente', Cunning Hired Knaves blog, 8 April 2013, https://hiredknaves.wordpress.com/2013/04/08/berated-and-garlanded-as-stupid-by-hugo-chave/

70. Simon Tisdall, 'Death of Hugo Chávez brings chance of fresh start for US and Latin America', *Guardian*, 5 March 2013, www.guardian.co.uk/world/2013/mar/05/hugo-chavez-dead-us-latin-america

71. David Usborne, 'Death of Venezuelan President Hugo Chávez leaves tears – and a nation divided', *Independent*, 6 March 2013, http://tinyurl.com/cd2edkt

72. 'Venezuela's President Hugo Chávez dies', BBC website, 5 March 2013, www.bbc.com/news/av/world-latin-america-20912436/venezuela-s-president-hugo-chavez-dies

73. 'Hugo Chávez: a look back at the Venezuelan President's life', *Telegraph*, 6 March 2013, www.telegraph.co.uk/news/worldnews/southamerica/

venezuela/9911920/Hugo-Chavez-dead-look-back-Venezuelan-Presidents-life.html

74. Virginia Lopez and Jonathan Watts, 'South American leaders fly to join Venezuelans mourning Chávez's death', *Guardian*, 6 March 2013, www.guardian.co.uk/world/2013/mar/06/south-american-leaders-venezuelans-chavez

75. David Usborne, 'Death of Venezuelan President Hugo Chávez leaves tears – and a nation divided', *Independent*, 6 March 2013, www.independent.co.uk/news/world/americas/death-of-venezuelan-president-hugo-chavez-leaves-tears–and-a-nation-divided-8521706.html

76. Leader, 'Hugo Chávez – an era of grand political illusion comes to an end', *Independent*, 6 March 2013, https://goo.gl/RktpPE

77. Salim Lamrani – Opera Mundi, '50 truths about Hugo Chávez and the Bolivarian revolution', 9 March 2013, https://venezuelanalysis.com/analysis/8133

78. The Economist Online, 'Venezuela after Chávez – Now for the reckoning', *The Economist*, 5 March 2013, http://tinyurl.com/d3ev9dk

4. Israel and Palestine:
'We Wait in Fear for the Phone Call from the Israelis'

1. Jeremy Bowen, email forwarded to Media Lens, 2 January 2009.

2. Ilan Pappé, *The Ethnic Cleansing of Palestine*, Oneworld Publications, Oxford, 2006, p. x.

3. Edward S. Herman and Grace Kwinjeh, 'Ethnic cleansing: constructive, benign, and nefarious (Kafka Era Studies, No. 1)', ZNet, 9 August 2006; www.informationclearinghouse.info/article14461.htm

4. Avi Shlaim, *The Iron Wall: Israel and the Arab World*, W. W. Norton & Company, New York, 2000, p. 31.

5. Ibid., p. 582.

6. Greg Philo and Mike Berry, *Bad News From Israel*, Pluto Books, London, 2004, p. 216.

7. Greg Philo and Mike Berry, *More Bad News From Israel*, Pluto Books, London, 2011, p. x.

8. Ibid., pp. 340–1.

9. Ibid., p. 341.

10. Ibid., p. 392.

11. Ibid., p. 390.

12. Tim Llewellyn, 'BBC is "confusing cause and effect" in its Israeli coverage', *Guardian*, 23 May 2011; www.theguardian.com/media/2011/may/23/bbc-israeli-conflict-coverage

13. Greg Philo,'More Bad News from Israel', SOAS, 19.5.11, YouTube, 21 May 2011; www.youtube.com/watch?v=wx7NaQsvUnE&t=3m12s

14. Peter Oborne, 'Dispatches: Inside Britain's Israel lobby 2009', Channel 4, published on YouTube, 1 September 2013; www.youtube.com/watch?v=lby-BP5xVRI

15. Peter Oborne and James Jones, 'The pro-Israel lobby in Britain: full text', openDemocracy, 13 November 2009; www.opendemocracy.net/ourkingdom/peter-oborne-james-jones/pro-israel-lobby-in-britain-full-text

16. Lisa O'Carroll, 'James Harding: ex-Times editor could become the story at the BBC', *Guardian*, 16 April 2013; www.theguardian.com/media/2013/apr/16/james-harding-times-bbc

17. 'Chomsky on the US, Israel, and Gaza', 8 January 2009; www.thecommentfactory.com /noam-chomsky-on-the-us-israel-and-gaza-1298

18. Noam Chomsky, *Fateful Triangle*, Pluto Press, London, 1999, p. 489.

19. Adam Rosgan, 'Hamas leader to JPost: We're ready for long-term cease-fire with Israel', *Jerusalem Post*, 6 September 2017; www.jpost.com/Arab-Israeli-Conflict/Hamas-leader-to-JPost-Were-ready-for-long-term-cease-fire-with-Israel-504435

20. Cited, Noam Chomsky, *Fateful Triangle*, Pluto Press, London, 1999, p. 75.

21. Noam Chomsky, 'Exterminate all the brutes: Gaza 2009', 19 January 2009; https://chomsky.info/20090119/

22. Ethan Bronner, 'Parsing gains of Gaza war,' *New York Times*, 18 January 2009.

23. Quoted, Noam Chomsky, *Hegemony or Survival*, Hamish Hamilton, 2003, p. 218.

24. Noam Chomsky, 'Exterminate all the brutes: Gaza 2009', 19 January 2009, https://chomsky.info/20090119/

25. Ibid.

26. Rory McCarthy, 'Gaza truce broken as Israeli raid kills six Hamas gunmen', *Guardian*, 5 November 2008, www.guardian.co.uk/world/2008/nov/05/israelandthepalestinians

27. Noam Chomsky, 'Exterminate all the brutes: Gaza 2009', 19 January 2009, https://chomsky.info/20090119/

28. Jonathan Cook, *Disappearing Palestine*, Zed Books, 2008, p. 70.

29. Ibid., pp. 149–50.

30. Edward S. Herman and Grace Kwinjeh, 'Ethnic cleansing: Constructive, benign, and nefarious (Kafka Era Studies, No. 1)', ZNet, 9 August 2006; www.informationclearinghouse.info/article14461.htm

31. Ibid.

32. Cook, *Disappearing Palestine,* p. 141.

33. Quoted, Bill Neely, then ITV News international editor, Twitter, 18 November 2012; https://twitter.com/BillNeelyNBC/status/270103700 104691712

34. Gilad Sharon, 'A decisive conclusion is necessary', *Jerusalem Post*, 18 November 2012; www.jpost.com/Opinion/Op-Ed-Contributors/ A-decisive-conclusion-is-necessary

35. 'Israel-Gaza crisis: Tel Aviv bomb blast on bus', BBC website, 21 November 2012; www.bbc.co.uk/news/world-middle-east-20425352

36. Bill Neely, Twitter, 21 November 2012; https://twitter.com/ BillNeelyNBC/status/271202650542985216

37. Bill Neely, Twitter, 21 November 2012; https://twitter.com/ BillNeelyNBC/status/271201123262685184

38. Media Lens, Twitter, 21 November 2012; https://twitter.com/ medialens/status/271203489076629505

39. Bill Neely, Twitter, 21 November 2012; https://twitter.com/ BillNeelyNBC/status/271318324682579968

40. Bill Neely, Twitter, 21 November 2012; https://twitter.com/ BillNeelyNBC/status/271372989390524416

41. Media Lens, Twitter, 21 November 2012; https://twitter.com/ medialens/status/271525148606214144

42. Bill Neely, Twitter, 21 November 2012; https://twitter.com/ BillNeelyNBC/status/271533073823318016

43. Media Lens, Twitter, 21 November 2012; https://twitter.com/ medialens/status/271534030976073728

44. Media Lens, Twitter, 21 November 2012; https://twitter.com/ medialens/status/271535186129342464

45. 'Blitz, Bombing and Total War', Channel 4, 15 January 2005.

46. Bill Neely, Twitter, 21 November 2012; https://twitter.com/ BillNeelyNBC/status/271539344802725888

47. Media Lens, Twitter, 21 November 2012; https://twitter.com/ medialens/status/271540192517689346

48. Ruth Eglash and William Branigin, 'Israeli army says three kidnapped teenagers found dead', *Washington Post*, 30 June 2014; http://wapo.st/2Er6CET

49. Quoted, Palestine Solidarity Campaign, Twitter, 14 July 2014 ; https://twitter.com/PSCupdates/status/488755538046754816

50. 'As it happened: Gaza conflict intensifies', BBC website, 20 July 2014; www.bbc.co.uk/news/world-middle-east-28391201

51. *Washington Post* graphic, July 22, 2014; http://wapo.st/2ErAH77

52. Media Lens, Twitter, 22 July 2014; https://twitter.com/medialens/status/491501083291025408

53. 'Gaza conflict: Abbas backs Hamas ceasefire demands', BBC website, 23 July 2014; www.bbc.co.uk/news/world-middle-east-28431945

54. BBC News (World), Twitter, 23 July 2014; https://twitter.com/BBCWorld/status/49180450683407974

55. Gaza conflict: Israel restarts air strikes amid rocket fire', BBC website, 15 July 2014; www.bbc.co.uk/news/world-middle-east-28314604

56. Jonathon Shafi, 'BBC Gaza', Bella Caledonia, 21 July 2014; http://bellacaledonia.org.uk/2014/07/21/bbc-gaza/

57. Anne Barnard, 'Boys drawn to Gaza Beach, and into center of Mideast strife', *New York Times*, 16 July 2014; www.nytimes.com/2014/07/17/world/middleeast/gaza-strip-beach-explosion-kills-children.html?_r=0

58. Meghan Kenneally, 'Inside a Gaza hospital under Israeli rocket fire', ABC News, 16 June 2014; http://abcnews.go.com/International/inside-gaza-hospital-israeli-rocket-fire/story?id=24592141

59. Jonathan Whittall, 'Opinion and debate: The limits of humanitarianism in Gaza', Médecins Sans Frontières/Doctors Without Borders (MSF) website, 14 July 2014; www.msf.org.uk/article/opinion-and-debate-limits-humanitarianism-gaza

60. 'Massacres that matter – Part 1 "Responsibility to protect" in Egypt, Libya And Syria', Media Lens media alert, 27 August 2013; www.medialens.org/index.php/alerts/alert-archive/alerts-2013/739-massacres-that-matter-responsibility-to-protect-in-egypt-libya-and-syria-part-1.html

61. Media Lens, Twitter, 10 July 2014; https://twitter.com/medialens/status/487156143375253504

62. Media Lens, Twitter, 11 July 2014; https://twitter.com/medialens/status/487512421528244224

63. Media Lens, Twitter, 11 July 2014; https://twitter.com/medialens/status/487538164618493952

64. John Plunkett, 'BBC defends coverage of Israeli air strikes in Gaza after bias accusations', *Guardian* website, 16 July 2014; www.theguardian.com/media/2014/jul/16/bbc-defends-coverage-israeli-airstrikes-gaza-palestinian

65. UNICEFpalestine, Twitter, 22 July 2014; https://twitter.com/UNICEFpalestine/status/491587547034710017

66. Nafeez Ahmed, 'IDF's Gaza assault is to control Palestinian gas, avert Israeli energy crisis', *Guardian* website, 9 July 2014; www.theguardian.com/environment/earth-insight/2014/jul/09/israel-war-gaza-palestine-natural-gas-energy-crisis

67. Nafeez Ahmed, 'Ukraine crisis is about Great Power oil, gas pipeline rivalry', *Guardian* website, March 6, 2014; www.theguardian.com/environment/earth-insight/2014/mar/06/ukraine-crisis-great-power-oil-gas-rivals-pipelines

68. Nafeez Ahmed, 'Why food riots are likely to become the new normal', *Guardian* website, March 6, 2013; www.theguardian.com/environment/blog/2013/mar/06/food-riots-new-normal

69. 'The 1000: London's most influential people 2014 – campaigners', *Evening Standard*, 16 October 2014; www.standard.co.uk/news/the1000/the-1000-londons-most-influential-people-2014-campaigners-9789797.html

70. Jonathan Cook, 'Why the *Guardian* axed Nafeez Ahmed's blog', Jonathan Cook's blog, 4 December 2014; www.jonathan-cook.net/blog/2014-12-04/why-the-guardian-axed-nafeez-ahmeds-blog/

71. Nafeez Ahmed, 'Palestine is not an environment story', *Medium*, 3 December 2014; https://medium.com/insurge-intelligence/palestine-is-not-an-environment-story-921d9167ddef

72. Nafeez Ahmed, 'Iraq blowback: Isis rise manufactured by insatiable oil addiction', *Guardian* website, 16 June 2014; www.theguardian.com/environment/earth-insight/2014/jun/16/blowback-isis-iraq-manufactured-oil-addiction

73. Jonathan Cook, 'Why the *Guardian* axed Nafeez Ahmed's blog', Jonathan Cook's blog, 4 4 December 2014; www.jonathan-cook.net/blog/2014-12-04/why-the-guardian-axed-nafeez-ahmeds-blog/

5. Libya: 'It is All About Oil'

1. Scott Ritter and William Rivers Pitt, *War On Iraq*, Profile Books, 2002, pp. 23 and 29.

2. Leader, 'Power, not oil, Mr Greenspan', *Sunday Times*, 16 September 2007.

3. 'More than 1,000 new wells at West Qurna 1', iraq-business news, 27 September 2010, www.iraq-businessnews.com/2010/09/27/more-than-1000-new-wells-at-west-qurna-1/

4. BP Global press release, 'Rumaila oilfield achieves 3 billion barrel production landmark', 20 December 2016, www.bp.com/en/global/corporate/media/press-releases/rumaila-oilfield-achieves-3-billion-barrel-production-landmark.html

5. 'Boris Johnson Libya "dead bodies" comment provokes anger', BBC website, www.bbc.com/news/uk-politics-41490174

6. Howard Zinn, 'The end of empire?', Tomgram, 1 April 2008, www.tomdispatch.com/post/174913/howard_zinn_the_end_of_empire_

7. John Norris, *Collision Course: NATO, Russia, and Kosovo*, Praeger, 2005, p. xiii.

8. Amnesty Press Release, 'Security Council and African Union failing Libyan people', 23 February 2011, www.amnesty.org/en/press-releases/2011/02/security-council-and-african-union-failing-libyan-people/

9. HRW, 'No mercenaries in eastern Libya', archive, February 2011, www.rnw.org/archive/hrw-no-mercenaries-eastern-libya

10. Maximilian Forte, *Slouching Towards Sirte – NATO's War on Libya and Africa*, Baraka Books, digital version, 2012, p. 637.

11. Forte, ibid., p. 641.

12. Moreno-Ocampo, cited, Maximilian Forte, 'The Top Ten Myths in the War Against Libya', CounterPunch, 31 August 2011, www.counterpunch.org/2011/08/31/the-top-ten-myths-in-the-war-against-libya/

13. Jim Miklaszewski, 'US intel: No evidence of Viagra as weapon in Libya', blog, 29 April 2011, https://redantliberationarmy.wordpress.com/2011/04/30/us-intel-no-evidence-of-viagra-as-weapon-in-libya/

14. Cherif Bassiouni, AFP, 'Libya rape claims "hysteria" – investigator', *Herald Sun*, 10 June 2011, www.heraldsun.com.au/news/breaking-news/libya-rape-claims-hysteria-investigator/story-e6frf7jx-1226072781882

15. Forte, *Slouching Towards Sirte*, p. 661.

16. Michael Moore, Twitter, 20 March 2011, 5:31 PM, http://twitter.com/MMFlint

17. Jonathan Freedland, 'Though the risks are very real, the case for intervention remains strong', *Guardian*, 22 March 2011, www.

theguardian.com/commentisfree/2011/mar/22/case-for-intervention-still-strong

18. Brian Whitaker, 'The difference with Libya', *Guardian*, 23 March 2011, www.theguardian.com/commentisfree/2011/mar/23/libya-bahrain-yemen-un-responsibility-protect

19. Menzies Campbell and Phillipe Sands, 'Our duty to protect the Libyan people', *Guardian*, 9 March 2011, www.theguardian.com/commentisfree/2011/mar/09/our-duty-protect-libyan-people

20. Leader, 'Libya: The west can't let Gaddafi destroy his people', *Observer*, 13 March 2011, www.theguardian.com/commentisfree/2011/mar/13/observer-editorial-libya

21. Boris Johnson, 'Libya: Taking on Colonel Gaddafi is a noble cause, but the risks are huge', *Telegraph*, 21 March 2011, www.telegraph.co.uk/comment/columnists/borisjohnson/8394605/Libya-Taking-on-Colonel-Gaddafi-is-a-noble-cause-but-the-risks-are-huge.html

22. David Aaronovitch, 'Those weapons had better be there ...', *Guardian*, 29 April 2003, www.theguardian.com/Columnists/Column/0,5673,945551,00.html

23. David Aaronovitch, 'Go for a no-fly zone or regret it', *The Times*, 24 February 2011, www.thetimes.co.uk/tto/opinion/columnists/davidaaronovitch/article2924184.ece

24. Editorial, 'At war in Libya', *New York Times*, 21 March 2011, www.nytimes.com/2011/03/22/opinion/22tue1.html

25. NATO Fact Sheet, 'Operation UNIFIED PROTECTOR Final Mission Stats', 2 November 2011, www.nato.int/nato_static/assets/pdf/pdf_2011_11/20111108_111107-factsheet_up_factsfigures_en.pdf

26. Editorial, 'Foreign policy: intervention after Libya', *Guardian*, 23 August 2011, www.theguardian.com/commentisfree/2011/aug/23/libya-foreign-policy-intervention

27. Simon Tisdall, 'Muammar Gaddafi's violent death leaves Libya at a crossroads', *Guardian*, 20 October 2011, www.theguardian.com/commentisfree/2011/oct/20/gaddafi-death-leaves-libya-crossroads

28. Editorial, 'An honourable intervention. A hopeful future', *Observer*, 28 August 2011, www.theguardian.com/commentisfree/2011/aug/28/observer-editorial-libya-needs-help-not-interference

29. Andrew Rawnsley, 'The right and the wrong lessons to draw from Libya's liberation', *Observer*, 28 August 2011, www.theguardian.com/commentisfree/2011/aug/28/andrew-rawnsley-libya-lessons

30. Andrew Rawnsley, 'The voices of doom were so wrong', *Observer*, 13 April 2003, www.theguardian.com/politics/2003/apr/13/iraq.iraq

31. Nick Robinson, BBC 'News at Six', 20 October 2011.

32. Norman Smith, BBC News online, 21 October 2011.

33. Ian Pannell, BBC News online, 21 October 2011.

34. Andrew Marr, BBC 'News at Ten', 9 April 2003. See Media Lens, YouTube, 27 September 2010, www.youtube.com/watch?v=5_JC371jxPI

35. John Humphrys, BBC Radio 4 'Today', 21 October 2011, http://news.bbc.co.uk/today/hi/today/newsid_9621000/9621014.stm

36. David Edwards, 'Unthinkable thoughts: An interview with Harold Pinter', Media Lens website, 13 January 2000, www.medialens.org/index.php/alerts/interviews/76-unthinkable-thoughts-an-interview-with-harold-pinter.html

37. Andrew Grice, 'Vindication for Cameron over the "armchair generals"', *Independent*, 20 October 2011, www.independent.co.uk/news/uk/politics/vindication-for-cameron-over-the-armchair-generals-2373793.html

38. Editorial, 'This grim end should serve as a warning', *Telegraph*, 20 October 2011, www.telegraph.co.uk/comment/telegraph-view/8838685/This-grim-end-should-serve-as-a-warning.html

39. Matthew d'Ancona, 'Libya is Cameron's chance to exorcise the ghost of Iraq', *Telegraph*, 26 March 2011, www.telegraph.co.uk/news/worldnews/africaandindianocean/libya/8408687/Libya-is-Camerons-chance-to-exorcise-the-ghost-of-Iraq.html

40. Leader, 'Libya – the mission that crept', *Independent*, 28 July 2011, www.independent.co.uk/voices/editorials/leading-article-libya-the-mission-that-crept-2327706.html

41. Leading article, 'Death of a dictator,' *The Times*, 21 October 2011, www.thetimes.co.uk/article/death-of-a-dictator-9jljnrozbwx

42. Simon Tisdall, Owen Bowcott, Richard Norton-Taylor and Nick Hopkins, 'Q&A: the Libyan ceasefire, the UN resolution and military tactics', *Guardian*, 18 March 2011, www.theguardian.com/world/2011/mar/18/libya-ceasefire-un-resolution-military-tactics?cat=world&type=article

43. Leading article, 'The challenge ahead,' *The Times*, 25 August 2011, www.thetimes.co.uk/article/the-challenge-ahead-tw52th9qqqc

44. Carlotta Gall, 'Libyan refugees stream to Tunisia for care, and tell of a home that is torn apart', *New York Times*, 9 September 2014, www.

nytimes.com/2014/09/10/world/africa/libya-refugees-tunisia-tripoli.
html

45. Nick Squires, 'Migrants tell of deepening chaos in Libya: "Everyone is armed now"', *Telegraph*, 22 February 2015, www.telegraph.co.uk/news/worldnews/africaandindianocean/libya/11427306/Migrants-tell-of-deepening-chaos-in-Libya-Everyone-is-armed-now.html

46. Ibid.

47. 'Libya: Examination of intervention and collapse and the UK's future policy options', 9 September 2016, https://publications.parliament.uk/pa/cm201617/cmselect/cmfaff/119/11902.htm

48. Juan Cole, 'Answer to Glenn Greenwald', informed COMMENT blog, 30 March 2011, www.juancole.com/2011/03/answer-to-glenn-greenwald.html

49. Robert Fisk, 'This slaughter will end only when words of condemnation are acted on', *Independent*, 8 August 2011, www.independent.co.uk/news/world/middle-east/robert-fisk-this-slaughter-will-end-only-when-words-of-condemnation-are-acted-on-2334157.html

50. Mehdi Hasan, 'Oh, what a liberal war!', *New Statesman*, 31 March 2011, www.newstatesman.com/international-politics/2011/03/military-gaddafi-civilians

51. Paul Mason, 'The Libya fallout shows how Theresa May has failed on terror', *Guardian*, 27 May 2011, www.theguardian.com/commentisfree/2017/may/27/libya-fallout-theresa-may-failed-terror

52. Noam Chomsky, *Making the Future: Occupations, Interventions, Empire and Resistance*, Hamish Hamilton, e-book, 2012, p. 372.

53. Owen Jones, 'The case against bombing Libya', *Left Futures*, March 2011, www.leftfutures.org/2011/03/the-case-against-bombing-libya/

54. John Pilger, 'Welcome to the violent world of Mr. Hopey Changey', blog, 26 May 2011, http://johnpilger.com/articles/welcome-to-the-violent-world-of-mr-hopey-changey

55. Seumas Milne, 'If the Libyan war was about saving lives, it was a catastrophic failure', *Guardian*, 26 October 2011, www.theguardian.com/commentisfree/2011/oct/26/libya-war-saving-lives-catastrophic-failure

56. Rupert Read, 'Exposed: The pro-Assad useful idiots in our midst', Left Foot Forward, 22 October 2011, http://leftfootforward.org/2011/10/pro-basher-al-assad-useful-idiots-exposed/

57. 'Libya: Examination of intervention and collapse and the UK's future policy options', 9 September 2016, https://publications.parliament.uk/pa/cm201617/cmselect/cmfaff/119/11902.htm

58. Ibid., 'The evidence base: our assessment', 9 September 2016, https://publications.parliament.uk/pa/cm201617/cmselect/cmfaff/119/11905.htm#_idTextAnchor023

59. Media Lens, ProQuest search, 15 February 2018.

60. 'Libya: Examination of intervention and collapse and the UK's future policy options,' 9 September 2016, https://publications.parliament.uk/pa/cm201617/cmselect/cmfaff/119/11902.htm

61. Alan J. Kuperman, 'False pretense for war in Libya?', *Boston Globe*, 14 April 2011, http://archive.boston.com/bostonglobe/editorial_opinion/oped/articles/2011/04/14/false_pretense_for_war_in_libya/

62. Baron Richards of Herstmonceux, 'UK military chief criticises Libya decision', BBC website, 14 September 2016, www.bbc.com/news/uk-politics-37359463

63. Steven Mufson, 'Conflict in Libya: U.S. oil companies sit on sidelines as Gaddafi maintains hold', *Washington Post*, 10 June 2011, https://goo.gl/140tZE

64. Johann Hari, 'We're not being told the truth on Libya', *Independent*, 7 April 2011, www.independent.co.uk/voices/commentators/johann-hari/johann-hari-were-not-being-told-the-truth-on-libya-2264785.html

65. Leaked cable, WikiLeaks, 'GROWTH OF RESOURCE NATIONAL-ISM IN LIBYA', 15 November 2007, https://wikileaks.org/plusd/cables/07TRIPOLI967_a.html

66. Glenn Greenwald, 'In a pure coincidence, Gaddafi impeded U.S. oil interests before the war', Salon, 6 November 2011, www.salon.com/2011/06/11/libya_9/

67. 'Libya: Examination of intervention and collapse and the UK's future policy options', 9 September 2016, https://publications.parliament.uk/pa/cm201617/cmselect/cmfaff/119/11902.htm

68. Paul Jay interview with Kevin G. Hall, 'WikiLeaks reveals US wanted to keep Russia out of Libyan oil', *The Real News*, 11 May 2011, http://therealnews.com/t2/index.php?option=com_content&task=view&id=31&Itemid=74&jumival=6759

69. Salma El Wardany, 'Libya restarts Wintershall oil fields to boost nation output', *Bloomberg Businessweek*, 22 January 2018, www.bloomberg.

com/news/articles/2018-01-22/libya-restarts-wintershall-s-oil-fields-to-boost-national-output

70. Polly Toynbee, 'Those out to demonise Hillary Clinton should be careful what they wish for', *Guardian*, 9 June 2016, www.theguardian.com/commentisfree/2016/jun/09/demonise-hillary-clinton-careful-us-president

71. Mark Landler, 'How Hillary Clinton became a hawk', *New York Times* magazine, 21 April 2016, www.nytimes.com/2016/04/24/magazine/how-hillary-clinton-became-a-hawk.html

72. David Sirota, 'Clinton foundation donors got weapons deals from Hillary Clinton's State Department', *International Business Times*, 26 May 2015, www.ibtimes.com/clinton-foundation-donors-got-weapons-deals-hillary-clintons-state-department-1934187

73. Jeffrey Sachs, 'Hillary is the candidate of the war machine', Huffington Post, 5 February 2017, www.huffingtonpost.com/jeffrey-sachs/hillary-is-the-candidate_b_9168938.html

74. Gareth Porter, 'US military leadership resisted Obama's bid for regime change in Syria, Libya', *Middle East Eye*, 4 January 2016, www.middleeasteye.net/columns/us-military-leadership-s-resistance-regime-change-1343405723#sthash.ofuBqSvC.dpuf

75. James Rubin, 'Why Hillary Clinton would make a better president than Obama', *Sunday Times*, 12 April 2015, www.thetimes.co.uk/article/why-hillary-clinton-would-make-a-better-president-than-obama-7hlk5992pgp

76. Mary Riddell, 'Hillary Clinton is not alone these days. Are women finally taking over the world?', *Telegraph*, 12 April 2015, https://goo.gl/pCxYWq

77. Jeffrey Sachs, Huffington Post, 5 February 2017.

78. Frank Morgan, 'Donald Trump is moving to the White House, and liberals put him there', *Guardian*, 9 November 2016, www.theguardian.com/commentisfree/2016/nov/09/donald-trump-white-house-hillary-clinton-liberals

79. CBS News interview, 'Hillary Clinton on Gaddafi: We came, we saw, he died', YouTube, 20 October 2011, www.youtube.com/watch?v=Fgcd1ghag5Y

80. Forte, *Slouching Towards Sirte*, pp. 359–60.

81. Zoe Williams, 'Why does nobody mention that Hillary Clinton is perfectly nice?', *Guardian*, 21 October 2017, www.theguardian.com/us-news/2017/oct/21/why-does-nobody-mention-that-hillary-clinton-is-perfectly-nice

82. Hadley Freeman, Twitter, 10 November 2016, https://twitter.com/HadleyFreeman/status/796704317008920576

83. Helena Horton, Twitter, 10 November 2016, https://twitter.com/horton_official/status/796814415588945920

84. Horton, Twitter, 12 October 2016, https://twitter.com/horton_official/status/797461950141792256

85. Horton, Twitter, 12 November 2016, https://twitter.com/horton_official/status/797462211132358659

86. Robert Webb, Twitter, 10 November 2016, https://twitter.com/arobertwebb/status/796809135597780992

87. Marina Hyde, Twitter, 25 August 2015, https://twitter.com/MarinaHyde/status/636114404094935040

88. Freeman, Twitter, 25 August 2015, https://twitter.com/HadleyFreeman/status/636134870436159488

89. Glenn Greenwald, Twitter, 25 August 2015, https://twitter.com/ggreenwald/status/636131030399909889

90. Greenwald, Twitter, 25 August 2015, https://twitter.com/ggreenwald/status/636131347019497473

91. Greenwald, Twitter, 25 August 2015, https://twitter.com/ggreenwald/status/636142901236473856

92. Greenwald, Twitter, 12 September 2012, https://twitter.com/ggreenwald/status/246205157338120192, now unavailable.

93. David Aaronovitch, Twitter, 13 September 2012, https://twitter.com/DAaronovitch/status/246282796207845377

94. Aaronovitch, Twitter, 13 September 2012, https://twitter.com/DAaronovitch/status/246278832070467585

95. @portraitinflesh, Twitter, 13 September 2012, https://twitter.com/portraitinflesh/status/246205615049945088

96. Greenwald, Twitter, 13 September 2012, https://twitter.com/ggreenwald/statuses/246218320880214016, now unavailable

97. Jonathan Cook, email to Media Lens, 14 September 2012.

6. Syria: Instant Certainty Promoting War

1. Ian Black, 'Syria's powerful allies thwart international attempts to halt violence', Guardian, 5 October 2011, www.guardian.co.uk/global/2011/oct/05/syria-protests-un-analysis

2. Stephen Gowans, 'The revolutionary distemper in Syria that wasn't', what's left blog, 22 October 2016, https://gowans.wordpress. com/2016/10/22/the-revolutionary-distemper-in-syria-that-wasnt/

3. Charles Glass, 'The U.S. and Russia ensure a balance of terror in Syria', *The Intercept*, 29 October 2016, https://theintercept.com/2016/10/29/ the-u-s-and-russia-ensure a balance-of-terror-in-syria/

4. Ian Black, 'Syria's powerful allies thwart international attempts to halt violence', *Guardian*, 5 October 2011, https://www.theguardian.com/ global/2011/oct/05/syria-protests-un-analysis

5. *Independent on Sunday*, 27 May 2012, archived cover, http://twicsy. com/i/66VHAb

6. David Randall, 'The President and his First Lady ... and their people', *Independent on Sunday*, 27 May 2012, www.independent.co.uk/news/ world/middle-east/exclusive-dispatch-assad-blamed-for-massacre-of-the-innocents-7791507.html

7. James Robbins, BBC 'News at Ten', 29 May 2012.

8. Herve Ladsous, cited, Joseph Logan, 'West expels envoys over massacre of Syrian children', Reuters, 29 May 2012, https://af.reuters.com/ article/worldNews/idAFBRE84S0P320120529

9. Jonny Dymond, 'Annan to visit Syria as UN condemns Houla massacre', BBC website, 28 May 2012, www.bbc.com/news/world-middle-east-18231502

10. 'Syria: Kofi Annan arrives in Damascus', Middle East Live, *Guardian*, 28 May 2012, www.theguardian.com/world/middle-east-live/2012/ may/28/syria-bashar-al-assad

11. Jon Williams, 'Reporting conflict in Syria', BBC website, 7 June 2012, www.bbc.co.uk/blogs/theeditors/2012/06/reporting_conflict_in_syria. html

12. Paul Danahar, 'Analysis – New "massacre" reported in Syria's Hama province', BBC website, 7 June 2012, www.bbc.com/news/world-middle-east-18348201

13. John Rosenthal, 'Report: Rebels responsible for Houla massacre', *National Review*, 9 June 2012, www.nationalreview.com/corner/ 302261/report-rebels-responsible-houla-massacre-john-rosenthal

14. Martin Rowson, cartoon, *Guardian*, 27 May 2012, www.theguardian. com/commentisfree/cartoon/2012/may/27/syria

15. Media Lens, Twitter, 28 May 2012, https://twitter.com/medialens/ status/207046652211638272

16. Martin Rowson, Twitter, 28 May 2012, https://twitter.com/MartinRowson/status/207061055480930304

17. Media Lens, Twitter, 28 May 2012, https://twitter.com/medialens/status/207062849430880256

18. Rowson, Twitter, 28 May 2012, https://twitter.com/MartinRowson/status/207061327372492803

19. Media Lens, Twitter, 28 May 2012, https://twitter.com/medialens/status/207064179964772353

20. Rowson, Twitter, 28 May 2012, https://twitter.com/MartinRowson/status/207068776456400896

21. Rowson, Twitter, 28 May 2012, https://twitter.com/MartinRowson/status/207069193764487168

22. Maj Gen Robert Mood, cited, 'Houla: How a massacre unfolded', BBC website, 8 June 2012, www.bbc.co.uk/news/world-middle-east-18233934

23. Mood, cited, Patrick Seale, 'In Syria, this is no plan for peace', *Guardian*, 27 May 2012, www.guardian.co.uk/commentisfree/2012/may/27/syria-no-plans-peace

24. Oral Update of the Independent International Commission of Inquiry on the Syrian Arab Republic, Human Rights Council Twentieth session Agenda item 4 Human, 26 June 2012, www.ohchr.org/Documents/HRBodies/HRCouncil/RegularSession/Session20/COI_OralUpdate_A.HRC.20.CRP.1.pdf

25. Media Lens search, LexisNexis, 5 July 2012.

26. UN News, 'Syrian Government and opposition forces responsible for war crimes – UN panel', 15 August 2012, www.un.org/apps/news/story.asp?NewsID=42687#.WNjhJKLRzv8 – this article contains a link to download the UN report

27. NBC, cited, Peter Hart, 'This time, trust anonymous WMD claims – they've got "Specific Intelligence"', FAIR, 7 December 2012, https://fair.org/media_criticism/this-time-trust-anonymous-wmd-claims-theyve-got-specific-intelligence/

28. FAIR, ibid.

29. Leading article, 'Assad's arsenal: The embattled Syrian regime may be preparing to use chemical weapons. That would be a catastrophe; it must be averted, whatever it takes', *The Times*, 5 December 2012.

30. Matt Williams and Martin Chulov, 'Barack Obama warns Syria of chemical weapons "consequences"', *Guardian*, 4 December 2012, www.

guardian.co.uk/world/2012/dec/04/barack-obama-syria-chemical-weapons-warning

31. Jonathan Marcus, 'Fears grow for fate of Syria's chemical weapons', BBC website, 5 December 2012, www.bbc.co.uk/news/world-middle-east-18483788

32. Robert Fisk, 'Bashar al-Assad, Syria, and the truth about chemical weapons', *Independent*, 8 December 2012, www.independent.co.uk/voices/comment/bashar-alassad-syria-and-the-truth-about-chemical-weapons-8393539.html

33. Alex Thomson, 'Syria, a weapon of mass deception?', Channel 4 blog, 7 December 2012, http://blogs.channel4.com/alex-thomsons-view/syria-weapon-mass-deception/3330

34. United Nations Mission to Investigate Allegations of the Use of Chemical Weapons in the Syrian Arab Republic: Final report, 13 December 2013, www.un.org/disarmament/content/slideshow/Secretary_General_Report_of_CW_Investigation.pdf

35. Editorial, 'Syria: chemical weapons with impunity', *Guardian*, 22 August 2013, www.theguardian.com/commentisfree/2013/aug/22/syria-chemical-weapons

36. Headline, 'Syria: air attacks loom as West finally acts', *Independent*, 26 August 2013.

37. Robert Fisk, 'Syria and sarin gas: US claims have a very familiar ring', *Independent*, 28 April 2013, www.independent.co.uk/news/world/middle-east/syria-and-sarin-gas-us-claims-have-a-very-familiar-ring-8591214.html

38. Roula Khalaf and Abigail Fielding Smith, 'Qatar bankrolls Syrian revolt with cash and arms', *Financial Times*, 16 May 2013, www.ft.com/intl/cms/s/0/86e3f28e-be3a-11e2-bb35-00144feab7de.html#axzz2h7fSxNZf

39. Martin Chulov and Ian Black, 'Syria: Jordan to spearhead Saudi Arabian arms drive', *Guardian*, 14 April 2013, www.theguardian.com/world/2013/apr/14/syria-jordan-spearhead-saudi-arms-drive

40. David Kenner, 'Why Is Saudi Arabia buying 15,000 U.S. anti-tank missiles for a war it will never fight? Hint: Syria', Foreign Policy, 12 December 2013, http://foreignpolicy.com/2013/12/12/why-is-saudi-arabia-buying-15000-u-s-anti-tank-missiles-for-a-war-it-will-never-fight/

41. Greg Miller and Karen DeYoung, 'Secret CIA effort in Syria faces large funding cut', *Washington Post*, 12 June 2015, www.washingtonpost.

com/world/national-security/lawmakers-move-to-curb-1-billion-cia-program-to-train-syrian-rebels/2015/06/12/b0f45a9e-1114-11e5-adec-e82f8395c032_story.html

42. Thomas Grove, 'Insight: Syria pays for Russian weapons to boost ties with Moscow', Reuters, 29 August 2013, www.reuters.com/article/2013/08/29/us-syria-crisis-russia-arms-insight-idUSBRE 97S0WW20130829

43. See our media alert: 'Structural inclinations – The leaning tower of propaganda: Chemical weapons attacks in Ghouta, Syria', Media Lens website, 9 October 2013, www.medialens.org/index.php/alerts/alert-archive/alerts-2013/744-structural-inclinations-the-chemical-weapons-attacks-in-ghouta-syria.html

44. Barack Obama, 'President Obama's Sept. 10 speech on Syria', *Washington Post*, 10 September 2013, www.washingtonpost.com/politics/running-transcript-president-obamas-sept-10-speech-on-syria/2013/09/10/a8826aa6-1a2e-11e3-8685-5021e0c41964_story.html?utm_term=.140b1ce5ab30

45. Seymour Hersh, 'Whose Sarin?', *London Review of Books*, 19 December 2013, www.lrb.co.uk/v35/n24/seymour-m-hersh/whose-sarin

46. William J. Broad, 'Weapons experts raise doubts about Israel's antimissile system', *New York Times*, 20 March 2013, https://goo.gl/8rUwvm

47. See our media alert, 'Projectile Dysfunction – Iron Dome, Israel, Trident, and the media', Media Lens website, 20 May 2010, www.medialens.org/index.php/alerts/alert-archive/2010/17-projectile-dysfunction-iron-dome-israel-trident-and-the-media.html

48. William J. Broad, 'Rockets in Syrian attack carried large payload of gas, experts say', *New York Times*, 4 September 2013, www.nytimes.com/2013/09/05/world/middleeast/rockets-in-syrian-attack-carried-large-payload-of-gas-experts-say.html

49. Link to Lloyd and Postol report PDF here: carinaragno, 'Possible implications of faulty US technical intelligence in the Damascus nerve agent attack of August 21', Dogma and Geopolitics blog, 18 January 2014, https://goo.gl/vKfQKB

50. Theodore Postol, cited, Matthew Schofield – McClatchy Foreign Staff, 'New analysis of rocket used in Syria chemical attack undercuts U.S. claim', *Star-Telegram*, 15 January 2014, www.star-telegram.com/2014/01/15/5488779/new-analysis-of-rocket-used-in.html

51. Ibid.

52. Roy Greenslade, 'US missile strike in Syria: morally right but done for the wrong reasons?' *Guardian*, 9 April 2017, www.theguardian.com/media/greenslade/2017/apr/09/us-trump-missile-strike-syria-morally-right-wrong-reasons-roy-greenslade-media

53. Adam Johnson, 'Out of 47 major editorials on Trump's Syria strikes, only one opposed', FAIR, 9 April 2017, http://fair.org/home/out-of-46-major-editorials-on-trumps-syria-strikes-only-one-opposed/

54. Leading article, 'Suffocating Syria: Assad and Isis are poisoning a once-proud nation. Both must be dislodged', *The Times*, 6 April 2012, www.thetimes.co.uk/article/suffocating-syria-nrlpn3q6z

55. Editorial, 'The US strike against Assad was justified – now for the hard part', *Independent*, 7 April 2017, www.independent.co.uk/voices/editorials/the-us-strike-against-assad-was-justified-now-for-the-hard-part-a7673206.html

56. Owen Jones, 'Syria and the disgusting dishonesty of John Rentoul', *Medium*, 9 April 2017, https://medium.com/@OwenJones84/syria-and-the-disgusting-dishonesty-of-john-rentoul-a3b26ae0151f

57. Monbiot, Twitter, 7 April 2017, https://twitter.com/GeorgeMonbiot/status/850350733727858690

58. Jonathan Freedland, 'Inaction over Syria has exacted a terrible price', *Guardian*, 5 April 2007, www.theguardian.com/commentisfree/2017/apr/05/inaction-syria-chemical-weapons-attack-terrible-price

59. 'Syria "chemical attack": Trump condemns "affront to humanity"', BBC website, 6 April 2017, www.bbc.com/news/world-middle-east-39508868

60. According to Newssniffer, 6 April 2017, link no longer functional www.newssniffer.co.uk/articles/1357208/diff/6/7

61. Jerry Smith, 'Syria chemical attack: reaction', Channel 4 News, 5 April 2017, www.channel4.com/news/syria-chemical-attack-reaction

62. Theodore Postol report, 'A quick turnaround assessment of the White House Intelligence Report issued on April 11, 2017 about the nerve agent attack in Khan Shaykhun, Syria', 17 April 2017, https://goo.gl/2AMFUt

63. Noam Chomsky in Dan Falcone interview: 'US is the "Most dangerous country in the world"', truthout, 24 April 2017, www.truth-out.org/opinion/item/40319-noam-chomsky-us-is-the-most-dangerous-country-in-the-world

64. Mike Whitney, 'Syria: Where the rubber meets the road', 12 April 2017, www.CounterPunch.org/2017/04/12/syria-where-the-rubber-meets-the-road/

65. Ibid.

66. Hans Blix, cited Teri Schultz, 'EU urges diplomacy in Syria as ex-weapons inspector says US acted without proof', DW website, 7 April 2017, http://m.dw.com/en/eu-urges-diplomacy-in-syria-as-ex-weapons-inspector-says-us-acted-without-proof/a-38345413

67. Scott Ritter, 'Wag the dog – How Al Qaeda played Donald Trump and the American media', *Huffington Post*, 9 April 2017, https://goo.gl/Z9jVXV

68. See our media alert: 'Nuclear deceit – The Times and Iran', Media Lens website, 14 January 2010, www.medialens.org/index.php/alerts/alert-archive/2010/39-nuclear-deceit-the-times-and-iran.html

69. Philip Giraldi, cited, Whitney, op. cit.

70. Jonathan Steele, 'Russia vetoes U.N. resolution on Syria as questions linger over deadly chemical attack', *Democracy Now!*, 13 April 2017, www.democracynow.org/2017/4/13/russia_vetoes_un_resolution_on_syria

71. 'Obama's battle against so-called Islamic State', BBC Radio 4, Best of Today, 20 August 2016, https://goo.gl/PKsVoA

72. Cited Noam Chomsky, '"What we say goes": The Middle East in the New World Order', Chomsky website, May 1991, https://chomsky.info/199105__/

73. Adam Johnson, 'Pundits, decrying the horrors of war in Aleppo, demand expanded war', *The Nation*, 24 August 2016, www.thenation.com/article/pundits-decrying-the-horrors-of-war-in-aleppo-demand-expanded-war/

74. John Simpson, 'Barack Obama's best years could still be ahead of him', BBC website, 29 October 2014, www.bbc.com/news/world-29735983

75. Greg Miller and Karen DeYoung, 'Secret CIA effort in Syria faces large funding cut', *Washington Post*, 12 June 2015, https://goo.gl/664uNC

76. Adam Johnson, 'The Syrian refugee crisis and the "do something" lie', FAIR, 5 September 2015, http://fair.org/home/the-syrian-refugee-crisis-and-the-do-something-lie/

77. Bassem, Twitter, 2 April 2017, https://twitter.com/BBassem7/status/848526738468491265

78. Zacks Investment Research, InvestorPlace, 'Raytheon company (RTN) approves 9% increase in quarterly dividend', 31 March 2017, https://goo.gl/5XCBUo

79. Gareth Porter, email to Media Lens, 22 August 2016.

80. Paul Mason, 'How the west slipped into powerlessness', Channel 4 blog, 20 February 2014, www.channel4.com/news/by/paul-mason/blogs/world-superpowers

81. Paul Mason, Twitter, 19 May 2014, https://twitter.com/paulmasonnews/status/468337860215459840

82. Media Lens, Twitter, 19 May 2014, https://twitter.com/medialens/status/468341366821752832

83. Mason, Twitter, 19 May 2014, https://twitter.com/paulmasonnews/status/468363982110474240

84. Media Lens, Twitter, 19 May 2014, https://twitter.com/medialens/status/468368004414459904

85. Glenn Greenwald, *No Place To Hide – Edward Snowden, the NSA and the Surveillance State*, Penguin, digital edition, 2014, p. 471.

86. Ibid., p. 474.

87. Mason, Twitter, 19 May 2014, https://twitter.com/paulmasonnews/status/468370645743841280

7. Yemen: Feeding the Famine

1. 'Syria: The world looks the other way. Will you?', front page of *Independent on Sunday*, May 27 2012; https://twitter.com/IndyOnSunday/status/206459463081795584/photo/1

2. 'Nayirah testimony', Wikipedia; https://en.wikipedia.org/wiki/Nayirah_(testimony); accessed 15 February 2018.

3. 'Saddam Hussein's alleged shredder', Wikipedia; https://en.wikipedia.org/wiki/Saddam_Hussein%27s_alleged_shredder; accessed 15 February 2018.

4. Media Lens, 'Disappearing genocide: The media and the death of Slobodan Milosevic', 20 March 2006; www.medialens.org/index.php/alerts/alert-archive/2006/440-disappearing-genocide.html

5. Patrick Wintour, 'West must confront Russia over Aleppo, emergency Commons debate to hear', *Guardian*, 11 October 2016 11.50 BST; www.theguardian.com/politics/2016/oct/11/west-must-confront-russia-over-aleppo-syria-emergency-commons-debate-to-hear

6. Boris Johnson, 'If we want to be taken seriously, we have to defend ourselves', *Telegraph*, 16 February 2015; www.telegraph.co.uk/news/uknews/defence/11414624/If-we-want-to-be-taken-seriously-we-have-to-defend-ourselves.html

7. Boris Johnson, 'Blair's Iraq invasion was a tragic error, and he's mad to deny it', *Telegraph*, 15 June 2014; www.telegraph.co.uk/news/worldnews/middleeast/iraq/10901651/Blairs-Iraq-invasion-was-a-tragic-error-and-hes-mad-to-deny-it.html

8. Felicity Arbuthnot, 'The unspoken war on Yemen, Anglo-American crimes against humanity, U.N. and media silence, complicity of "The International Community", destruction of an entire country…', *Global Research*, 8 September 2016; www.globalresearch.ca/the-unspoken-war-on-yemen-anglo-american-crimes-against-humanity-u-n-and-media-silence-complicity-of-the-international-community-destruction-of-an-entire-country/5544706

9. 'Journalist Iona Craig: The U.S. could stop refueling Saudis & end devastating war in Yemen tomorrow', Democracy Now!, 15 December 2016; www.democracynow.org/2016/12/15/journalist_iona_craig_the_us_could

10. Saleh was killed by Houthi rebels in December 2017, seemingly for switching sides and seeking peace with Saudi Arabia. Patrick Wintour, 'Yemen Houthi rebels kill former president Ali Abdullah Saleh', *Guardian* website, 4 December 2017; www.theguardian.com/world/2017/dec/04/former-yemen-president-saleh-killed-in-fresh-fighting

11. Gareth Porter, 'The media misses the point on "proxy war"', Middle East Eye, 4 May 2015; www.middleeasteye.net/columns/media-misses-point-proxy-war-1956459570

12. Peter Foster and Almigdad Mojalli, 'UK "will support Saudi-led assault on Yemeni rebels – but not engaging in combat"',*Telegraph*, 27 March 2015; www.telegraph.co.uk/news/worldnews/middleeast/yemen/11500518/UK-will-support-Saudi-led-assault-on-Yemeni-rebels-but-not-engaging-in-combat.html

13. Emma Graham-Harrison, 'UK in denial over Saudi arms sales being used in Yemen, claims Oxfam', *Guardian*, 23 August 2016; www.theguardian.com/world/2016/aug/23/uk-in-denial-over-saudi-arms-sales-being-used-in-yemen-claims-oxfam

14. Jon Stone, 'Britain is now the second biggest arms dealer in the world', *Independent*, 7 September 2016; www.independent.co.uk/news/uk/

home-news/britain-is-now-the-second-biggest-arms-dealer-in-the-world-a7225351.html

15. Graham-Harrison, 'UK in denial over Saudi arms sales being used in Yemen, claims Oxfam', *Guardian*, 23 August 2016; www.theguardian.com/world/2016/aug/23/uk-in-denial-over-saudi-arms-sales-being-used-in-yemen-claims-oxfam

16. 'Journalist Iona Craig', Democracy Now!, 15 December 2016; www.democracynow.org/2016/12/15/journalist_iona_craig_the_us_could

17. Samuel Osborne, 'Saudi Arabia delaying aid to Yemen is "killing children", warns Save the Children', *Independent*, 1 March 2017; www.independent.co.uk/news/world/middle-east/saudi-arabia-yemen-aid-delay-killing-children-save-the-children-warn-a7606411.html

18. Ibid.

19. Amnesty International, 'Yemen: Children among civilians killed and maimed in cluster bomb "minefields"', 23 May 2016; www.amnesty.org/en/latest/news/2016/05/yemen-children-among-civilians-killed-and-maimed-in-cluster-bomb-minefields/

20. Amnesty International UK, 'Why the UK must stop arms sales to Saudi Arabia', 7 June 2016; www.amnesty.org.uk/why-uk-must-stop-arms-sales-saudi-arabia

21. Amnesty International, 'Suspend Saudi Arabia from UN Human Rights Council', 29 June 2016; www.amnesty.org/en/latest/news/2016/06/suspend-saudi-arabia-from-un-human-rights-council/

22. Ben Kentish, 'Saudi-led coalition in Yemen accused of "genocide" after airstrike on funeral hall kills 140', *Independent*, 9 October 2016; www.independent.co.uk/news/world/middle-east/yemen-air-strike-bomb-kills-140-saudi-arabia-usa-white-house-a7352386.html

23. Neil Connery, 'ITV News sees evidence British-made cluster bombs used in Yemen attacks', ITV, 26 October 2016; www.itv.com/news/2016-10-26/itv-news-sees-evidence-british-made-cluster-bombs-used-in-yemen-attacks/

24. May Bulman, 'Yemen's Prime Minister accuses UK of war crimes', *Independent*, 13 December 2016; www.independent.co.uk/news/world/asia/yemen-prime-minister-uk-war-crimes-abdulaziz-bin-habtour-a7473001.html

25. Con Coughlin, 'UK must keep supporting Yemen campaign to prevent terror in West, says Saudi foreign minister', *Telegraph*, 6 September 2016; www.telegraph.co.uk/news/2016/09/06/uk-must-keep-supporting-yemen-campaign-to-prevent-terror-in-west/

26. Louis Charbonneau and Michelle Nichols, 'U.N. chief blasts Saudi pressure after Yemen coalition blacklisting', Reuters, 19 June 2016; www.reuters.com/article/us-yemen-security-saudi-un-idUSKCN0 YV1UQ

27. Lizzie Dearden, 'UN blacklists Saudi Arabia-led coalition for "killing and maiming" children in Yemen air strikes', Independent, 3 June 2016; www.independent.co.uk/news/world/middle-east/un-blacklists-saudi-arabia-led-coalition-for-killing-and-maiming-children-in-yemen-air-strikes-a7063681.html

28. 'Yemen conflict: UN accuses Saudis of pressure over blacklist', BBC News, 9 June 92016; www.bbc.co.uk/news/world-middle-east-36494598

29. Kayleigh Lewis, 'UN "blackmailed" into removing Saudi Arabia from blacklist after just a week', Independent, 9 June 2016; www.independent.co.uk/news/world/middle-east/un-saudi-arabia-blackmail-blacklist-removed-after-one-week-a7073046.html

30. David Aaronovitch, 'It's because we're rich that we must impose peace for others', Independent, 25 March 1999.

31. David Aaronovitch, 'My country needs me', Independent, 6 April 1999.

32. David Aaronovitch, 'Stop trying to stop the war, Start trying to win the peace', Independent, 16 November 2001.

33. David Aaronovitch, 'Why the Left must tackle the crimes of Saddam: With or without a second UN resolution, I will not oppose action against Iraq', Observer, 2 February 2003.

34. David Aaronovitch, 'Go for a no fly zone over Libya or regret it', The Times, 24 February 2011.

35. David Aaronovitch, 'Remember Bosnia, seedbed of radical Islam; The people of Syria wonder why the West will not help', The Times, 31 May 2012.

36. David Aaronovitch, 'Forget the past. Iraqi Kurds need our help now; The 2003 invasion is irrelevant to what is happening in Mosul now. What matters is preventing the advance of Isis', The Times, 12 June 2014.

37. Daniel Wickham, Twitter, 28 January 2016; https://twitter.com/DanielWickham93/status/692765929760018432

38. David Aaronovitch, Twitter, 28 January 2016; https://twitter.com/DAaronovitch/status/692766357402849280

39. Editorial, 'The Guardian view on famine: sitting by as disaster unfolds. Millions face starvation, but the world is turning away. We are too late

to prevent this severe food crisis – but we can and must act now to save lives', *Guardian*, 23 February 2017 19.45 GMT; www.theguardian.com/commentisfree/2017/feb/23/the-Guardian-view-on-famine-sitting-by-as-disaster-unfolds

40. Adam Johnson, 'Downplaying US contribution to potential Yemen famine', FAIR, 27 February 2017; http://fair.org/home/downplaying-us-contribution-to-potential-yemen-famine

41. Peter Oborne and Nawal Al-Maghafi, 'A calamity is unfolding in Yemen and it's time the world woke up', *Middle East Eye*, 31 August 2016; www.middleeasteye.net/essays/yemen-war-saudi-arabia-houthi-sanaa-peter-oborne-820075995

42. '"Corrosive, Shallow, Herd-Like and Gross" – Peter Oborne and the corporate media', Media Lens media alert, 25 February 2015; www.medialens.org/index.php/alerts/alert-archive/2015/787-peter-oborne.html

43. Noam Chomsky, 'East Timor Retrospective', *Le Monde Diplomatique*, October 1999; https://chomsky.info/199910__/

44. Noam Chomsky, *Rogue States*, Pluto Books, 2000, p. 232.

45. Peter Oborne and Nawal Al-Maghafi, 'A calamity is unfolding in Yemen and it's time the world woke up', *Middle East Eye*, 31 August 2016; www.middleeasteye.net/essays/yemen-war-saudi-arabia-houthi-sanaa-peter-oborne-820075995

46. BBC News, 'Labour MP urges probe into Philip Hammond's Yemen answers', 29 July 2016; www.bbc.co.uk/news/uk-politics-36924137

47. Ian Johnston, 'Anger as Saudi Arabia blocks UN inquiry into "war crimes" in Yemen', *Independent*, 1 October 2015; www.independent.co.uk/travel/middle-east/un-inquiry-into-saudi-arabia-war-crimes-in-yemen-shelved-after-saudi-opposition-a6676141.html

48. Peter Oborne, 'Yemen's war: The destruction of Sanaa', YouTube, 1 September 2016; www.youtube.com/watch?v=EoZsjagnKPs

49. Patrick Wintour, 'Boris Johnson defends UK arms sales to Saudi Arabia', *Guardian* website, September 5, 2016; www.theguardian.com/world/2016/sep/05/mps-to-urge-ban-on-uk-arms-sales-to-saudi-arabia

50. 'Sick sophistry – BBC News on the Afghan hospital "mistakenly" bombed by the United States', Media Lens media alert, 20 October 2015; www.medialens.org/index.php/alerts/alert-archive/2015/804-sick-sophistry-bbc-news-on-the-afghan-hospital-mistakenly-bombed-by-the-united-states.html

51. 'Kunduz killers go free', Media Lens media alert, 31 March 2016; www. medialens.org/index.php/alerts/alert-archive/2016/815-kunduz-killers-go-free.html

52. '"I would have refused such an order" – Former RAF pilot gives his view of US bombing of MSF hospital In Kunduz', Media Lens media alert, 28 October 2015; www.medialens.org/index.php/alerts/alert-archive/2015/805-i-would-have-refused-such-an-order-former-raf-pilot-gives-his-view-of-us-bombing-of-msf-hospital-in-kunduz.html

53. Patrick Wintour, 'Saudi Arabia makes plea for Britain not to ban arms sales', *Guardian*, 6 September 2016; www.theguardian.com/world/2016/sep/06/saudi-arabia-makes-plea-for-britain-not-to-ban-arms-sales

54. Rowena Mason and Euan MacAskill, 'Saudis dropped British-made cluster bombs in Yemen, Fallon tells Commons', *Guardian*, 20 December 2016; www.theguardian.com/world/2016/dec/19/saudis-dropped-british-cluster-bombs-in-yemen-fallon-tells-commons

55. Aisha Gani, 'Theresa May says the UK will keep selling weapons To Saudi Arabia', *Buzzfeed*, 14 December 2016; www.buzzfeed.com/aishagani/theresa-may-says-the-uk-will-keep-selling-weapons-to-saudi-a?utm_term=.mjDrZNB7x#.yrOOA04wo

56. House of Commons Hansard, 26 October 2016; https://hansard.parliament.uk/Commons/2016-10-26/debates/61DFF92D-1BE0-4909-8020-76FC80CA5136/Yemen

57. Emma Graham-Harrison and agencies, 'Yemen famine feared as starving children fight for lives in hospital', *Guardian*, 4 October 2016; www.theguardian.com/world/2016/oct/04/yemen-famine-feared-as-starving-children-fight-for-lives-in-hospital

58. Robert Fisk, 'Saudi Arabia "deliberately targeting impoverished Yemen's farms and agricultural industry"', *Independent*, 23 October 2016; www.independent.co.uk/news/world/middle-east/saudi-arabia-s-bombing-of-yemeni-farmland-is-a-disgraceful-breach-of-the-geneva-conventions-a7376576.html

59. Ben Norton, 'Famine looms in Yemen, as U.S.-backed Saudi bombing intentionally targets food production', *Salon*, 27 October 2016; www.salon.com/2016/10/27/famine-looms-in-yemen-as-u-s-backed-saudi-bombing-intentionally-targets-food-production/

60. Ewen MacAskill and Paul Torpey, 'One in three Saudi air raids on Yemen hit civilian sites, data shows', *Guardian*, 16 September 2016;

www.theguardian.com/world/2016/sep/16/third-of-saudi-airstrikes-on-yemen-have-hit-civilian-sites-data-shows

61. House of Commons Hansard, Division 72, October 26, 2016; https://hansard.parliament.uk/Commons/2016-10-26/division/6ABA6BF7-9182-4F50-A430-7BCA9FCEE6B1/Yemen?outputType=Name

62. John Woodcock, 'Empty gesture politics will only make the crisis in Yemen worse', *LabourList*, 26 October 2016; http://labourlist.org/2016/10/john-woodcock-the-crisis-in-yemen-must-not-be-ignored/

63. 'Parliamentarians listed on the final guest list and seating plan for the ADS Annual Defence Dinner, 3 February 2015', Campaign Against Arms Trade, www.caat.org.uk/issues/influence/resources/2015-02-03.ads.dinner-parliamentarians.pdf

64. Kate McCann, 'Labour MP posts pro-Trident leaflets on colleagues' doors in parliament', *Telegraph*, 24 November 2015; www.telegraph.co.uk/news/politics/12013950/Labour-MP-posts-pro-Trident-leaflets-on-colleagues-doors-in-parliament.html

65. Laura Hughes, 'Labour will support Trident renewal despite Jeremy Corbyn's opposition', *Telegraph*, 14 October 2016; www.telegraph.co.uk/news/2016/10/14/labour-will-support-trident-renewal-despite-jeremy-corbyns-oppos/

66. Peter Oborne, 'How Britain's party of war gave the green light to Saudi in Yemen', *Middle East Eye*, 28 October 2016; www.middleeasteye.net/columns/reign-british-neo-cons-and-party-war-128790447

67. David Wearing, 'The Labour rebels who didn't back the Yemen vote have blood on their hands', *Guardian*, 28 October 2016; www.theguardian.com/commentisfree/2016/oct/28/emily-thornberry-labour-mps-blood-hands-yemen-conflict-saudi-arabia

68. Editorial, 'The *Guardian* view on parliamentary business: the importance of absence', *Guardian*, 28 October 2016; www.theguardian.com/commentisfree/2016/oct/28/the-Guardian-view-on-parliamentary-business-the-importance-of-absence

69. Rafat Al-Alkahli, 'The West must get all sides in Yemen to reach a deal – or face an overwhelming humanitarian catastrophe', *Telegraph*, 29 October 2016; www.telegraph.co.uk/news/2016/10/29/the-west-must-get-all-sides-in-yemen-to-reach-a-deal--or-face-a/

70. 'Trump in Saudi Arabia: First foreign trip starts as home troubles mount', BBC website, 20 May 2017; www.bbc.co.uk/news/world-us-canada-39984903

71. 'Extremely high number of deaths expected as Yemen slides into Cholera epidemic', *SBS News*, 22 May 2017; www.sbs.com.au/news/extremely-high-number-of-deaths-expected-as-yemen-slides-into-cholera-epidemic

72. Ibid.

73. Gareth Porter, Twitter, 27 May 2017; https://twitter.com/GarethPorter/status/868488396947283968

74. BBC News screenshot, Media Lens, Twitter, 21 May 2017; https://twitter.com/medialens/status/866165024179597312

75. Mark Curtis, Twitter, 18 May 2017; https://twitter.com/markcurtis30/status/865142900824432640

76. Mark Curtis, 'UK General Election: What are the foreign policy implications?', *New Internationalist*, 18 May 2017; https://newint.org/blog/2017/05/18/uk-general-election-what-are-the-foreign-policy-implications/

77. Nicholas Wilson, 'Amber Rudd shuts down my speech about HSBC and Saudi Arabia', YouTube, 4 June 2017; www.youtube.com/watch?v=TEcMW6RmC_w

78. Nicholas Wilson, 'When will BBC censorship of HSBC end?, Mr Ethical website, 14 September 2016; http://nicholaswilson.com/when-will-bbc-censorship-of-hsbc-end/

79. Laura Kuenssberg, 'General Election 2017: Jeremy Corbyn doubles down on defence', BBC website, 12 May 2017; www.bbc.co.uk/news/election-2017-39894297

8. The BBC as a Propaganda Machine

1. Interview with Jon Snow, 9 January 2001; www.medialens.org/index.php/alerts/interviews/81-interview-with-jon-snow.html

2. Interview with Alan Rusbridger, 8 December 2001; www.medialens.org/index.php/alerts/interviews/80-interview-with-alan-rusbridger-editor-the-Guardian.html

3. 'Smearing Chomsky – The *Guardian* in the gutter', Media Lens media alert, 4 November 2005; http://medialens.org/index.php/alerts/alert-archive/2005/419-smearing-chomsky-the-Guardian-in-the-gutter.html

4. '"No great way to die" – but the generals love napalm', Media Lens media alert, 30 March 2005; http://medialens.org/index.php/alerts/

alert-archive/2005/387-qno-great-way-to-die-but-the-generals-love-napalm.html

5. 'BBC still ignoring evidence of war crimes', Media Lens media alert, 24 May 2005; http://medialens.org/index.php/alerts/alert-archive/2005/396-bbc-still-ignoring-evidence-of-war-crimes.html

6. 'Impartiality is in our genes', Helen Boaden, BBC website, 18 September 2010; www.bbc.co.uk/blogs/theeditors/2010/09/impartiality_is_in_our_genes.html

7. Gavin Lewis, 'The broken BBC: from public service to corporate power', *Monthly Review*, 1 April 2016; https://monthlyreview.org/2016/04/01/the-broken-bbc/

8. Steve Rushton, 'The fantastic corruption of the Broadcasting British Class', *Novara Media*, 12 June 2016; http://novara.media/2gq7MR9

9. Sarah O'Connell, 'The BBC has lost touch: here's how it could re-connect', openDemocracy, 24 May 2016; www.opendemocracy.net/ourbeeb/sarah-oconnell/bbc-has-lost-touch

10. Jon Sopel, 'Trump lambasts media for questioning veteran donations', BBC website, 31 May 2016; www.bbc.co.uk/news/election-us-2016-36422611

11. 'BBC values: James Harding', BBC website, 2 July 2013; www.bbc.co.uk/academy/journalism/values/article/art20130702112133786

12. 'James Harding: BBC News and Current Affairs – our stories', BBC website, 4 December 2013; www.bbc.co.uk/mediacentre/speeches/2013/james-harding.html

13. Charlotte Higgins, 'The future of the BBC: you either believe in it or you don't', *Guardian* website, 20 August 2014; www.theguardian.com/media/2014/aug/20/-sp-bbc-report-future-charter-renewal

14. Glenn Greenwald, 'Cowardly firing of Australian state-funded TV journalist highlights the West's real religion', *The Intercept*, 30 April 2015; https://theintercept.com/2015/04/30/cowardly-firing-australian-tv-journalists-highlights-west-religion/

15. Charlotte Higgins, 'The future of the BBC: you either believe in it or you don't', *Guardian* website, 20 August 2014; www.theguardian.com/media/2014/aug/20/-sp-bbc-report-future-charter-renewal

16. Jenni Russell, 'Could Newsnight's editor really have acted alone on the Jimmy Savile story?', *Guardian* website, 23 October 2012; www.theguardian.com/commentisfree/2012/oct/23/newsnight-editor-jimmy-savile-story

17. 'BBC complaints process "too complex", Lords says', BBC website, 29 June 2011; www.bbc.co.uk/news/uk-politics-13949966

18. Francis Elliott, 'Media Diary: Helen the hidden', *Independent* website, 26 November 2006; www.independent.co.uk/news/media/the-tossers-who-could-win-for-the-tories-425799.html

19. John Simpson, 'Barack Obama's best years could still be ahead of him', BBC website, October 29, 2014; www.bbc.co.uk/news/world-29735983

20. Name withheld, email to Media Lens, 13 November 2014.

21. 'Chomsky on Trump's climate denialism: He wants us to march toward the destruction of the species', *Democracy Now!*, 16 May 2016; www.democracynow.org/2016/5/16/chomsky_on_trump_s_climate_denialism

22. Nick Bryant, 'The decline of US power', BBC website, 10 July 2015; www.bbc.co.uk/news/world-us-canada-33440287

23. 'Happy new year? The world's getting slowly more cheerful', BBC website, 30 December 2013; www.bbc.co.uk/news/world-25496299

24. Glenn Greenwald, 'To defend Iran deal, Obama boasts that he's bombed seven countries', *The Intercept*, 6 August 2015; https://theintercept.com/2015/08/06/obama-summarizes-record/

25. 'Drone warfare', The Bureau of Investigative Journalism, accessed 13 February 2018; www.thebureauinvestigates.com/projects/drone-war

26. 'Army chief calls for investment to keep up with Russia', BBC website, 22 January 2018; www.bbc.co.uk/news/uk-42770208

27. Dave Majumdar, 'Newly declassified documents: Gorbachev told NATO wouldn't move past East German border', 12 December 2017; http://nationalinterest.org/blog/the-buzz/newly-declassified-documents-gorbachev-told-NATO-wouldnt-23629

28. Jules Defour, 'The worldwide network of US military sases', *Global Research*, 1 July 2007; www.globalresearch.ca/the-worldwide-network-of-us-military-bases/5564

29. 'Chomsky: Obama "dangerously escalating tensions along the Russian border"', *Sputnik News*, 2 June 2006; https://sputniknews.com/us/201606021040693785-chomsky-russia-obama/

30. William Blum, 'Overthrowing other people's governments: The master list', William Blum's website, accessed 13 February 2018; https://williamblum.org/essays/read/overthrowing-other-peoples-governments-the-master-list

31. Blum, 'United States bombings of other countries', William Blum's website, accessed 13 February 2018; https://williamblum.org/chapters/rogue-state/united-states-bombings-of-other-countries

32. John Pilger, 'Inside the invisible government: war, propaganda, Clinton & Trump', *CounterPunch*, 28 October 2016; www.counterpunch.org/2016/10/28/inside-the-invisible-government-war-propaganda-clinton-trump/

33. @AAZios, Twitter, 23 January 2018; https://twitter.com/AAZios/status/955914628353200130

34. Jonathan Beale, Twitter, 23 January 2018; https://twitter.com/bealejonathan/status/955927296132763648

35. Beale, Twitter, 22 January 2018; https://twitter.com/bealejonathan/status/955548060427407366

36. Glenn Greenwald, 'A Clinton fan manufactured fake news that MSNBC personalities spread to discredit WikiLeaks docs', *The Intercept*, 9 December 2016; https://theintercept.com/2016/12/09/a-clinton-fan-manufactured-fake-news-that-msnbc-personalities-spread-to-discredit-wikileaks-docs/

37. Carole Cadwalladr, 'Google, democracy and the truth about internet search', *Observer*, 4 December 2016; www.theguardian.com/technology/2016/dec/04/google-democracy-truth-internet-search-facebook

38. Rory Cellan-Jones, 'Was it Facebook "wot won it"?', 10 November 2016, www.bbc.co.uk/news/technology-37936225

39. John Pilger, 'Inside the invisible government: war, propaganda, Clinton & Trump', *CounterPunch*, 28 October 2016; www.counterpunch.org/2016/10/28/inside-the-invisible-government-war-propaganda-clinton-trump/

40. 'BBC's Laura Kuenssberg named Journalist of the Year', *Press Gazette*, 6 December 2016; www.pressgazette.co.uk/bbcs-laura-kuenssberg-named-journalist-of-the-year-full-list-of-2016-british-journalism-awards-winners/

41. Freddy Mayhew, 'Interview with Journalist of the Year Laura Kuenssberg: "I would die in a ditch for the impartiality of the BBC"', *Press Gazette*, 9 December 2016; www.pressgazette.co.uk/interview-with-journalist-of-the-year-laura-kuenssberg-i-would-die-in-a-ditch-for-the-impartiality-of-the-bbc/

42. Brian Wheeler, 'Dyke in BBC "conspiracy" claim', BBC website, 20 September 2009; http://news.bbc.co.uk/1/hi/uk_politics/8265628.stm

43. Rowena Mason, 'BBC may have shown bias against Corbyn, says former trust chair', *Guardian* website, 12 May 2016; www.theguardian.com/media/2016/may/12/bbc-bias-labour-sir-michael-lyons

44. Craig Murray, 'The establishment rallies around Kuenssberg', Craig Murray's blog, 10 May 2016; www.craigmurray.org.uk/archives/2016/05/establishment-rallies-around-keunssberg/

45. Freddy Mayhew, 'Interview with Journalist of the Year Laura Kuenssberg: "I would die in a ditch for the impartiality of the BBC"', December 9, 2016; www.pressgazette.co.uk/interview-with-journalist-of-the-year-laura-kuenssberg-i-would-die-in-a-ditch-for-the-impartiality-of-the-bbc/

46. Des Freedman, 'Laura Kuenssberg wins "journalist of the year"', *Counterfire*, 7 December 2016; www.counterfire.org/news/18658-laura-kuenssberg-wins-journalist-of-the-year

9. Dismantling the National Health Service

1. Noam Chomsky, 'The corporate assault on public education', *AlterNet*, 8 March 2013; www.alternet.org/education/chomsky-corporate-assault-public-education

2. Andrew Grice, 'My family depends on NHS so it's safe in my hands, says Cameron', *Independent*, 3 October 2006; www.independent.co.uk/news/uk/politics/my-family-depends-on-nhs-so-its-safe-in-my-hands-says-cameron-418621.html

3. 'NHS reforms protest – Wednesday 7 March', The NHS Reforms blog, 7 March 2012; www.theguardian.com/society/blog/2012/mar/07/nhs-reforms-live-blog-thousands-to-attend-westminster-protest-rall

4. Randeep Ramesh, 'NHS among developed world's most efficient health systems, says study', *Guardian*, 7 August 2011; www.theguardian.com/society/2011/aug/07/nhs-among-most-efficient-health-services

5. Denis Campbell, 'NHS reform bill "complex, incoherent and not fit for purpose", say doctors', *Guardian*, 1 March 2012; www.theguardian.com/politics/2012/mar/01/nhs-reform-bill-incoherent-doctors

6. Richard Horton, 'Lancet editor and doctors write: The fight for our NHS goes on', *Red Pepper*, 22 March 2012; www.redpepper.org.uk/nhs-fight-goes-on/

7. Denis Campbell, 'Royal College of Surgeons condemns NHS reforms', *Guardian*, 9 March 2012; www.theguardian.com/society/2012/mar/09/royal-college-surgeons-nhs-reforms

8. Dr Laurence Buckman, 'BMA letter opposing NHS reforms', *Guardian*, 1 March 2012; www.theguardian.com/society/2012/mar/01/bma-letter-opposing-nhs-reforms

9. Tim Hardy, 'Doctors of tomorrow add voices to call to drop the bill', Beyondclicktivism, 15 March 2012; https://beyondclicktivism.com/2012/03/15/doctors-of-tomorrow-add-voices-to-call-to-drop-the-bill/

10. Jane Kirby, 'Nurses chief rejects Andrew Lansley's claims', *Independent*, 19 January 2012; www.independent.co.uk/news/uk/politics/nurses-chief-rejects-andrew-lansleys-claims-6291663.html

11. Jane Martinson, 'Happy, touchy-feely and driven by God', *Guardian*, 24 February 2006; www.theguardian.com/business/2006/feb/24/columnists

12. Max Pemberton, '"Healthy competition" in the NHS is a sick joke', *Telegraph*, 9 April 2012; www.telegraph.co.uk/news/features/9193015/Healthy-competition-in-the-NHS-is-a-sick-joke.html

13. Dr John Lister, 'It didn't have to be this way', *Labour Briefing*, April 2012, p. 5.

14. E.g. Denis Campbell, 'Save our NHS rally: thousands march in health bill protest', *Guardian*, 8 March 2012; www.theguardian.com/society/2012/mar/07/save-nhs-rally-health-bill

15. Ellen Graubart, 'The great NHS swindle', Counterfire, 5 December 2013; www.counterfire.org/articles/analysis/16852-the-great-nhs-swindle

16. '333 donations from private healthcare sources totalling £8.3 million gifted to the Tories', *Dorset Eye*, www.dorseteye.com/south/articles/333-donations-from-private-healthcare-sources-totalling-8-3-million-gifted-to-the-tories; accessed 29 August 2017

17. Andrew Robertson, 'NHS privatisation: Compilation of financial and vested interests', Social Investigations blog, 18 February 2012; http://socialinvestigations.blogspot.co.uk/2012/02/nhs-privatisation-compilation-of.html

18. Colin Lawson, 'The revolving door between healthcare companies, lobbyists, think tanks, special advisers and government', Reason and Reality blog, 30 January 2012; www.reasonandreality.org/?p=384

19. BBC, 'Editorial Guidelines', Section 4: Impartiality; www.bbc.co.uk/editorialguidelines/guidelines/impartiality; accessed 29 August 2017

20. Tim Hardy, 'Doctors of Tomorrow Add Voices to Call to Drop the Bill', Beyondclicktivism, March 15, 2012; https://beyondclicktivism.com/2012/03/15/doctors-of-tomorrow-add-voices-to-call-to-drop-the-bill/

21. Email to Media Lens, name withheld, 23 March 2012.

22. RT, 27 March 2012; www.rt.com/news/uk-health-service-reforms-519/

23. Isobel Weinberg, 'BBC coverage of the NHS bill', *Storify*, 19 March 2012; https://storify.com/isobelweinberg/bbc-coverage-of-the-nhs-bill

24. Clive Peedell, Twitter, 27 March 2012; https://twitter.com/cpeedell/status/184701963823357952

25. Dorothy Bishop, 'BBC's "extensive coverage" of the NHS bill', 9 April 2012; http://deevybee.blogspot.co.uk/2012/04/bbcs-extensive-coverage-of-nhs-bill.html

26. Liz Panton, 'NHS bill – complaint to BBC about BBCQT – not one question!', Giving Voice blog, 23 March 2012; http://salt-mine.net/blog/2012/03/23/complaint-bbcqt-no-question-nhs-bill/

27. 'Dr Phil Hammond attacks Andrew Lansley's anti-NHS bill on Question Time', 'Question Time', Thursday, 13 October 2011; YouTube, www.youtube.com/watch?v=2OIei5dqS1w

28. Ian Sinclair, 'The BBC is neither independent or impartial: interview with Tom Mills', openDemocracy, 25 January 2017; www.opendemocracy.net/ourbeeb/ian-sinclair-tom-mills/bbc-is-neither-independent-or-impartial-interview-with-tom-mills

29. 'Dr Mike Lynch OBE, former non-executive director', BBC website; www.bbc.co.uk/aboutthebbc/insidethebbc/managementstructure/biographies/lynch_mike; accessed 29 August 2017

30. For more info, see 'Why did the BBC ignore the NHS bill?', Rusty Light blog, 31 March 2012; http://rustylight.blogspot.co.uk/2012/03/why-did-bbc-ignore-nhs-bill.html

31. Andrew Robertson, 'BBC chief Lord Patten of Barnes, Bridgepoint and the conflicts of interest', Social Investigations blog, 22 March 2012; http://socialinvestigations.blogspot.co.uk/2012/03/lord-patten-of-barnes-bridgepoint-and.html

32. David Edwards, Interview with Alan Rusbridger, Editor, *Guardian*, 8 December 2000; http://medialens.org/index.php/alerts/interviews/80-interview-with-alan-rusbridger-editor-the-guardian.html

33. Colin Lawson, 'The revolving door between healthcare companies, lobbyists, think tanks, special advisers and government', Reason and Reality blog, January 30, 2012; www.reasonandreality.org/?p=384

34. Taxpayers' Alliance, 'New research: BBC and S4C spend millions on private healthcare', 27 May 2011; www.taxpayersalliance.com/new_research_bbc_and_s4c_spend_millions_on_private_healthcare

35. 'Medical insurance for 500 BBC bosses', *Telegraph*, 12 March 2012.

36. Marcus Chown, Twitter, 23 March 2012; https://twitter.com/marcus chown/status/183192773158113281

37. Email to Marcus Chown, published on Twitter, 23 March 2012; https://twitter.com/marcuschown/status/183192773158113281.

38. Email to Media Lens, 3 April 2012.

39. Email to Media Lens, 24 April 2012.

40. Raymond Tallis, 'The NHS: creeping privatisation, spending cuts, media storms and a simple lack of understanding', iNews, 12 September 2016; https://inews.co.uk/opinion/comment/jeremy-hunt-health-secretary-blood-on-his-hands-raymond-tallis-essay-nhs/

41. Rachel Clarke, 'I am a doctor, not a border control officer – Jeremy Hunt won't stop me treating my patients', *Independent* website, 6 February 2017; www.independent.co.uk/voices/nhs-crisis-jeremy-hunt-health-tourism-theresa-may-a7564846.html

42. Daniel Margrain, 'The government's deliberate destruction of our NHS', Scisco media, 15 February 2017; https://sciscomedia.co.uk/government-deliberate-destruction-nhs/

43. Kerry-anne Mendoza, 'We need to talk about what happened on BBC Newsnight last night, because it was not OK', *The Canary*, 22 February 2017; www.thecanary.co/2017/02/22/bbc-newsnight-last-night-video/

10. Scottish Independence: An 'Amazing Litany' of Bias

1. Craig Murray blog, 'The three amigos ride to Scotland', Craig Murray blog, 9 September 2014; www.craigmurray.org.uk/archives/2014/09/the-three-amigos-ride-to-scotland/

2. Andrew Critchlow, 'Scottish homeowners face mortgage meltdown if Yes campaign wins', *Telegraph*, 7 September 2014; www.telegraph.co.uk/finance/newsbysector/banksandfinance/11080611/Scottish-homeowners-face-mortgage-meltdown-if-Yes-campaign-wins.html

3. Boris Johnson, 'Scottish independence: Decapitate Britain, and we kill off the greatest political union ever', *Telegraph*, 8 September 2014;

www.telegraph.co.uk/news/uknews/scotland/11080893/Scottish-independence-Decapitate-Britain-and-we-kill-off-the-greatest-political-union-ever.html

4. 'Signifying much', *The Times*, 8 September 2014.

5. Larry Elliott, 'What would independence really mean for Scotland's economy?', *Guardian*, 7 September 2014; www.theguardian.com/politics/2014/sep/07/what-would-independence-mean-for-scotland-economy

6. Jonathan Freedland, 'If Britain loses Scotland it will feel like an amputation', *Guardian*, 5 September 2014; www.theguardian.com/commentisfree/2014/sep/05/britain-scotland-independence

7. 'The *Guardian* view on the Scottish referendum: Britain deserves another chance', *Guardian*, 12 September 2014; www.theguardian.com/commentisfree/2014/sep/12/-view-scottish-independence

8. Suzanne Moore, 'The Scottish independence debate has given politicians what they say they want – engagement', 10 September 2014; www.theguardian.com/commentisfree/2014/sep/10/-sp-the-scottish-independence-debate-has-given-politicians-what-they-say-they-want-engagement

9. Will Hutton, 'We have 10 days to find a settlement to save the union', *Observer*, 6 September 2014; www.theguardian.com/commentisfree/2014/sep/06/will-hutton-10-days-to-save-the-union-scottish-independence

10. Mike Small, 'Too little too late', Bella Caledonia, 6 September 2014; http://bellacaledonia.org.uk/2014/09/06/too-little-too-late/

11. George Monbiot, 'A yes vote in Scotland would unleash the most dangerous thing of all – hope', *Guardian* website, 9 September 2014; www.theguardian.com/commentisfree/2014/sep/09/yes-vote-in-scotland-most-dangerous-thing-of-all-hope

12. John Robertson, 'Fairness in the first year? BBC and ITV Coverage of the Scottish Referendum Campaign from September 2012 to September 2013', University of the West of Scotland, 20 January 2014; https://issuu.com/creative_futur/docs/robertson2014fairnessinthefirstyear; available directly at: http://worldofstuart.excellentcontent.com/repository/FairnessInTheFirstYear.pdf; see also, John Robertson, 'BBC bias and the Scots referendum – new report', openDemocracy, 21 February 2014; www..net/ourkingdom/john-robertson/bbc-bias-and-scots-referendum-new-report

13. Email from John Robertson, 18 March 2014.

14. Craig Murray blog, 'BBC the new hammer of the Scots', Craig Murray blog, 29 April 2013; www.craigmurray.org.uk/archives/2013/04/bbc-the-new-hammer-of-the-scots/

15. BBC News, 26 April 2013; www.bbc.co.uk/news/uk-scotland-22314646

16. BBC News, 22 April 2013; www.bbc.co.uk/news/uk-scotland-scotland-politics-22246176

17. BBC News, 14 March 2013; www.bbc.co.uk/news/uk-scotland-scotland-politics-21776602

18. BBC News, 2 December 2012; www.bbc.co.uk/news/uk-scotland-scotland-business-20562203

19. BBC News, 10 December 2013; www.bbc.co.uk/news/uk-scotland-20666146

20. BBC News, 15 January 2013; www.bbc.co.uk/news/uk-scotland-scotland-politics-21016047

21. BBC News, 25 March 2012; www.bbc.co.uk/news/uk-scotland-scotland-politics-17505302

22. Derek Bateman, 'Breaking news...BBC threatens academic', Derek Bateman blog, 22 January 2014; https://derekbateman1.wordpress.com/2014/01/22/breaking-newsbbc-threatens-academic/

23. Quoted, 'BBC blasted in UWS response', Derek Bateman blog, 2 February 2014; http://derekbateman.scot/2014/02/02/bbc-blasted-in-uws-response/

24. 'Academic condemns BBC Scotland', YouTube, 11 March 2014; www.youtube.com/watch?v=HkHURxtyH14

25. John Robertson, 'UWS academic responds to BBC Scotland criticism of indy news study', Newsnet.scot, 2 February 2017; http://newsnet.scot/archive/uws-academic-responds-to-bbc-scotland-criticism-of-indy-news-study/

26. Search for 'John Mullin' in our free online archive of media alerts; http://medialens.org/index.php/alerts.html

27. 'BBC Scotland chiefs appear in front of Culture Committee', YouTube, 11 March 2014; www.youtube.com/watch?v=RmuoZVJTc-Y

28. Derek Bateman, 'Journalists at work', Derek Bateman blog, March 14, 2014; https://derekbateman1.wordpress.com/2014/03/14/journalists-at-work

29. Toby Helm and Daniel Boffey, 'Scottish referendum: Shock new poll says Scots set to vote for independence', *Observer*, 7 September 2014; www.theguardian.com/politics/2014/sep/06/scots-radical-new-deal-save-the-union

30. 'Scottish independence: Timetable on new Scots powers to be outlined "in days"', BBC News, 7 September 2014; www.bbc.co.uk/news/uk-scotland-29099431

31. Jamie Ross, 'Scottish independence: Osborne's further powers plan "not against purdah rules"', BBC News, 7 September 2014; www.bbc.co.uk/news/uk-scotland-29100372

32. 'Better Together "new" powers claim collapses within hours', Newsnet Scotland, 7 September 2014; http://newsnet.scot/archive/better-together-new-powers-claim-collapses-within-hours/

33. 'The BBC is killing democracy', YouTube, 11 September 2014; www.youtube.com/watch?v=5EMLOTsimSs&feature=youtu.be

34. 'Ultimate Smackdown', YouTube, 11 September 2014; www.youtube.com/watch?v=rHmLb-RIbrM

35. Kyle Arnold, Facebook post, 11 September 2014; www.facebook.com/kyle.rh.arnold/videos/10152229101841105/

36. 'BBC protest – Scottish Independence Referendum 2014', YouTube, 14 September 2017; www.youtube.com/watch?v=dEkY6Z2VZW4

37. RT '"Sack Nick Robinson!" Pro-indy Scots denounce "liar" BBC journo in protest', YouTube, 15 September 2014; www.youtube.com/watch?v=sodlIuiZ15c.

38. '"Stick your license fee up your a***!" Pro-indy Scots denounce "liar" BBC journo in protest', RT, 15 September 2014; www.rt.com/uk/187864-scottish-independence-bbc-protest/

39. Severin Carrell, 'Alex Salmond backs protests against "bias" shown by BBC's Nick Robinson', Guardian, 15 September 2014; www.theguardian.com/politics/2014/sep/15/alex-salmond-bbc-protest-nick-robinson

40. 'BBC News at Six and Ten, BBC One, 11 September, 2014', BBC Complaints, 2015 (undated); www.bbc.co.uk/complaints/complaint/alexsalmondrbsquestion/

41. Press Association, 'BBC's Nick Robinson attacks "bullying" over Scottish referendum coverage', Guardian website, 21August 2015; www.theguardian.com/media/2015/aug/21/bbc-nick-robinson-bullying-scottish-referendum-alex-salmond

42. Jane Martinson, 'Nick Robinson: "What was ignored was that Salmond picked the fight, not me"', Guardian, 21 June 2015; www.theguardian.com/media/2015/jun/21/nick-robinson-bbc-lung-cancer-cybernats

43. 'The comic book simplicity of propaganda', Media Lens media alert, 1 October 2014; www.medialens.org/index.php/alerts/alert-archive/2014/777-the-comic-book-simplicity-of-propaganda.html

44. 'Where journalism collides with state "security": BBC News, MI5 and the mantra of "keeping people safe"', Media Lens media alert, 14 October 2013; www.medialens.org/index.php/alerts/alert-archive/alerts-2013/745-where-journalism-collides-with-state-security-bbc-news-mi5-and-the-mantra-of-keeping-people-safe.html

45. Dave Lord, 'EXCLUSIVE: "Insulting, embarrassing and shameful" Alex Salmond lashes out over BBC coverage of the independence referendum', *Courier*, 23 August 2015; www.thecourier.co.uk/news/scotland/254098/exclusive-insulting-embarrassing-and-shameful-alex-salmond-lashes-out-over-bbc-coverage-of-the-independence-referendum/

46. Nick Robinson, 'The BBC must resist Alex Salmond's attempt to control its coverage', *Guardian*, 24 August 2015; www.theguardian.com/media/2015/aug/24/the-bbc-must-resist-alex-salmonds-attempt-to-control-its-coverage

47. Jane Martinson, 'BBC's Nick Robinson heats up row with SNP's Alex Salmond', *Guardian*, 24 August 2015; www.theguardian.com/media/2015/aug/24/bbcs-nick-robinson-heats-up-row-with-snps-alex-salmond

48. George Monbiot, Twitter, 21 August 2015; https://twitter.com/GeorgeMonbiot/status/634633973189242880

49. Nick Robinson, '"Remember the last time you shouted like that?" I asked the spin-doctor', *The Times*, 16 July 2004.

50. Glenn Greenwald, Twitter, 27 January 2014; https://twitter.com/ggreenwald/status/427793325068783616

51. Nick Robinson, '"Remember the last time you shouted like that?" I asked the spin-doctor', *The Times*, July 16, 2004.

52. Nick Robinson, Twitter, 2 July 2015; https://twitter.com/bbcnickrobinson/status/616556234100113408

11. *Climate Chaos: An Inconvenient Emergency*

1. '"Planetary emergency" due to Arctic melt', news24, 20 September 2012; www.news24.com/SciTech/News/Planetary-emergency-due-to-Arctic-melt-20120920

2. Damian Carrington and Michael Slezak, 'February breaks global temperature records by "shocking" amount', *Guardian* website, 14 March 2016; www.theguardian.com/science/2016/mar/14/february-breaks-global-temperature-records-by-shocking-amount

3. Roz Pidcock, 'World's major climate agencies confirm 2016 as hottest year on record', Carbon Brief, 18 January 2017; www.carbonbrief.org/worlds-major-climate-agencies-confirm-2016-hottest-year-on-record

4. Damian Carrington, 'Record-breaking climate change pushes world into "uncharted territory"', *Guardian*, 21 March 2017; www.theguardian.com/environment/2017/mar/21/record-breaking-climate-change-world-uncharted-territory

5. Ibid.

6. John Vidal, '"Extraordinarily hot" Arctic temperatures alarm scientists', *Guardian* website, 22 November 2016; www.theguardian.com/environment/2016/nov/22/extraordinarily-hot-arctic-temperatures-alarm-scientists

7. Fiona Harvey, 'Arctic ice melt could trigger uncontrollable climate change at global level', *Guardian* website, 25 November 2016; www.theguardian.com/environment/2016/nov/25/arctic-ice-melt-trigger-uncontrollable-climate-change-global-level

8. Ian Johnston, 'Global warming could cause sea levels to rise higher than the height of a three-storey building, study suggests', *Independent*, 19 January 2017; www.independent.co.uk/environment/sea-level-rise-global-warming-climate-change-9-metres-study-science-a7536136.html

9. Ibid.

10. Andrew Simms, '"A cat in hell's chance" – why we're losing the battle to keep global warming below 2C', *Guardian*, 19 January 2017; www.theguardian.com/environment/2017/jan/19/cat-in-hells-chance-why-losing-battle-keep-global-warming-2c-climate-change

11. Ian Johnston, 'Climate change may be escalating so fast it could be "game over", scientists warn', *Independent*, 9 November 2016; www.independent.co.uk/news/science/climate-change-game-over-global-warming-climate-sensitivity-seven-degrees-a7407881.html

12. Ibid.

13. Quoted, Peter Kristoff, 'Are you ready for a four degree world?', The Conversation, 4 August 2011; http://theconversation.com/are-you-ready-for-a-four-degree-world-2452

14. Oliver Milman, 'Rate of environmental degradation puts life on Earth at risk, say scientists', *Guardian* website, 15 January 2015; www.theguardian.com/environment/2015/jan/15/rate-of-environmental-degradation-puts-life-on-earth-at-risk-say-scientists

15. Ibid.

16. Jon Queally, 'That was easy: in just 60 years, neoliberal capitalism has nearly broken Planet Earth', Common Dreams, 16 January 2015; www.commondreams.org/news/2015/01/16/was-easy-just-60-years-neoliberal-capitalism-has-nearly-broken-planet-earth

17. Quoted, Jo Confino, 'It is profitable to let the world go to hell', *Guardian* website, 19 January 2015; www.theguardian.com/sustainable-business/2015/jan/19/davos-climate-action-democracy-failure-jorgen-randers

18. 'Doomsday Clock moved to just two minutes to "apocalypse"', BBC website, 25 January 2018; www.bbc.co.uk/news/world-42823734

19. Bulletin of the Atomic Scientists, 'It is now two minutes to midnight', 2018 Doomsday Clock Statement, Science and Security Board, Bulletin of the Atomic Scientists, 25 January 2018; https://thebulletin.org/2018-doomsday-clock-statement

20. Jason Samenow, 'Harvey is a 1,000-year flood event unprecedented in scale', *Washington Post*, 31 August 2017; www.washingtonpost.com/news/capital-weather-gang/wp/2017/08/31/harvey-is-a-1000-year-flood-event-unprecedented-in-scale/?utm_term=.1459d0f8b29c

21. Marianna Parraga and Gary McWilliams, 'Funding battle looms as Texas sees Harvey damage at up to $180 billion', 3 September 2017, Reuters; www.reuters.com/article/us-storm-harvey/funding-battle-looms-as-texas-sees-harvey-damage-at-up-to-180-billion-idUSKCN1BE0TL

22. Jason Samenow, 'Harvey is a 1,000-year flood event unprecedented in scale', *Washington Post*, 31 August 2017; www.washingtonpost.com/news/capital-weather-gang/wp/2017/08/31/harvey-is-a-1000-year-flood-event-unprecedented-in-scale/?utm_term=.1459d0f8b29c

23. Eric Holthaus, 'Harvey is what climate change looks like', *Politico Magazine*, 28 August 2017; www.politico.com/magazine/story/2017/08/28/climate-change-hurricane-harvey-215547

24. Rupam Jain and Tommy Wilkes, 'Worst floods to hit South Asia in decade expose lack of monsoon planning', Reuters, 1 September 2017; www.reuters.com/article/us-southasia-floods/worst-floods-to-hit-

south-asia-in-decade-expose-lack-of-monsoon-planning-idUSK
CN1BC4QI

25. 'Mumbai mayhem: How heavy rains brought the city to its knees',
Times of India, 30 August 2017; https://timesofindia.indiatimes.com/
city/mumbai/mumbai-mayhem-how-heavy-rains-brought-the-city-
to-its-knees/articleshow/60287516.cms

26. David Roberts, 'Climate change did not "cause" Harvey or Irma, but it's
a huge part of the story', Vox, 11 September 2017; www.vox.com/
energy-and-environment/2017/8/28/16213268/harvey-climate-change

27. Matt McGrath, 'Hurricane Harvey: The link to climate change', BBC
website, 29 August 2017; www.bbc.co.uk/news/science-environment-
41082668

28. Eric Holthaus, 'Harvey and Irma aren't natural disasters. They're
climate change disasters', Grist, 11 September 2017; https://grist.org/
article/harvey-and-irma-arent-natural-disasters-theyre-climate-
change-disasters/

29. Naomi Klein, 'Harvey didn't come out of the blue. Now is the time to
talk about climate change', *The Intercept*, 28 August 2017; https://
theintercept.com/2017/08/28/harvey-didnt-come-out-of-the-blue-
now-is-the-time-to-talk-about-climate-change/

30. 'Biological annihilation: Earth's sixth mass extinction event is under
way', *The Real News Network*, 1 August 2017; http://therealnews.com/
t2/index.php?option=com_content&task=view&id=31&Itemid=
74&jumival=19607

31. Barry Saxifrage, 'These "missing charts" may change the way you think
about fossil fuel addiction', *National Observer*, 13 July 2017; www.
nationalobserver.com/2017/07/13/analysis/these-missing-charts-may-
change-way-you-think-about-fossil-fuel-addiction

32. Amitav Ghosh, *The Great Derangement: Climate Change and the
Unthinkable*, University of Chicago Press, 2016.

33. Bill McKibben, 'The new battle plan for the planet's climate crisis',
Rolling Stone, 24 January 2017; www.rollingstone.com/politics/
features/bill-mckibbens-battle-plan-for-the-planets-climate-
crisis-w462680

34. Ibid.

35. Jeff Goodell, 'Will we miss our last chance to save the world from
climate change?', *Rolling Stone*, 22 December 2016; www.rollingstone.
com/politics/features/will-we-miss-our-last-chance-to-survive-
climate-change-w456917

36. Editorial, 'The *Guardian* view on Obama's legacy: yes he did make a difference', *Guardian* website, 19 January 2017; www.theguardian.com/commentisfree/2017/jan/19/the-Guardian-view-on-obamas-legacy-yes-he-did-make-a-difference

37. Ian Sinclair, 'Obama: The sham environmentalist', *Morning Star*, 25 January 2017; https://morningstaronline.co.uk/a-f298-obama-the-sham-environmentalist-1

38. Ian Johnston and Tom Batchelor, 'Government "tried to bury" its own alarming report on climate change', *Independent*, 22 January 2017; www.independent.co.uk/environment/climate-change-risk-assessment-global-warming-government-accused-burying-report-a7540726.html

39. Ibid.

40. Ibid.

41. Leonid Bershidsky, 'The numbers are in: fake news didn't work', *Bloomberg*, 23 January 2017; www.bloomberg.com/view/articles/2017-01-23/the-numbers-are-in-fake-news-didn-t-work

42. Piers Robinson, 'Fake news, propaganda and threats to journalism', Spinwatch, 21 January 2017; www.spinwatch.org/index.php/issues/propaganda/item/5942-fake-news-propaganda-and-threats-to-journalism

43. Quoted, video clip, Caroline Lucas, Twitter, 7 September 2017; https://twitter.com/CarolineLucas/status/905785888483016704

44. 'Where journalism collides with state "security": BBC News, MI5 and the mantra of "keeping people safe"', Media Lens media alert, 14 October 2013; www.medialens.org/index.php/alerts/alert-archive/alerts-2013/745-where-journalism-collides-with-state-security-bbc-news-mi5-and-the-mantra-of-keeping-people-safe.html

45. 'Flagship of fearmongering: The *Guardian*, MI5 and state propaganda', Media Lens media alert, 8 November 2016; www.medialens.org/index.php/alerts/alert-archive/2016/831-flagship-of-fearmongering-the-Guardian-mi5-and-state-propaganda.html

46. Amitav Ghosh, 'The Great Derangement: Climate Change and the Unthinkable', University of Chicago Press, 2016, p. 143; our emphasis.

47. Senator Sheldon Whitehouse, 'Time to wake up: The climate denial beast', YouTube, 4 February 2014; www.youtube.com/watch?v=Iu4HLr4hIUk

48. Robert Brulle, 'Institutionalizing delay: foundation funding and the creation of U.S. climate change counter-movement organizations',

Climatic Change, 21 December 2013; drexel.edu/~/media/Files/now/pdfs/Institutionalizing%20Delay%20-%20Climatic%20Change.ashx

49. Alex McKechnie, 'Not just the Koch Brothers: new Drexel study reveals funders behind the climate change denial effort', *Drexel Now*, 20 December 2013; http://drexel.edu/now/archive/2013/December/Climate-Change/

50. Bob Ward, 'Secret funding of climate sceptics is not restricted to the US', *Guardian* website, 15 February 2013; www.theguardian.com/environment/2013/feb/15/secret-funding-climate-sceptics-not-restricted-us

51. Kyla Mandel, 'A new special relationship for America and Britain emerges with climate science deniers linked to Trump and Brexit', DeSmog UK, 16 January 2017; www.desmog.uk/2017/01/16/mapped-new-special-relationship-america-and-britain-emerges-between-climate-science-deniers-trump-and-brexit

52. Alex McKechnie, 'Not Just the Koch Brothers: New Drexel Study Reveals Funders Behind the Climate Change Denial Effort', Drexel Now, December 20, 2013; http://drexel.edu/now/archive/2013/December/Climate-Change/

53. 'The 97% consensus on global warming', Skeptical Science website, accessed 11 September 2017; https://skepticalscience.com/global-warming-scientific-consensus.htm

54. Katherine Ellen Foley, 'Those 3% of scientific papers that deny climate change? A review found them all flawed', Quartz, 5 September 2017; https://qz.com/1069298/the-3-of-scientific-papers-that-deny-climate-change-are-all-flawed/

55. NASA, 'Scientific consensus: Earth's climate is warming', 16 March 2017; http://climate.nasa.gov/scientific-consensus/

56. Cheryl Jones, 'Frank Fenner sees no hope for humans', *Australian*, 16 June 2010; http://bit.ly/2EFZd3H

57. Paul Kingsnorth, 'The new environmentalism: where men must act "as gods" to save the planet', *Guardian* website, 1 August 2012; www.theguardian.com/commentisfree/2012/aug/01/neogreens-science-business-save-planet

58. Suzanne Goldenberg, 'Conservative groups spend up to $1bn a year to fight action on climate change', *Guardian* website, 20 December 2013; www.theguardian.com/environment/2013/dec/20/conservative-groups-1bn-against-climate-change

59. Personal communication, 14 February 2014.

60. Douglas Fischer, 'Coverage of climate change tumbles again in 2011', ClimateCentral, 3 January 2012; www.climatecentral.org/news/partner-news/climate-coverage-down-again-in-2011

61. Justin Lewis, 'Cycle of silence: the strange case of disappearing environmental issues', *The Conversation*, 12 January 2015; https://theconversation.com/cycle-of-silence-the-strange-case-of-disappearing-environmental-issues-36306

62. 'Bias towards power *is* corporate media "objectivity": Journalism, floods and climate silence', Media Lens media alert, 13 February 2014; http://medialens.org/index.php/alerts/alert-archive/2014/755-bias-towards-power-is-corporate-media-objectivity-journalism-floods-and-climate-silence.html

63. Quoted, Sharon Beder, *Global Spin – The Corporate Assault on Environmentalism*, Green Books, 1997, p. 22.

64. Ed Pilkington, 'Put oil firm chiefs on trial, says leading climate change scientist', *Guardian*, 23 June 2008; www.theguardian.com/environment/2008/jun/23/fossilfuels.climatechange

65. 'The UK General Election of 2017: the campaigns, media and polls', Centre for Research in Communication and Culture, Loughborough University, 7 July 2017; http://blog.lboro.ac.uk/crcc/general-election/; see also: Media Lens, Twitter, 16 May 2017; https://twitter.com/medialens/status/864488653183234049

66. 'Report into BBC's science coverage likely to suggest corporation needs to avoid false balance on climate', *Carbon Brief*, 19 July 2011; www.carbonbrief.org/report-into-bbcs-science-coverage-likely-to-suggest-corporation-needs-to-avoid-false-balance-on-climate

67. Ian Sinclair, 'The BBC is neither independent or impartial: interview with Tom Mills', 25 January 2017; www.opendemocracy.net/ourbeeb/ian-sinclair-tom-mills/bbc-is-neither-independent-or-impartial-interview-with-tom-mills

68. Mark Sweney, 'Sir David Clementi confirmed as new BBC chair', *Guardian* website, 10 January 2017; www.theguardian.com/media/2017/jan/10/sir-david-clementi-bbc-chair-unitary-board-trust-bank-of-england

69. 'Global Warning: 24 hours on the climate change frontline as Trump becomes president – as it happened', *Guardian* website, 20 January 2017; www.theguardian.com/environment/live/2017/jan/19/global-warning-live-from-the-climate-change-frontline-as-trump-becomes-president

70. Maeve Shearlaw, 'So you want to be a climate campaigner? Here's how', *Guardian* website, 23 January 2017; www.theguardian.com/environment/2017/jan/23/climate-campaigner-heres-how-activsim-green

71. Screenshot of *Guardian* website frontpage, 19 January 2017, Media Lens Facebook page; http://bit.ly/2EohjUt

72. '"Grievous censorship" by the *Guardian*: Israel, Gaza and the termination of Nafeez Ahmed's Blog', Media Lens media alert, 9 December 2014; www.medialens.org/index.php/alerts/alert-archive/2014/782-grievous-censorship-by-the-guardian-israel-gaza-and-the-termination-of-nafeez-ahmed-s-blog.html

73. Nafeez Ahmed, 'Death, drugs, and HSBC: Fraudulent blood money makes the world go round', Medium, 2 March 2015; https://medium.com/insurge-intelligence/death-drugs-and-hsbc-355ed9ef5316#.uy3gm5hps

74. George Monbiot, 'Newspapers must stop taking advertising from environmental villains', *Guardian* website, 5 June 2009; www.theguardian.com/environment/georgemonbiot/2009/jun/05/climate-change-corporatesocialresponsibility

75. 'Melting ice sheets and media contradictions', Media Lens media alert, 4 July 2007; http://medialens.org/index.php/alerts/alert-archive/2007/513-melting-ice-sheets-and-media-contradictions.html

76. Ian Sinclair, Twitter, 20 January 2017; https://twitter.com/IanJSinclair/status/822524417188237314

77. Ian Sinclair, Twitter, 20 January 2017; https://twitter.com/IanJSinclair/status/822523376644354052

78. 'Keep it in the ground campaign: Q&A with Alan Rusbridger – as it happened', *Guardian* website, 19 March 2015; www.theguardian.com/environment/keep-it-in-the-ground-blog/live/2015/mar/18/keep-it-in-the-ground-campaign-live-q-and-a-with-alan-rusbridger; also tweeted here by Guardian Environment: Twitter, 19 March 2015; https://twitter.com/Guardianeco/status/578540844522815488

79. Lee Glendinning, 'In this new world, now is the time to support fearless, independent journalism', *Guardian* website, 9 November 2016; www.theguardian.com/membership/2016/nov/09/with-trump-victorious-time-to-support-fearless-independent-journalism

80. Jonathan Porritt, 'It is "impossible" for today's big oil companies to adapt to climate change', *Guardian* website, 15 January 2015; www.

theguardian.com/environment/2015/jan/15/it-is-impossible-todays-big-oil-companies-adapt-climate-change-jonathon-porritt

81. 'kalahari', reader comment, *Guardian* website, 16 January 2015; www.theguardian.com/environment/2015/jan/15/it-is-impossible-todays-big-oil-companies-adapt-climate-change-jonathon-porritt#comment-46208978

82. Lisa Hymas, 'E. O. Wilson wants to know why you're not protesting in the streets', *Grist*, 30 April 2012; http://grist.org/article/e-o-wilson-wants-to-know-why-youre-not-protesting-in-the-streets/

83. Ralph Nader, interview with Paul Jay, *The Real News Network*, 4 November 2008; http://therealnews.com/t2/index.php?option=com_content&task=view&id=31&Itemid=74&jumival=2718

12. 'Fake News', Objective Journalism and the No-Business Model

1. Oxford Dictionaries, 'Word of the Year 2016 is ...', https://en.oxforddictionaries.com/word-of-the-year/word-of-the-year-2016

2. Reinhold Niebuhr cited, Noam Chomsky, 'Force and opinion', *Z Magazine*, July-August, 1991, https://chomsky.info/199107__/

3. 'Fake news website', Wikipedia, accessed 19 February 2018, https://en.wikipedia.org/wiki/Fake_news_website

4. 'Filter Bubble', Wikipedia, accessed 23 May 2018, https://en.wikipedia.org/wiki/Filter_bubble

5. Kate Connolly, Angelique Chrisafis, Poppy McPherson, Stephanie Kirchgaessner, Benjamin Haas, Dominic Phillips, Elle Hunt and Michael Safi, 'Fake news: an insidious trend that's fast becoming a global problem', *Guardian*, 2 December 2016, www.theguardian.com/media/2016/dec/02/fake-news-facebook-us-election-around-the-world

6. Philip Giraldi, cited Gareth Porter, 'U.S. intelligence found Iran nuke document was forged', Inter Press Service, 28 December 2009, www.ipsnews.net/2009/12/politics-us-intelligence-found-iran-nuke-document-was-forged/

7. Andrew Smith, 'The pedlars of fake news are corroding democracy', *Guardian*, 25 November 2016, www.theguardian.com/commentisfree/2016/nov/25/pedlars-fake-news-corroding-democracy-social-networks

8. Editorial, 'The *Guardian* view on Charlie Hebdo: those guns were trained on free speech', *Guardian*, 7 June 2015, www.theguardian.com/

commentisfree/2015/jan/07/Guardian-view-charlie-hebdo-guns-trained-free-speech

9. Adam Johnson, 'WaPo spreading own falsehoods shows real power of fake news', FAIR, 4 January 2017, http://fair.org/home/wapo-spreading-own-falsehoods-shows-real-power-of-fake-news/

10. Glenn Greenwald, 'Yet another major Russia story falls apart. Is skepticism permissible yet?', The Intercept, 28 September 2017, https://theintercept.com/2017/09/28/yet-another-major-russia-story-falls-apart-is-skepticism-permissible-yet/

11. *Time* magazine cover, Boris Yeltsin, *Time*, 15 July 1996, http://content.time.com/time/covers/0,16641,19960715,00.html

12. Julia Carrie Wong, Sam Levin and Olivia Solon, 'Bursting the Facebook bubble: we asked voters on the left and right to swap feeds', *Guardian*, 16 November 2016, www.theguardian.com/us-news/2016/nov/16/facebook-bias-bubble-us-election-conservative-liberal-news-feed

13. Craig Timberg, 'Russian propaganda effort helped spread "fake news" during election, experts say', *Washington Post*, 24 November 2016, www.washingtonpost.com/business/economy/russian-propaganda-effort-helped-spread-fake-news-during-election-experts-say/2016/11/24/793903b6-8a40-4ca9-b712-716af66098fe_story.html?utm_term=.4b3c76d5f300

14. Matt Taibbi, 'The "Washington Post" "Blacklist" story is shameful and disgusting', *Rolling Stone*, 28 November 2016, www.rollingstone.com/politics/features/washington-post-blacklist-story-is-shameful-disgusting-w452543

15. Ibid.

16. Aaron Bastani, Twitter, 20 January 2017, https://twitter.com/AaronBastani/status/822458608365563904

17. Jonathan Cook, Twitter, 8 December 2014, https://twitter.com/Jonathan_K_Cook/status/541909096254173184

18. George Monbiot, Twitter, 8 December 2014, https://twitter.com/GeorgeMonbiot/status/541909889694851072

19. Owen Jones, Twitter, 10 December 2014, https://twitter.com/OwenJones84/status/542767232393424896

20. Jones, Twitter, 10 December 2014, https://twitter.com/OwenJones84/status/542767948474376192

21. Jones, Twitter, 20 March 2015, https://twitter.com/OwenJones84/status/578967597921779712

22. Jones, Twitter, 19 November 2017, https://twitter.com/OwenJones84/status/932281552238718976

23. Zoe Williams, Twitter, 19 November 2017, https://twitter.com/zoesqwilliams/status/932271742319505408

24. Naomi Klein, Twitter, 17 November 2017, https://twitter.com/Naomi AKlein/status/931513331864821762

25. Katharine Viner, 'A mission for journalism in a time of crisis', *Guardian*, 16 November 2017, www.theguardian.com/news/2017/nov/16/a-mission-for-journalism-in-a-time-of-crisis

26. Mehdi Hasan, Twitter, 7 March 2013, https://twitter.com/mehdir hasan/status/309607808356204544

27. Media Lens, Twitter, 7 March 2013, https://twitter.com/medialens/status/309608737411330048

28. Jon Rappoport, 'The fake news business exposed', *Event Chronicle*, 25 January 2017, www.theeventchronicle.com/fake-news-agenda/fake-news-business-exposed-reporters-tell-truth-off-record/

29. Jonathan Cook, 'Clinton's defeat and the "fake news" conspiracy', blog, 18 December 2016, www.jonathan-cook.net/blog/2016-12-18/its-clinton-who-rejects-the-democratic-vote/#sthash.o5umZkjw.dpuf

30. Andre Damon and Niles Niemuth, 'New Google algorithm restricts access to left-wing, progressive web sites', WSWS website, 27 July 2017, www.wsws.org/en/articles/2017/07/27/goog-j27.html

31. Propaganda model, Wikipedia, accessed 19 February 2018, https://en.wikipedia.org/wiki/Propaganda_model

32. James Twitchell, cited, Sharon Beder, *Global Spin*, Green Books, 1997, p. 181.

33. Glenn Greenwald, 'More on the media's Pentagon-subservient WikiLeaks coverage', *Salon*, 27 October 2010, www.salon.com/2010/10/27/burns_4/

34. Andrew Marr, Notebook, *Daily Telegraph*, 10 January 2001; https://www.telegraph.co.uk/comment/4258447/Notebook.html

35. Nick Robinson, '"Remember the last time you shouted like that?" I asked the spin doctor', *The Times*, 16 July 2004.

36. Glenn Greenwald, Twitter, 27 January 2014, https://twitter.com/ggreenwald/status/427793325068783616

37. Nick Robinson, Twitter, 7 November 2017, https://twitter.com/bbcnickrobinson/status/927969188668411904

38. Matt Taibbi, 'Hey, MSM: All journalism is advocacy journalism', *Rolling Stone*, 27 June 2013, www.rollingstone.com/politics/news/hey-msm-all-journalism-is-advocacy-journalism-20130627

39. Andrew Marr, BBC 1, 'News at Ten', 9 April 2003. See YouTube clip www.youtube.com/watch?v=5_JC371jxPI

40. Nick Robinson, ITN News, 8 September 2003.

41. Taibbi, *Rolling Stone*, 27 June 2013.

42. Erich Fromm, *Man For Himself*, Ark edition, Routledge & Kegan Paul, 1986, p. 105.

43. Ibid., pp. 105–6, original emphasis.

44. Ibid., p. 110.

45. Shantideva, *The Way of the Bodhisattva*, Shambhala, 1997, p. 123.

46. Ibid., p. 49.

47. Osho, 'From sex to superconsciousness', Osho world website, 1979, available as a free pdf, https://goo.gl/NT50D9

48. Jean-Jacques Rousseau, *Reveries of the Solitary Walker*, Penguin Classics, 1979, p. 94.

49. Schopenhauer, *Essays and Aphorisms*, Penguin Books, 1981, p. 199.

50. Erich Fromm, *On the Art of Being*, Continuum, 1992, p. 6.

51. Rousseau, *Reveries*, p. 94.

52. Ibid., p. 96.

53. Craig Murray, 'Save Craig Murray', 6 September 2017, blog, www.craigmurray.org.uk/archives/2017/09/save-craig-murray/

Index

Randers, Jørgen 194
Randerson, James 74
rape rumour (Libya) 79–80, 88
Rappoport, Jon 222–3
Rawnsley, Andrew 5, 82–3
Raytheon 121
Real News 91, 115
Reay, David 192
Rentoul, John 34
responsibility to protect 18–19, 72,
    80, 97, 107, 124, 135–8
Rice, Susan 80
Richards, David 89
Richardson, Bill 90
Riddell, Mary 93
Riefenstahl, Leni *xiii*
Ritter, Scott 76, 116
Robbins, James 100
Roberts, David 196
Robertson, Andrew 161–2
Robertson, John 178–84
Robinson, Nick 83, 118–19, 121,
    169, 185–90, 226–7
Rolling Stone 218–19, 227–8
Rousseau, Jean-Jacques 230, 234–5
Rowson, Martin 102–3
Royal College of GPs 158
Royal College of Midwives 158
Royal Dutch Shell 92
Rubin, James 93
Rudd, Amber 139–40
Rusbridger, Alan 142, 167, 209, 220
Rushton, Steve 144
Russell, Jenni 147
Russia
    elections and 217
    Syria and 97, 98, 100–1, 108,
        115, 119
    as threat 149–52

Sachs, Jeffrey 93
Salmond, Alex 178, 185–9, 187–8
Sambrook, Richard 142
Sandbrook, Dominic 54
Sands, Philippe 80
Sarkozy, Nicolas 89, 91
Saudi Arabia 108, 126–40
Save the Children 127–8, 138
Saxifrage, Barry 197–8
Sayeed, Theodore 13
Schellnhuber, John 193
Schopenhauer, Arthur 233
Scotsman 32
Scottish independence referendum
    173–90
self-censorship *viii–ix*, 14–15,
    170–1, 226, 228
September 11 attacks 24
Serbia 78, 130
SERCO 159
Shafi, Jonathon 71
Shah, Naz 4–6, 7, 10–11
Shamir, Yitzhak 66
Shantideva (Buddhist sage) 229–30
Sharon, Ariel 67
Sharon, Gilad 68
Shlaim, Avi 60
Sikora, Karol 172
Simpson, John 41, 118, 119–22,
    148
Sinclair, Ian 122–3, 199
Sirota, David 93
Small, Mike 177
Smith, Andrew 215–16
Smith, Jerry 113
Smith, Joan 45, 53
Smith, Norman 83
Snow, Jon 34, 141–2
Snowden, Edward 54

The Pluto Press Newsletter

Hello friend of Pluto!

Want to stay on top of the best radical books
we publish?

Then sign up to be the first to hear about our
new books, as well as special events,
podcasts and videos.

You'll also get 50% off your first order with us
when you sign up.

Come and join us!

Go to bit.ly/PlutoNewsletter